THE PLAYS OF

ANTON CHEKOV

Nine Plays including *The Sea-Gull*, *The Cherry Orchard*, *The Three Sisters* and Others.

CAXTON HOUSE, INC.,

New York, N. Y.

PRINTED IN THE UNITED STATES OF AMERICA
AMERICAN BOOK—STRATFORD PRESS, INC., NEW YORK

CONTENTS

THE SEA–GULL

A Comedy in Four Acts

First performed at St. Petersburg,
October 17, 1896

CHARACTERS IN THE PLAY

IRINA NIKOLAYEVNA ARKADIN (MADAME TREPLEV) (*an Actress*).

KONSTANTIN GAVRILOVITCH TREPLEV (*her son, a young man*).

PYOTR NIKOLAYEVITCH SORIN (*her brother*).

NINA MIHAILOVNA ZARETCHNY (*a young girl, the daughter of a wealthy Landowner*).

ILYA AFANASYEVITCH SHAMRAEV (*a retired Lieutenant,* SORIN'S *Steward*).

POLINA ANDREYEVNA (*his wife*).

MASHA (*his daughter*).

BORIS ALEXEYEVITCH TRIGORIN (*a literary man*).

YEVGENY SERGEYEVITCH DORN (*a Doctor*).

SEMYON SEMYONOVITCH MEDVEDENKO (*a Schoolmaster*).

YAKOV (*a Labourer*).

A MAN COOK.

A HOUSEMAID.

The action takes place in SORIN'S *house and garden. Between the Third and Fourth Acts there is an interval of two years.*

ACT I

Part of the park on SORIN'S *estate. Wide avenue leading away from the specta-
tors into the depths of the park towards the lake is blocked up by a platform roughly put together for private theatricals, so that the lake is not
visible. To right and left of the platform, bushes. A few chairs, a little
table.*

The sun has just set. YAKOV *and other labourers are at work on the platform
behind the curtain; there is the sound of coughing and hammering.*
MASHA *and* MEDVEDENKO *enter on the left, returning from a walk.*

MEDVEDENKO. Why do you always wear black?

MASHA. I am in mourning for my life. I am unhappy.

MEDVEDENKO. Why? (*Pondering*) I don't understand . . . You are in
good health; though your father is not very well off, he has got enough. My
life is much harder than yours. I only get twenty-three roubles a month, and
from that they deduct something for the pension fund, and yet I don't wear
mourning. (*They sit down.*)

MASHA. It isn't money that matters. A poor man may be happy.

MEDVEDENKO. Theoretically, yes; but in practice it's like this: there are
my two sisters and my mother and my little brother and I, and my salary is
only twenty-three roubles. We must eat and drink, mustn't we? One must
have tea and sugar. One must have tobacco. It's a tight fit.

MASHA (*looking round at the platform*). The play will soon begin.

MEDVEDENKO. Yes. Miss Zaretchny will act: it is Konstantin Gavrilitch's
play. They are in love with each other and to-day their souls will be united
in the effort to realise the same artistic effect. But your soul and mine have
not a common point of contact. I love you. I am so wretched I can't stay at
home. Every day I walk four miles here and four miles back and I meet with
nothing but indifference from you. I can quite understand it. I am without
means and have a big family to keep. . . . Who would care to marry a man
who hasn't a penny to bless himself with?

MASHA. Oh, nonsense! (*Takes a pinch of snuff*) Your love touches me, but
I can't reciprocate it—that's all. (*Holding out the snuff-box to him*) Help
yourself.

MEDVEDENKO. I don't feel like it (*a pause*).

15

MASHA. How stifling it is! There must be a storm coming. . . . You're always discussing theories or talking about money. You think there is no greater misfortune than poverty, but to my mind it is a thousand times better to go in rags and be a beggar than . . . But you wouldn't understand that, though. . . .

(SORIN *and* TREPLEV *enter on the right.*)

SORIN (*leaning on his walking-stick*). I am never quite myself in the country, my boy, and, naturally enough, I shall never get used to it. Last night I went to bed at ten and woke up this morning at nine feeling as though my brain were glued to my skull, through sleeping so long (*laughs*). And after dinner I accidentally dropped off again, and now I am utterly shattered and feel as though I were in a nightmare, in fact. . . .

TREPLEV. Yes, you really ought to live in town. (*Catches sight of* MASHA *and* MEDVEDENKO) When the show begins, my friends, you will be summoned, but you mustn't be here now. You must please go away.

SORIN (*to* MASHA). Marya Ilyinishna, will you be so good as to ask your papa to tell them to take the dog off the chain?—it howls. My sister could not sleep again last night.

MASHA. Speak to my father yourself; I am not going to. Please don't ask me. (*To* MEDVEDENKO) Come along!

MEDVEDENKO (*to* TREPLEV). So you will send and let us know before it begins. (*Both go out.*)

SORIN. So I suppose the dog will be howling all night again. What a business it is! I have never done as I liked in the country. In old days I used to get leave for twenty-eight days and come here for a rest and so on, but they worried me so with all sorts of trifles that before I had been here two days I was longing to be off again (*laughs*). I've always been glad to get away from here. . . . But now I am on the retired list, and I have nowhere else to go, as a matter of fact. I've got to live here whether I like it or not. . . .

YAKOV (*to* TREPLEV). We are going to have a bathe, Konstantin Gavrilitch.

TREPLEV. Very well; but don't be more than ten minutes (*looks at his watch*). It will soon begin.

YAKOV. Yes, sir (*goes out*).

TREPLEV (*looking round the stage*). Here is our theatre. The curtain, then the first wing, then the second, and beyond that—open space. No scenery of any sort. There is an open view of the lake and the horizon. We shall raise the curtain at exactly half-past eight, when the moon rises.

SORIN. Magnificent.

TREPLEV. If Nina is late it will spoil the whole effect. It is time she was here. Her father and her stepmother keep a sharp eye on her, and it is as hard for her to get out of the house as to escape from prison (*puts his uncle's cravat straight*). Your hair and your beard are very untidy. They want clipping or something. . . .

SORIN (*combing out his beard*). It's the tragedy of my life. Even as a young man I looked as though I had been drinking for days or something of the sort. I was never a favourite with the ladies (*sitting down*). Why is your mother out of humour?

TREPLEV. Why? Because she is bored (*sitting down beside him*). She is jealous. She is set against me, and against the performance, and against my play because Nina is acting in it, and she is not. She does not know my play, but she hates it.

SORIN (*laughs*). What an idea!

TREPLEV. She is annoyed to think that even on this little stage Nina will have a triumph and not she (*looks at his watch*). My mother is a psychological freak. Unmistakably talented, intelligent, capable of sobbing over a book, she will reel off all Nekrassov by heart; as a sick nurse she is an angel; but just try praising Duse in her presence! O-ho! You must praise no one but herself, you must write about her, make a fuss over her, be in raptures over her extraordinary acting in "La Dame aux Camélias" or the "Ferment of Life"; but she has none of this narcotic in the country, she is bored and cross, and we are all her enemies—we are all in fault. Then she is superstitious—she is afraid of three candles, of the number thirteen. She is stingy. She has got seventy thousand roubles in a bank at Odessa—I know that for a fact—but ask her to lend you some money, and she will burst into tears.

SORIN. You imagine your mother does not like your play, and you are already upset and all that. Don't worry; your mother adores you.

TREPLEV (*pulling the petals off a flower*). Loves me, loves me not; loves me, loves me not; loves me, loves me not (*laughs*). You see, my mother does not love me. I should think not! She wants to live, to love, to wear light blouses; and I am twenty-five, and I am a continual reminder that she is no longer young. When I am not there she is only thirty-two, but when I am there she is forty-three, and for that she hates me. She knows, too, that I have no belief in the theatre. She loves the stage, she fancies she is working for humanity, for the holy cause of art, while to my mind the modern theatre is nothing but tradition and conventionality. When the curtain goes up, and by artificial light, in a room with three walls, these great geniuses, the devotees of holy art, represent how people eat, drink, love, move about, and wear their jackets; when from these commonplace sentences and pictures they try to draw a moral —a petty moral, easy of comprehension and convenient for domestic use; when in a thousand variations I am offered the same thing over and over again—I run away as Maupassant ran away from the Eiffel Tower which weighed upon his brain with its vulgarity.

SORIN. You can't do without the stage.

TREPLEV. We need new forms of expression. We need new forms, and if we can't have them we had better have nothing (*looks at his watch*). I love my mother—I love her very much—but she leads a senseless sort of life, always taken up with this literary gentleman, her name is always trotted out in the papers—and that wearies me. And sometimes the simple egoism of an ordinary mortal makes me feel sorry that my mother is a celebrated actress, and I fancy that if she were an ordinary woman I should be happier. Uncle, what could be more hopeless and stupid than my position? She used to have visitors, all celebrities—artists and authors—and among them all I was the only one who was nothing, and they only put up with me because I was her son. Who am I? What am I? I left the University in my third year—owing to circumstances "for which we accept no responsibility," as the editors say; I have no talents. I haven't a penny of my own, and on my passport I am described as an artisan of Kiev. You know my father was an artisan of Kiev, though he too was a well-known actor. So, when in her drawing-room all these artists and authors graciously noticed me, I always fancied from their faces that they were taking the measure of my insignificance—I guessed their thoughts and suffered from the humiliation. . . .

SORIN. And, by the way, can you tell me, please, what sort of man this literary gentleman is? There's no making him out. He never says anything.

TREPLEV. He is an intelligent man, good-natured and rather melancholy, you know. A very decent fellow. He is still a good distance off forty, but he is already celebrated and has enough and to spare of everything. As for his writings . . . what shall I say? They are charming, full of talent, but . . . after Tolstoy or Zola you do not care to read Trigorin.

SORIN. Well, I am fond of authors, my boy. At one time I had a passionate desire for two things: I wanted to get married, and I wanted to become an author; but I did not succeed in doing either. Yes, it is pleasant to be even a small author, as a matter of fact.

TREPLEV (listens). I hear steps . . . (embraces his uncle). I cannot live without her. . . . The very sound of her footsteps is lovely. . . . I am wildly happy (goes quickly to meet NINA ZARETCHNY as she enters). My enchantress —my dream. . . .

NINA (in agitation). I am not late. . . . Of course I am not late. . . .

TREPLEV (kissing her hands). No, no, no!

NINA. I have been uneasy all day. I was so frightened. I was afraid father would not let me come. . . . But he has just gone out with my stepmother. The sky is red, the moon is just rising, and I kept urging on the horse (laughs). But I am glad (shakes SORIN's hand warmly).

SORIN (laughs). Your eyes look as though you have been crying. . . . Fie, fie! That's not right!

NINA. Oh, it was nothing. . . . You see how out of breath I am. I have to go in half an hour. We must make haste. I can't stay, I can't! For God's sake don't keep me! My father doesn't know I am here.

TREPLEV. It really is time to begin. We must go and call the others.

SORIN. I'll go this minute (goes to the right, singing "To France two grenadiers." Looks round). Once I sang like that, and a deputy prosecutor said to me, "You have a powerful voice, your Excellency"; then he thought a little and added, "but not a pleasant one" (laughs and goes off).

NINA. My father and his wife won't let me come here. They say it is so Bohemian here . . . they are afraid I shall go on the stage. . . . But I feel drawn to the lake here like a sea-gull. . . . My heart is full of you (*looks round*).

TREPLEV. We are alone.

NINA. I fancy there is someone there.

TREPLEV. There's nobody. (*They kiss.*)

NINA. What tree is this?

TREPLEV. An elm.

NINA. Why is it so dark?

TREPLEV. It's evening; everything is getting dark. Don't go away early, I entreat you!

NINA. I must.

TREPLEV. And if I come to you, Nina, I'll stand in the garden all night, watching your window.

NINA. You can't; the watchman would notice you. Trésor is not used to you, and he would bark.

TREPLEV. I love you!

NINA. Sh-h. . . .

TREPLEV (*hearing footsteps*). Who is there? You, Yakov?

YAKOV (*behind the stage*). Yes, sir.

TREPLEV. Take your places. It's time to begin. Is the moon rising?

YAKOV. Yes, sir.

TREPLEV. Have you got the methylated spirit? Have you got the sulphur? When the red eyes appear there must be a smell of sulphur. (*To* NINA) Go, it's all ready. Are you nervous?

NINA. Yes, awfully! Your mother is all right—I am not afraid of her—but there's Trigorin . . . I feel frightened and ashamed of acting before him . . . a celebrated author. . . . Is he young?

TREPLEV. Yes.

NINA. How wonderful his stories are.

TREPLEV (*coldly*). I don't know. I haven't read them.

NINA. It is difficult to act in your play. There are no living characters in it.

TREPLEV. Living characters! One must depict life not as it is, and not as it ought to be, but as we see it in our dreams.

NINA. There is very little action in your play—nothing but speeches. And to my mind there ought to be love in a play. (*Both go behind the stage.*)

(*Enter* POLINA ANDREYEVNA *and* DORN.)

POLINA. It is getting damp. Go back and put on your goloshes.

DORN. I am hot.

POLINA. You don't take care of yourself. It's obstinacy. You are a doctor, and you know perfectly well that damp air is bad for you, but you want to make me miserable; you sat out on the verandah all yesterday evening on purpose. . . .

DORN (*hums*). "Do not say that youth is ruined."

POLINA. You were so absorbed in conversation with Irina Nikolayevna . . . you did not notice the cold. Own up . . . you are attracted by her.

DORN. I am fifty-five.

POLINA. Nonsense! That's not old for a man. You look very young for your age, and are still attractive to women.

DORN. Well, what would you have?

POLINA. All you men are ready to fall down and worship an actress, all of you!

DORN (*hums*). "Before thee once again I stand." If artists are liked in society and treated differently from merchants, for example, that's only in the nature of things. It's idealism.

POLINA. Women have always fallen in love with you and thrown themselves on your neck. Is that idealism too?

DORN (*shrugs his shoulders*). Well, in the attitude of women to me there has been a great deal that was good. What they principally loved in me was a first-rate doctor. You remember that ten or fifteen years ago I was the only decent accoucheur in the district. Then, too, I have always been an honest man.

POLINA (*seizes him by the hand*). Dearest!

DORN. Sh-h! They are coming.

(*Enter* MADAME ARKADIN *arm in arm with* SORIN, TRIGORIN, SHAMRAEV, MEDVEDENKO *and* MASHA.)

SHAMRAEV. In the year 1873 she acted marvellously at the fair at Poltava. It was a delight! She acted exquisitely! Do you happen to know, madam, where Pavel Semyonitch Tchadin, a comic actor, is now? His Rasplyuev was inimitable, even finer than Sadovsky's, I assure you, honoured lady. Where is he now?

MADAME ARKADIN. You keep asking me about antediluvians. How should I know? (*Sits down.*)

SHAMRAEV (*with a sigh*). Pashka Tchadin! There are no such actors now. The stage has gone down, Irina Nikolayevna! In old days there were mighty oaks, but now we see nothing but stumps.

DORN. There are few actors of brilliant talents nowadays, that's true; but the average level of acting is far higher than it was.

SHAMRAEV. I can't agree with you. But, of course, it's a matter of taste. *De gustibus aut bene aut nihil.*

(TREPLEV *comes out from behind the stage.*)

MADAME ARKADIN (*to her son*). My dear son, when is it going to begin?

TREPLEV. In a minute. I beg you to be patient.

MADAME ARKADIN (*recites from* "Hamlet").

"Oh, Hamlet, speak no more!
Thou turn'st mine eyes into my very soul;
And there I see such black and grained spots
As will not leave their tinct."

TREPLEV (*from* "Hamlet").
"And let me wring your heart, for so I shall,
If it be made of penetrable stuff."
(*A horn is sounded behind the stage.*)

TREPLEV. Ladies and gentlemen, we begin! I beg you to attend (*a pause*). I begin (*taps with a stick and recites aloud*). Oh, you venerable old shadows that float at nighttime over this lake, lull us to sleep and let us dream of what will be in two hundred thousand years!

SORIN. There will be nothing in two hundred thousand years.

TREPLEV. Then let them present that nothing to us.

MADAME ARKADIN. Let them. We are asleep.

(*The curtain rises; the view of the lake is revealed; the moon is above the horizon, its reflection in the water;* NINA ZARETCHNY, *all in white, is sitting on a big stone.*)

NINA. Men, lions, eagles and partridges, horned deer, geese, spiders, silent fish that dwell in the water, starfishes and creatures which cannot be seen by the eye—all living things, all living things, all living things, having completed their cycle of sorrow, are extinct. . . . For thousands of years the earth has borne no living creature on its surface, and this poor moon lights its lamp in vain. On the meadow the cranes no longer waken with a cry, and there is no sound of the May beetles in the lime trees. It is cold, cold, cold! Empty, empty, empty! Dreadful, dreadful, dreadful! (*a pause*). The bodies of living creatures have vanished into dust, and eternal matter has transformed them into rocks, into water, into clouds, while the souls of all have melted into one. That world-soul I am—I. . . . In me is the soul of Alexander the Great, of Cæsar, of Shakespeare and of Napoleon, and of the lowest leech. In me the consciousness of men is blended with the instincts of the animals, and I remember all, all, all! And I live through every life over again in myself! (*Will-of-the-wisps appear.*)

MADAME ARKADIN (*softly*). It's something decadent.

TREPLEV (*in an imploring and reproachful voice*). Mother!

NINA. I am alone. Once in a hundred years I open my lips to speak, and my voice echoes mournfully in the void, and no one hears. . . . You too, pale lights, hear me not. . . . The stagnant marsh begets you before daybreak and you wander until dawn, but without thought, without will, without the tremor of life. For fear that life should spring up in you the father of eternal matter, the devil, keeps the atoms in you, as in the stones and in the water, in continual flux, and you are changing perpetually. For in all the universe nothing remains permanent and unchanged but the spirit (*a pause*). Like a prisoner cast into a deep, empty well I know not where I am and what awaits me. All is hidden from me but that in the cruel, persistent struggle with the devil— the principle of the forces of matter—I am destined to conquer, and, after that, matter and spirit will be blended in glorious harmony and the Kingdom of the Cosmic Will will come. But that will come only little by little, through long, long thousands of years when the moon and the bright Sirius and the earth are changed to dust. . . . Till then—terror, terror . . . (*a pause; two red spots appear upon the background of the lake*). Here my powerful foe, the devil, is approaching. I see his dreadful crimson eyes. . . .

MADAME ARKADIN. There's a smell of sulphur. Is that as it should be?

TREPLEV. Yes.

MADAME ARKADIN (*laughs*). Oh, it's a stage effect!

TREPLEV. Mother!

NINA. He is dreary without man——

POLINA (*to* DORN). You have taken your hat off. Put it on or you will catch cold.

MADAME ARKADIN. The doctor has taken his hat off to the devil, the father of eternal matter.

TREPLEV (*firing up, aloud*). The play is over! Enough! Curtain!

MADAME ARKADIN. What are you cross about?

TREPLEV. Enough! The curtain! Let down the curtain! (*stamping*). Curtain! (*The curtain falls.*) I am sorry! I lost sight of the fact that only a few of the elect may write plays and act in them. I have infringed the monopoly. I . . . I . . . (*Tries to say something more, but with a wave of his hand goes out on left.*)

MADAME ARKADIN. What's the matter with him?

SORIN. Irina, you really must have more consideration for youthful vanity, my dear.

MADAME ARKADIN. What did I say to him?

SORIN. You hurt his feelings.

MADAME ARKADIN. He told us beforehand that it was a joke, and I regarded his play as a joke.

SORIN. All the same . . .

MADAME ARKADIN. Now it appears that he has written a great work. What next! So he has got up this performance and smothered us with sulphur not as a joke but as a protest. . . . He wanted to show us how to write and what to act. This is getting tiresome! These continual sallies at my expense—these continual pin-pricks would put anyone out of patience, say what you like. He is a vain, whimsical boy!

SORIN. He meant to give you pleasure.

MADAME ARKADIN. Really? He did not choose an ordinary play, however, but made us listen to this decadent delirium. For the sake of a joke I am ready to listen to delirium, but here we have pretensions to new forms and a new view of art. To my thinking it's no question of new forms at all, but simply bad temper.

TRIGORIN. Everyone writes as he likes and as he can.

MADAME ARKADIN. Let him write as he likes and as he can, only let him leave me in peace.

DORN. Jupiter! you are angry. . . .

MADAME ARKADIN. I am not Jupiter—I am a woman (*lights a cigarette*).

I am not angry—I am only vexed that a young man should spend his time so drearily. I did not mean to hurt his feelings.

MEDVEDENKO. No one has any grounds to separate spirit from matter, seeing that spirit itself may be a combination of material atoms. (*With animation, to* TRIGORIN) But you know someone ought to write a play on how we poor teachers live, and get it acted. We have a hard, hard life.

MADAME ARKADIN. That's true, but don't let us talk either of plays or of atoms. It is such a glorious evening! Do you hear? There is singing! (*listens*). How nice it is!

POLINA. It's on the other side of the lake (*a pause*).

MADAME ARKADIN (*to* TRIGORIN). Sit down beside me. Ten or fifteen years ago there were sounds of music and singing on that lake continually almost every night. There are six country houses on the shores of the lake. I remember laughter, noise, shooting, and love affairs without end. . . . The *jeune premier* and the idol of all those six households was in those days our friend here, the doctor (*motions with her head towards* DORN), Yevgeny Sergeitch. He is fascinating still, but in those days he was irresistible. But my conscience is beginning to trouble me. Why did I hurt my poor boy's feelings? I feel worried. (*Aloud*) Kostya! Son! Kostya!

MASHA. I'll go and look for him.

MADAME ARKADIN. Please do, my dear.

MASHA (*going to the left*). Aa-oo! Konstantin Gavrilitch! Aa-oo! (*goes off*).

NINA (*coming out from behind the stage*). Apparently there will be no going on, and I may come out. Good evening! (*Kisses* MADAME ARKADIN *and* POLINA ANDREYEVNA.)

SORIN. Bravo! Bravo!

MADAME ARKADIN. Bravo! Bravo! We admired you. With such an appearance, with such a lovely voice, you really cannot stay in the country; it is a sin. You must have talent. Do you hear? It's your duty to go on the stage.

NINA. Oh, that's my dream! (*sighing*) But it will never be realised.

MADAME ARKADIN. Who knows? Here, let me introduce Boris Alexeyevitch Trigorin.

NINA. Oh, I am so glad . . . (*overcome with embarrassment*). I am always reading your . . .

MADAME ARKADIN (*making her sit down beside them*). Don't be shy, my dear. He is a celebrity, but he has a simple heart. You see, he is shy himself.

DORN. I suppose we may raise the curtain; it's rather uncanny.

SHAMRAEV (*aloud*). Yakov, pull up the curtain, my lad. (*The curtain goes up.*)

NINA (*to* TRIGORIN). It is a queer play, isn't it?

TRIGORIN. I did not understand it at all. But I enjoyed it. You acted so genuinely. And the scenery was delightful (*a pause*). There must be a lot of fish in that lake.

NINA. Yes.

TRIGORIN. I love angling. There is nothing I enjoy so much as sitting on the bank of a river in the evening and watching the float.

NINA. But I should have thought that for anyone who has known the enjoyment of creation, no other enjoyment can exist.

MADAME ARKADIN (laughing). Don't talk like that. When people say nice things to him he is utterly floored.

SHAMRAEV. I remember one evening in the opera theatre in Moscow the celebrated Silva took the lower C! As it happened, there was sitting in the gallery the bass of our church choir, and all at once—imagine our intense astonishment—we heard from the gallery "Bravo, Silva!" a whole octave lower—like this: (in a deep bass) "Bravo, Silva!" The audience sat spellbound (a pause).

DORN. The angel of silence has flown over us.

NINA. It's time for me to go. Good-bye.

MADAME ARKADIN. Where are you off to? Why so early? We won't let you go.

NINA. My father expects me.

MADAME ARKADIN. What a man, really . . . (kisses her). Well, there is no help for it. I am sorry—I am sorry to let you go.

NINA. If you knew how grieved I am to go.

MADAME ARKADIN. Someone ought to see you home, my little dear.

NINA (frightened). Oh, no, no!

SORIN (to her, in an imploring voice). Do stay!

NINA. I can't, Pyotr Nikolayevitch.

SORIN. Stay for an hour. What is there in that?

NINA (thinking a minute, tearfully). I can't! (Shakes hands and hurriedly goes off.)

MADAME ARKADIN. Unfortunate girl she is, really. They say her mother left her father all her immense property—every farthing of it—and now the girl has got nothing, as her father has already made a will leaving everything to his second wife. It's monstrous!

DORN. Yes, her father is a pretty thorough scoundrel, one must do him the justice to say so.

SORIN (rubbing his cold hands). Let us go too, it's getting damp. My legs ache.

MADAME ARKADIN. They seem like wooden legs, you can hardly walk. Let us go, unlucky old man! (Takes his arm.)

SHAMRAEV (offering his arm to his wife). Madame?

SORIN. I hear that dog howling again. (To SHAMRAEV) Be so kind, Ilya Afanasyitch, as to tell them to let it off the chain.

SHAMRAEV It's impossible, Pyotr Nikolayevitch, I am afraid of thieves getting into the barn. Our millet is there. (To MEDVEDENKO who is walking beside him) Yes, a whole octave lower: "Bravo, Silva!" And he not a singer—simply a church chorister!

MEDVEDENKO. And what salary does a chorister get? (*All go out except* DORN.)

DORN (*alone*). I don't know, perhaps I know nothing about it, or have gone off my head, but I like the play. There is something in it. When that girl talked about loneliness and afterwards when the devil's eyes appeared, I was so excited that my hands trembled. It is fresh, naïve. . . '. Here he comes, I believe. I want to say all the nice things I can to him.

TREPLEV (*enters*). They have all gone.

DORN. I am here.

TREPLEV. Mashenka is looking for me all over the park. Insufferable creature she is!

DORN. Konstantin Gavrilitch, I liked your play extremely. It's a strange thing, and I haven't heard the end, and yet it made a strong impression! You are a gifted man—you must persevere.

(TREPLEV *presses his hand warmly and embraces him impulsively.*)

DORN. Fie, what an hysterical fellow! There are tears in his eyes! What I mean is this. You have taken a subject from the realm of abstract ideas. So it should be, for a work of art ought to express a great idea. A thing is only fine when it is serious. How pale you are!

TREPLEV. So you tell me to persevere?

DORN. Yes. . . But write only of what is important and eternal. You know, I have had varied experiences of life, and have enjoyed it; I am satisfied, but if it had been my lot to know the spiritual heights which artists reach at the moment of creation, I should, I believe, have despised my bodily self and all that appertains to it and left all things earthly as far behind as possible.

TREPLEV. Excuse me, where is Nina?

DORN. And another thing. In a work of art there ought to be a clear definite idea. You ought to know what is your aim in writing, for if you go along that picturesque route without a definite goal you will be lost and your talent will be your ruin.

TREPLEV (*impatiently*). Where is Nina?

DORN. She has gone home.

TREPLEV (*in despair*). What am I to do? I want to see her . . . I must see her. . . . I must go. . . .

(*Enter* MASHA.)

DORN (*to* TREPLEV). Calm yourself, my boy.

TREPLEV. But I am going all the same. I must go.

MASHA. Come indoors, Konstantin Gavrilitch. Your mother wants you. She is worried.

TREPLEV. Tell her that I have gone away. And I beg you—all of you—leave me in peace! Let me alone! Don't follow me about!

DORN. Come, come, come, dear boy. . . . You can't go on like that. . . . That's not the thing.

TREPLEV (*in tears*). Good-bye, doctor. Thank you . . . (*goes off*).

DORN (*with a sigh*). Youth! youth!

MASHA. When people have nothing better to say, they say, "Youth! youth!"
. . . (*Takes a pinch of snuff.*)

DORN (*takes her snuff-box from her and flings it into the bushes*). That's
disgusting! (*a pause*). I believe they are playing the piano indoors. We must
go in.

MASHA. Wait a little.

DORN. What is it?

MASHA. I want to tell you once more. I have a longing to talk . . (*growing
agitated*). I don't care for my father . . . but I feel drawn to you. For some
reason I feel with all my heart that you are very near me. . . . Help me. Help
me, or I shall do something silly, I shall make a mock of my life and ruin it.
. . . I can't go on. . . .

DORN. What is it? Help you in what?

MASHA. I am miserable. No one, no one knows how miserable I am! (*Laying her head on his breast, softly*) I love Konstantin!

DORN. How hysterical they all are! How hysterical! And what a lot of love.
. . . Oh, the sorcery of the lake! (*Tenderly*) But what can I do, my child?
What? What?

CURTAIN.

ACT II

*A croquet lawn. The house with a big verandah in the background on the
right, on the left is seen the lake with, the blazing sun reflected in it.
Flower beds. Midday. Hot. MADAME ARKADIN, DORN and MASHA are sitting
on a garden seat in the shade of an old lime tree on one side of the croquet lawn. DORN has an open book on his knee.*

MADAME ARKADIN (*to MASHA*). Come, let us stand up. (*They both get up.*)
Let us stand side by side. You are twenty-two and I am nearly twice as old.
Yevgeny Sergeitch, which of us looks the younger?

DORN. You, of course.

MADAME ARKADIN. There! And why is it? Because I work, I feel I am always on the go, while you stay always in the same place and have no life at all.
. . . And it is my rule never to look into the future. I never think about old
age or death. What is to be, will be.

MASHA. And I feel as though I had been born long, long ago; I trail my
life along like an endless train. . . . And often I have not the slightest desire
to go on living (*sits down*). Of course, that's all nonsense. I must shake myself
and throw it all off.

DORN (*hums quietly*). "Tell her, my flowers."

MADAME ARKADIN. Then I am as particular as an Englishman. I keep myself in hand, as they say, my dear, and am always dressed and have my hair done *comme il faut.* Do I allow myself to go out of the house even into the garden in a dressing-gown, or without my hair being done? Never! What has preserved me is that I have never been a dowdy, I have never let myself go, as some women do . . . (*walks about the lawn with her arms akimbo*). Here I am, as brisk as a bird. I could take the part of a girl of fifteen.

DORN. Nevertheless, I shall go on (*takes up the book*). We stopped at the corn merchant and the rats. . . .

MADAME ARKADIN. And the rats. Read (*sits down*). But give it to me, I'll read. It is my turn (*takes the book and looks in it*). And rats. . . . Here it is. . . . (*Reads*) "And of course for society people to spoil novelists and to attract them to themselves is as dangerous as for a corn merchant to rear rats in his granaries. And yet they love them. And so, when a woman has picked out an author whom she desires to captivate, she lays siege to him by means of compliments, flattery and favours . . ." Well, that may be so with the French, but there is nothing like that with us, we have no set rules. Among us, before a woman sets to work to captivate an author, she is generally head over ears in love herself, if you please. To go no further, take Trigorin and me. . . .

(*Enter* SORIN, *leaning on his stick and with him* NINA; MEDVEDENKO *wheels an empty bath-chair in after them.*)

SORIN (*in a caressing tone, as to a child*). Yes? We are delighted, aren't we? We are happy to-day at last? (*To his sister*) We are delighted! Our father and stepmother have gone off to Tver, and we are free now for three whole days.

NINA (*sits down beside* MADAME ARKADIN *and embraces her*). I am happy! Now I belong to you.

SORIN (*sits down in his bath-chair*). She looks quite a beauty to-day.

MADAME ARKADIN. Nicely dressed and interesting. . . . That's a good girl (*kisses* NINA). But we mustn't praise you too much for fear of ill-luck. Where is Boris Alexeyevitch?

NINA. He is in the bathing-house, fishing.

MADAME ARKADIN. I wonder he doesn't get sick of it! (*is about to go on reading*).

NINA. What is that?

MADAME ARKADIN. Maupassant's "Sur l'eau," my dear (*reads a few lines to herself*). Well, the rest isn't interesting or true (*shuts the book*). I feel uneasy. Tell me, what's wrong with my son? Why is he so depressed and ill-humoured? He spends whole days on the lake and I hardly ever see him.

MASHA. His heart is troubled. (*To* NINA, *timidly*) Please, do read us something out of his play!

NINA (*shrugging her shoulders*). Would you like it? It's so uninteresting.

MASHA (*restraining her enthusiasm*). When he reads anything himself his eyes glow and his face turns pale. He has a fine mournful voice, and the gestures of a poet.

(*There is a sound of* SORIN *snoring.*)

DORN. Good night!

MADAME ARKADIN. Petrusha!

SORIN. Ah?

MADAME ARKADIN. Are you asleep?

SORIN. Not a bit of it (*a pause*).

MADAME ARKADIN. You do nothing for your health, brother, and that's not right.

SORIN. I should like to take something, but the doctor won't give me anything.

DORN. Take medicine at sixty!

SORIN. Even at sixty one wants to live!

DORN (*with vexation*). Oh, very well, take valerian drops!

MADAME ARKADIN. It seems to me it would do him good to go to some mineral springs.

DORN. Well, he might go. And he might not.

MADAME ARKADIN. What is one to make of that?

DORN. There's nothing to make of it. It's quite clear (*a pause*).

MEDVEDENKO. Pyotr Nikolayevitch ought to give up smoking.

SORIN. Nonsense!

DORN. No, it's not nonsense. Wine and tobacco destroy the personality. After a cigar or a glass of vodka, you are not Pyotr Nikolayevitch any more but Pyotr Nikolayevitch plus somebody else; your ego is diffused and you feel towards yourself as to a third person.

SORIN (*laughs*). It's all very well for you to argue! You've lived your life, but what about me? I have served in the Department of Justice for twenty-eight years, but I haven't lived yet, I've seen and done nothing as a matter of fact, and very naturally I want to live very much. You've had enough and you don't care, and so you are inclined to be philosophical, but I want to live, and so I drink sherry at dinner and smoke cigars and so on. That's all it comes to.

DORN. One must look at life seriously, but to go in for cures at sixty and to regret that one hasn't enjoyed oneself enough in one's youth is frivolous, if you will forgive my saying so.

MASHA (*gets up*). It must be lunch-time (*walks with a lazy, lagging step*). My leg is gone to sleep (*goes off*).

DORN. She will go and have a couple of glasses before lunch.

SORIN. She has no personal happiness, poor thing.

DORN. Nonsense, your Excellency.

SORIN. You argue like a man who has had all he wants.

MADAME ARKADIN. Oh, what can be more boring than this sweet country boredom! Hot, still, no one ever doing anything, everyone airing their theories.

. . . It's nice being with you, my friends, charming to listen to you, but . . .
to sit in a hotel room somewhere and learn one's part is ever so much better.

NINA (*enthusiastically*). Delightful! I understand you.

SORIN. Of course, it's better in town. You sit in your study, the footman
lets no one in unannounced, there's a telephone . . . in the streets there are
cabs and everything. . . .

DORN (*hums*). "Tell her, my flowers."

(ENTER SHAMRAEV, *and after him* POLINA ANDREYEVNA.)

SHAMRAEV. Here they are! Good morning! (*kisses* MADAME ARKADIN's *hand
and then* NINA's). Delighted to see you in good health. (*To* MADAME ARKA-
DIN) My wife tells me that you are proposing to drive into town with her
to-day. Is that so?

MADAME ARKADIN. Yes, we are thinking of it.

SHAMRAEV. Hm! that's splendid, but how are you going, honoured lady?
They are carting the rye to-day; all the men are at work. What horses are you
to have, allow me to ask?

MADAME ARKADIN. What horses? How can I tell which?

SORIN. We've got carriage horses.

SHAMRAEV (*growing excited*). Carriage horses! But where am I to get
collars for them? Where am I to get collars? It's a strange thing! It passes
my understanding! Honoured lady! forgive me, I am full of reverence for
your talent. I would give ten years of my life for you, but I cannot let you
have the horses!

MADAME ARKADIN. But if I have to go! It's a queer thing!

SHAMRAEV. Honoured lady! you don't know what farming means.

MADAME ARKADIN (*flaring up*). That's the old story! If that's so, I go back
to Moscow to-day. Give orders for horses to be hired for me at the village,
or I'll walk to the station.

SHAMRAEV (*flaring up*). In that case I resign my position! You must look
for another steward (*goes off*).

MADAME ARKADIN. It's like this every summer; every summer I am insulted
here! I won't set my foot in the place again (*goes off at left where the bathing
shed is supposed to be; a minute later she can be seen entering the house.*
TRIGORIN *follows her, carrying fishing rods and tackle, and a pail*).

SORIN (*flaring up*). This is insolence! It's beyond everything. I am thoroughly sick of it. Send all the horses here this minute!

NINA (*to* POLINA ANDREYEVNA). To refuse Irina Nikolayevna, the famous
actress! Any wish of hers, any whim even, is of more consequence than all your
farming. It's positively incredible!

POLINA (*in despair*). What can I do? Put yourself in my position: what can
I do?

SORIN (*to* NINA). Let us go to my sister. We will all entreat her not to go
away. Won't we? (*Looking in the direction in which* SHAMRAEV *has gone.*)
Insufferable man! Despot!

NINA (*preventing him from getting up*). Sit still, sit still. We will wheel you in. (*She and* MEDVEDENKO *push the bath-chair.*) Oh, how awful it is!

SORIN. Yes, yes, it's awful. But he won't leave, I'll speak to him directly. (*They go out;* DORN *and* POLINA ANDREYEVNA *are left alone on the stage.*)

DORN. People are tiresome. Your husband ought to be simply kicked out, but it will end in that old woman Pyotr' Nikolayevitch and his sister begging the man's pardon. You will see!

POLINA. He has sent the carriage horses into the fields too! And there are misunderstandings like this every day. If you only knew how it upsets me! It makes me ill; see how I am trembling. . . . I can't endure his rudeness. (*In an imploring voice*) Yevgeny, dearest, light of my eyes, my darling, let me come to you. . . . Our time is passing, we are no longer young, and if only we could lay aside concealment and lying for the end of our lives, anyway . . . (*a pause*).

DORN. I am fifty-five; it's too late to change my life.

POLINA. I know you refuse me because there are other women too who are as near to you. You can't take them all to live with you. I understand. Forgive me, you are tired of me.

(NINA *appears near the house; she is picking flowers.*)

DORN. No, it's all right.

POLINA. I am wretched from jealousy. Of course you are a doctor, you can't avoid women. I understand.

DORN (*to* NINA, *who comes up to them*). How are things going?

NINA. Irina Nikolayevna is crying and Pyotr Nikolayevitch has an attack of asthma.

DORN (*gets up*). I'd better go and give them both valerian drops.

NINA (*gives him the flowers*). Please take these.

DORN. *Merci bien* (*goes towards the house*).

POLINA (*going with him*). What charming flowers! (*Near the house, in a smothered voice*) Give me those flowers! Give me those flowers! (*On receiving them tears the flowers to pieces and throws them away; both go into the house.*)

NINA (*alone*). How strange it is to see a famous actress cry, and about such a trivial thing! And isn't it strange? A famous author, adored by the public, written about in all the papers, his photographs for sale, his works translated into foreign languages—and he spends the whole day fishing and is delighted that he has caught two gudgeon. I thought famous people were proud, unapproachable, that they despised the crowd, and by their fame and the glory of their name, as it were, revenged themselves on the vulgar herd for putting rank and wealth above everything. But here they cry and fish, play cards, laugh and get cross like everyone else!

TREPLEV (*comes in without a hat on, with a gun and a dead sea-gull*). Are you alone here?

NINA. Yes.

(TREPLEV *lays the sea-gull at her feet.*)

NINA. What does that mean?

TREPLEV. I was so mean as to kill this bird to-day. I lay it at your feet.

NINA. What is the matter with you? (*Picks up the bird and looks at it.*)

TREPLEV (*after a pause*). Soon I shall kill myself in the same way.

NINA. You have so changed, I hardly know you.

TREPLEV. Yes, ever since the day when I hardly knew you. You have changed to me, your eyes are cold, you feel me in the way.

NINA. You have become irritable of late, you express yourself so incomprehensibly, as it were in symbols. This bird is a symbol too, I suppose, but forgive me, I don't understand it (*lays the sea-gull on the seat*). I am too simple to understand you.

TREPLEV. This began from that evening when my play came to grief so stupidly. Women never forgive failure. I have burnt it all; every scrap of it. If only you knew how miserable I am! Your growing cold to me is awful, incredible, as though I had woken up and found this lake had suddenly dried up or sunk into the earth. You have just said that you are too simple to understand me. Oh, what is there to understand? My play was not liked, you despise my inspiration, you already consider me commonplace, insignificant, like so many others . . . (*stamping*). How well I understand it all, how I understand it! I feel as though I had a nail in my brain, damnation take it together with my vanity which is sucking away my life, sucking it like a snake . . . (*sees* TRIGORIN, *who comes in reading a book*). Here comes the real genius, walking like Hamlet and with a book too. (*Mimics*) "Words, words, words." . . . The sun has scarcely reached you and you are smiling already, your eyes are melting in its rays. I won't be in your way (*goes off quickly*).

TRIGORIN (*making notes in his book*). Takes snuff and drinks vodka. Always in black. The schoolmaster is in love with her. . . .

NINA. Good morning, Boris Alexeyevitch!

TRIGORIN. Good morning. Circumstances have turned out so unexpectedly that it seems we are setting off to-day. We are hardly likely to meet again. I am sorry. I don't often have the chance of meeting young girls, youthful and charming; I have forgotten how one feels at eighteen or nineteen and can't picture it to myself, and so the young girls in my stories and novels are usually false. I should like to be in your shoes just for one hour to find out how you think, and altogether what sort of person you are.

NINA. And I should like to be in your shoes.

TRIGORIN. What for?

NINA. To know what it feels like to be a famous, gifted author. What does it feel like to be famous? How does it affect you, being famous?

TRIGORIN. How? Nohow, I believe. I have never thought about it. (*After a moment's thought*) It's one of two things: either you exaggerate my fame, or it never is felt at all.

NINA. But if you read about yourself in the newspapers?

TRIGORIN. When they praise me I am pleased, and when they abuse me I feel out of humour for a day or two.

NINA. What a wonderful world! If only you knew how I envy you! How different people's lots in life are! Some can scarcely get through their dull, obscure existence, they are all just like one another, they are all unhappy; while others—you, for instance—you are one out of a million, have an interesting life full of brightness and significance. You are happy.

TRIGORIN. I? (shrugging his shoulders) Hm. . . . You talk of fame and happiness, of bright interesting life, but to me all those fine words, if you will forgive my saying so, are just like a sweetmeat which I never taste. You are very young and very good-natured.

NINA. Your life is splendid!

TRIGORIN. What is there particularly nice in it? (Looks at his watch) I must go and write directly. Excuse me, I mustn't stay . . . (laughs). You have stepped on my favourite corn, as the saying is, and here I am beginning to get excited and a little cross. Let us talk though. We will talk about my splendid bright life. . . . Well, where shall we begin? (After thinking a little) There are such things as fixed ideas, when a man thinks days and night, for instance, of nothing but the moon. And I have just such a moon. I am haunted day and night by one persistent thought: I ought to be writing, I ought to be writing, I ought . . . I have scarcely finished one novel when, for some reason, I must begin writing another, then a third, after the third a fourth. I write incessantly, post haste, and I can't write in any other way. What is there splendid and bright in that, I ask you? Oh, it's an absurd life! Here I am with you; I am excited, yet every moment I remember that my unfinished novel is waiting for me. Here I see a cloud that looks like a grand piano. I think that I must put into a story somewhere that a cloud sailed by that looked like a grand piano. There is a scent of heliotrope. I hurriedly make a note: a sickly smell, a widow's flower, to be mentioned in the description of a summer evening. I catch up myself and you at every sentence, every word, and make haste to put those sentences and words away into my literary treasure-house— it may come in useful! When I finish work I race off to the theatre or to fishing; if only I could rest in that and forget myself. But no, there's a new subject rolling about in my head like a heavy iron cannon ball, and I am drawn to my writing table and must make haste again to go on writing and writing. And it's always like that, always. And I have no rest from myself, and I feel that I am eating up my own life, and that for the sake of the honey I give to someone in space I am stripping the pollen from my best flowers, tearing up the flowers themselves and trampling on their roots. Don't you think I am mad? Do my friends and acquaintances treat me as though I were sane? "What are you writing? What are you giving us?" It's the same thing again and again, and it seems to me as though my friends' notice, their praises, their enthusiasm—that it's all a sham, that they are deceiving me as an invalid and I am somehow afraid that they will steal up to me from behind, snatch me and carry me off and put me in a mad-house. And in those years, the best years of my youth, when I was beginning, my writing was unmixed torture. A small writer, particularly when he is not successful, seems to himself clumsy, awkward, unnecessary; his nerves are strained and overwrought. He can't resist hanging about people connected with literature and art, unrecognised and unnoticed by anyone, afraid to look anyone boldly in the face, like a passionate gambler without any money. I hadn't seen my reader, but for some reason I always imagined him hostile, and mistrustful. I was afraid of the public, it alarmed me, and when I had to produce my first play it always seemed to me that all the dark people felt hostile and all the fair ones were coldly indifferent. Oh, how awful it was! What agony it was!

NINA. But surely inspiration and the very process of creation give you moments of exalted happiness?

TRIGORIN. Yes. While I am writing I enjoy it. And I like reading my proofs, but . . . as soon as it is published I can't endure it, and I see that it is all wrong, a mistake, that it ought not to have been written at all, and I feel vexed and sick about it . . . (laughing). And the public reads it and says: "Yes, charming, clever. Charming, but very inferior to Tolstoy," or, "It's a fine thing, but Turgenev's 'Fathers and Children' is finer." And It will be the same to my dying day, only charming and clever, charming and clever—and nothing more. And when I die my friends, passing by my tomb, will say, "Here lies Trigorin. He was a good writer, but inferior to Turgenev."

NINA. Forgive me, but I refuse to understand you. You are simply spoiled by success.

TRIGORIN. What success? I have never liked myself; I dislike my own work. The worst of it is that I am in a sort of delirium, and often don't understand what I am writing. I love this water here, the trees, the sky. I feel nature, it arouses in me a passionate, irresistible desire to write. But I am not simply a landscape painter; I am also a citizen. I love my native country, my people; I feel that if I am a writer I am in duty bound to write of the people, of their sufferings, of their future, to talk about science and the rights of man and so on, and so on, and I write about everything. I am hurried and flustered, and on all sides they whip me up and are angry with me; I dash about from side to side like a fox beset by hounds. I see life and culture continually getting farther and farther away while I fall farther and farther behind like a peasant too late for the train; and what it comes to is that I feel I can only describe scenes and in everything else I am false to the marrow of my bones.

NINA. You are overworked and have not the leisure nor the desire to appreciate your own significance. You may be dissatisfied with yourself, but for others you are great and splendid! If I were a writer like you, I should give up my whole life to the common herd, but I should know that there could be no greater happiness for them than to rise to my level, and they would harness themselves to my chariot.

TRIGORIN. My chariot, what next! Am I an Agamemnon, or what? (*Both smile.*)

NINA. For such happiness as being a writer or an artist I would be ready to endure poverty, disappointment, the dislike of those around me; I would live in a garret and eat nothing but rye bread, I would suffer from being dissatisfied with myself, from recognising my own imperfections, but I should ask in return for fame . . . real, resounding fame. . . . (*covers her face with her hands*). It makes me dizzy. . . . Ough!

(*The voice of* MADAME ARKADIN *from the house.*)

MADAME ARKADIN. Boris Alexeyevitch!

TRIGORIN. They are calling for me. I suppose it's to pack. But I don't want to leave here. (*Looks round at the lake.*) Just look how glorious it is! It's splendid!

NINA. Do you see the house and garden on the other side of the lake?

TRIGORIN. Yes.

NINA. That house was my dear mother's. I was born there. I have spent all my life beside this lake and I know every little islet on it.

TRIGORIN. It's very delightful here! (*Seeing the sea-gull*) And what's this?

NINA. A sea-gull. Konstantin Gavrilitch shot it.

TRIGORIN. A beautiful bird. Really, I don't want to go away. Try and persuade Irina Nikolayevna to stay (*makes a note in his book*).

NINA. What are you writing?

TRIGORIN. Oh, I am only making a note. A subject struck me (*putting away the note-book*). A subject for a short story: a young girl, such as you, has lived all her life beside a lake; she loves the lake like a sea-gull, and is as free and happy as a sea-gull. But a man comes by chance, sees her, and having nothing better to do, destroys her like that sea-gull here (*a pause*).

(MADAME ARKADIN *appears at the window.*)

MADAME ARKADIN. Boris Alexeyevitch, where are you?

TRIGORIN. I am coming (*goes and looks back at* NINA. *To* MADAME ARKADIN *at the window*) What is it?

MADAME ARKADIN. We are staying.

(TRIGORIN *goes into the house.*)

NINA (*advances to the footlights; after a few moments' meditation*) It's a dream!

CURTAIN.

ACT III

The dining-room in SORIN'S *house. Doors on right and on left. A sideboard.
A medicine cupboard. A table in the middle of the room. A portmanteau
and hat-boxes; signs of preparation for departure.* TRIGORIN *is having
lunch;* MASHA *stands by the table.*

MASHA. I tell all this to you as a writer. You may make use of it. I am
telling you the truth: if he had hurt himself seriously I would not have gone
on living another minute. But I have pluck enough all the same. I just made
up my mind that I would tear this love out of my heart, tear it out by the
roots.

TRIGORIN. How are you going to do that?

MASHA. I am going to be married. To Medvedenko.

TRIGORIN. That's the schoolmaster?

MASHA. Yes.

TRIGORIN. I don't understand what's the object of it.

MASHA. To love without hope, to spend whole years waiting for something.
. . . But when I marry, there will be no time left for love, new cares will
smother all the old feelings. And, anyway, it will be a change, you know. Shall
we have another?

TRIGORIN. Won't that be too much?

MASHA. Oh, come! (*fills two glasses*). Don't look at me like that! Women
drink much oftener than you imagine. Only a small proportion drink openly
as I do, the majority drink in secret. Yes. And it's always vodka or brandy.
(*Clinks glasses*) My best wishes! You are a good-hearted man; I am sorry to
be parting from you. (*They drink.*)

TRIGORIN. I don't want to go myself.

MASHA. You should beg her to stay.

TRIGORIN. No, she won't stay now. Her son is behaving very tactlessly. First,
he shoots himself, and now they say he is going to challenge me to a duel. And
whatever for? He sulks, and snorts, and preaches new forms of art. . . . But
there is room for all—new and old—why quarrel about it?

MASHA. Well, there's jealousy too. But it is nothing to do with me.

(*A pause.* YAKOV *crosses from right to left with a portmanteau.* NINA
enters and stands by the window.)

MASHA. My schoolmaster is not very brilliant, but he is a good-natured
man, and poor, and he is very much in love with me. I am sorry for him. And
I am sorry for his old mother. Well, let me wish you all happiness. Don't
remember evil against me (*shakes hands with him warmly*). I am very grateful for your friendly interest. Send me your books and be sure to put in an

inscription. Only don't write, "To my honoured friend," but write simply, "To Marya who belongs nowhere and has no object in life." Good-bye! (*Goes out.*)

NINA (*stretching out her arm towards* TRIGORIN, *with her fist clenched*). Odd or even?

TRIGORIN. Even.

NINA (*with a sigh*). Wrong. I had only one pea in my hand. I was trying my fortune whether to go on the stage or not. I wish someone would advise me.

TRIGORIN. It's impossible to advise in such a matter (*a pause*).

NINA. We are parting and . . . perhaps we shall never meet again. Won't you please take this little medallion as a parting gift? I had your initials engraved on one side of it . . . and on the other the title of your book, "Days and Nights."

TRIGORIN. How exquisite! (*kisses the medallion*). A charming present!

NINA. Think of me sometimes.

TRIGORIN. I shall think of you. I shall think of you as you were on that sunny day—do you remember?—a week ago, when you were wearing a light dress . . . we were talking . . . there was a white sea-gull lying on the seat.

NINA (*pensively*). Yes, a sea-gull . . (*a pause*). We can't talk any more, there's someone coming. . . . Let me have two minutes before you go, I entreat you . . . (*goes out on the left*).

(*At the same instant* MADAME ARKADIN, SORIN *in a dress coat with a star of some order on it, then* YAKOV, *occupied with the luggage, enter on the right.*)

MADAME ARKADIN. Stay at home, old man. With your rheumatism you ought not to go gadding about (*To* TRIGORIN) Who was that went out? Nina?

TRIGORIN. Yes.

MADAME ARKADIN. *Pardon*, we interrupted you (*sits down*). I believe I have packed everything. I am worn out.

TRIGORIN (*reads on the medallion*). " 'Days and Nights,' page 121, lines 11 and 12."

YAKOV (*clearing the table*). Am I to pack your fishing things too, sir?

TRIGORIN. Yes, I shall want them again. You can give away the hooks.

YAKOV. Yes, sir.

TRIGORIN (*to himself*). Page 121, lines 11 and 12. What is there in those lines? (*To* MADAME ARKADIN) Are there copies of my books in the house?

MADAME ARKADIN. Yes, in my brother's study, in the corner bookcase.

TRIGORIN. Page 121 . . . (*goes out*).

MADAME ARKADIN. Really, Petrusha, you had better stay at home.

SORIN. You are going away; it will be dreary for me at home without you.

MADAME ARKADIN. And what is there in the town?

SORIN. Nothing particular, but still . . . (*laughs*). There will be the laying of the foundation-stone of the Zemstvo-hall, and all that sort of thing. One longs to shake oneself free from this stagnant existence, if only for an hour or two. I've been too long on the shelf like some old cigarette-holder. I have ordered the horses for one o'clock; we'll set off at the same time.

MADAME ARKADIN (*after a pause*). Come, stay here, don't be bored and don't catch cold. Look after my son. Take care of him. Give him good advice (*a pause*). Here I am going away and I shall never know why Konstantin tried to shoot himself. I fancy jealousy was the chief cause, and the sooner I get Trigorin away from here, the better.

SORIN. What can I say? There were other reasons too. It's easy to understand; he is young, intelligent, living in the country, in the wilds, with no money, no position and no future. He has nothing to do. He is ashamed of his idleness and afraid of it. I am very fond of him indeed, and he is attached to me, yet in spite of it all he feels he is superfluous in the house, that he is a dependent, a poor relation. It's easy to understand, it's *amour propre*. . . .

MADAME ARKADIN. He is a great anxiety to me! (*Pondering*) He might go into the service, perhaps.

SORIN (*begins to whistle, then irresolutely*). I think that quite the best thing would be if you were to . . . let him have a little money. In the first place he ought to be able to be dressed like other people and all that. Just look at him, he's been going about in the same wretched jacket for the last three years and he has no overcoat . . . (*laughs*). It would do him no harm to have a little fun . . . to go abroad or something. . . . It wouldn't cost much.

MADAME ARKADIN. But all the same . . . I might manage the suit, perhaps, but as for going abroad . . . No, just at the moment I can't even manage the suit. (*Resolutely*) I have no money!

(SORIN *laughs*.)

MADAME ARKADIN. No!

SORIN (*begins to whistle*). Quite so. Forgive me, my dear, don't be cross. I believe you. . . . You are a generous, noble-hearted woman.

MADAME ARKADIN (*weeping*). I have no money.

SORIN. If I had money, of course I would give him some myself, but I have nothing, not a half-penny (*laughs*). My steward takes all my pension and spends it all on the land and the cattle and the bees, and my money is all wasted. The bees die, and the cows die, they never let me have horses. . . .

MADAME ARKADIN. Yes, I have money, but you see I am an actress; my dresses alone are enough to ruin me.

SORIN. You are a kind, good creature . . . I respect you. . . . Yes . . . but there, I got a touch of it again . . . (*staggers*). I feel dizzy (*clutches at the table*). I feel ill and all that.

MADAME ARKADIN (*alarmed*). Petrusha! (*trying to support him*). Petrusha, my dear! (*Calling*) Help! help!

(*Enter* TREPLEV *with a bandage round his head and* MEDVEDENKO.)

MADAME ARKADIN. He feels faint!

SORIN. It's all right, it's all right! (*smiles and drinks some water*). It's passed off . . . and all that.

TREPLEV (*to his mother*). Don't be frightened, mother, it's not serious. Uncle often has these attacks now. (*To his uncle*) You must lie down, uncle.

SORIN. For a little while, yes. . . . But I am going to the town all the same. . . . I'll lie down a little and then set off. . . . It's quite natural (*goes out leaning on his stick*).

MEDVEDENKO (*gives him his arm*). There's a riddle: in the morning on four legs, at noon on two, in the evening on three. . . .

SORIN (*laughs*). Just so. And at night on the back. Thank you, I can manage alone. . . .

MEDVEDENKO. Oh come, why stand on ceremony! (*Goes out with* SORIN.)

MADAME ARKADIN. How he frightened me!

TREPLEV. It is not good for him to live in the country. He gets depressed. If you would be generous for once, mother, and lend him fifteen hundred or two thousand roubles, he could spend a whole year in town.

MADAME ARKADIN. I have no money. I am an actress, not a banker (*a pause*).

TREPLEV. Mother, change my bandage. You do it so well.

MADAME ARKADIN (*takes out of the medicine cupboard some iodoform and a box with bandaging material*). The doctor is late.

TREPLEV. He promised to be here at ten, and it is midday already.

MADAME ARKADIN. Sit down (*takes the bandage off his head*). It's like a turban. Yesterday a stranger asked in the kitchen what nationality you were. But you have almost completely healed. There is the merest trifle left (*kisses him on the head*). You won't do anything naughty again while I am away, will you?

TREPLEV. No, mother. It was a moment of mad despair when I could not control myself. It won't happen again. (*Kisses her hand*) You have such clever hands. I remember, long ago, when you were still acting at the Imperial Theatre—I was little then—there was a fight in our yard and a washerwoman, one of the tenants, was badly beaten. Do you remember? She was picked up senseless . . . you looked after her, took her remedies and washed her children in a tub. Don't you remember?

MADAME ARKADIN. No (*puts on a fresh bandage*).

TREPLEV. Two ballet dancers lived in the same house as we did at the time . . . They used to come to you and have coffee. . . .

MADAME ARKADIN. I remember that.

TREPLEV. They were very pious (*a pause*). Just lately, these last days, I have loved you as tenderly and completely as when I was a child. I have no one left now but you. Only why, why do you give yourself up to the influence of that man?

MADAME ARKADIN. You don't understand him, Konstantin. He is a very noble character. . . .

TREPLEV. And yet when he was told I was going to challenge him, the nobility of his character did not prevent him from funking it. He is going away. Ignominious flight!

MADAME ARKADIN. What nonsense! It is I who am asking him to go.

TREPLEV. A very noble character! Here you and I are almost quarrelling over him, and at this very moment he is somewhere in the drawing-room or the garden laughing at us . . . developing Nina, trying to convince her finally that he is a genius.

MADAME ARKADIN. You take a pleasure in saying unpleasant things to me. I respect that man and beg you not to speak ill of him before me.

TREPLEV. And I don't respect him. You want me to think him a genius too, but forgive me, I can't tell lies, his books make me sick.

MADAME ARKADIN. That's envy. There's nothing left for people who have pretension without talent but to attack real talent. Much comfort in that, I must say!

TREPLEV (*ironically*). Real talent! (*Wrathfully*) I have more talent than all of you put together if it comes to that! (*tears the bandage off his head*). You, with your hackneyed conventions, have usurped the supremacy in art and consider nothing real and legitimate but what you do yourselves; everything else you stifle and suppress. I don't believe in you! I don't believe in you or in him!

MADAME ARKADIN. Decadent!

TREPLEV. Get away to your charming theatre and act there in your paltry, stupid plays!

MADAME ARKADIN. I have never acted in such plays. Let me alone! You are not capable of writing even a wretched burlesque! You are nothing but a Kiev shopman! living on other people!

TREPLEV. You miser!

MADAME ARKADIN. You ragged beggar!

(TREPLEV *sits down and weeps quietly.*)

MADAME ARKADIN. Nonentity! (*walking up and down in agitation*). Don't cry. . . . You mustn't cry (*weeps*). Don't . . . (*kisses him on the forehead, on the cheeks and on the head*). My dear child, forgive me. . . . Forgive your sinful mother. Forgive me, you know I am wretched.

TREPLEV (*puts his arms round her*). If only you knew! I have lost everything! She does not love me, and now I cannot write . . . all my hopes are gone. . .

MADAME ARKADIN. Don't despair . . Everything will come right. He is going away directly, she will love you again (*wipes away his tears*). Give over. We have made it up now.

TREPLEV (*kisses her hands*). Yes, mother.

MADAME ARKADIN (*tenderly*). Make it up with him too. You don't want a duel, do you?

TREPLEV. Very well. Only, mother, do allow me not to meet him. It's pain-

ful to me—it's more than I can bear. (*Enter* TRIGORIN.) Here he is . . . I am
going . . . (*rapidly puts away the dressings in the cupboard*). The doctor
will do the bandaging now.

TRIGORIN (*looking in a book*). Page 121 . . . lines 11 and 12. Here it is
(*Reads*): "If ever my life can be of use to you, come and take it."

(TREPLEV *picks up the bandage from the floor and goes out.*)

MADAME ARKADIN (*looking at her watch*). The horses will soon be here.

TRIGORIN (*to himself*). "If ever my life can be of use to you, come and take
it."

MADAME ARKADIN. I hope all your things are packed?

TRIGORIN (*impatiently*). Yes, yes. (*Musing*) Why is it that I feel so much
sorrow in that appeal from a pure soul and that it wrings my heart so pain-
fully? "If ever my life can be of use to you, come and take it." (*To* MADAME
ARKADIN) Let us stay one day longer.

(MADAME ARKADIN *shakes her head.*)

TRIGORIN. Let us stay!

MADAME ARKADIN. Darling, I know what keeps you here. But have control
over yourself. You are a little intoxicated, try to be sober.

TRIGORIN. You be sober too, be sensible and reasonable, I implore you; look
at it all as a true friend should. (*Presses her hand*) You are capable of sacrifice. Be a friend to me, let me be free!

MADAME ARKADIN (*in violent agitation*). Are you so enthralled?

TRIGORIN. I am drawn to her! Perhaps it is just what 1 need.

MADAME ARKADIN. The love of a provincial girl? Oh, how little you know
yourself!

TRIGORIN. Sometimes people sleep as they talk—that's how it is with me, I
am talking to you and yet I am asleep and dreaming of her. . . . I am possessed by sweet, marvellous dreams. . . . Let me be free. . . .

MADAME ARKADIN (*trembling*). No, no! I am an ordinary woman, you
can't talk like that to me. Don't torture me, Boris. It terrifies me.

TRIGORIN. If you cared to, you could be not ordinary. Love—youthful,
charming, poetical, lifting one into a world of dreams—that's the only thing in
life that can give happiness! I have never yet known a love like that. . . . In
my youth I never had time, I was always hanging about the editors' offices,
struggling with want. Now it is here, that love, it has come, it beckons to me.
What sense is there in running away from it?

MADAME ARKADIN (*wrathfully*). You have gone mad!

TRIGORIN. Well, let me?

MADAME ARKADIN. You are all in a conspiracy together to torment me
to-day! (*weeps*).

TRIGORIN (*clutching at his heart*). She does not understand! She won't
understand!

MADAME ARKADIN. Am I so old and ugly that you don't mind talking of
other women to me? (*Puts her arms round him and kisses him.*) Oh, you are

mad! My wonderful, splendid darling. . . . You are the last page of my life! (*falls on her knees*). My joy, my pride, my bliss! . . . (*embraces his knees*). If you forsake me even for one hour I shall not survive it, I shall go mad, my marvellous, magnificent one, my master. . .

TRIGORIN. Someone may come in (*helps her to get up*).

MADAME ARKADIN. Let them, I am not ashamed of my love for you (*kisses his hands*). My treasure, you desperate boy, you want to be mad, but I won't have it, I won't let you . . . (*laughs*). You are mine . . . mine. . . . This forehead is mine, and these eyes, and this lovely silky hair is mine too . . . you are mine all over. You are so gifted, so clever, the best of all modern writers, you are the one hope of Russia. . . . You have so much truthfulness, simplicity, freshness, healthy humour. . . . In one touch you can give all the essential characteristics of a person or a landscape, your characters are living. One can't read you without delight! You think this is exaggerated? That I am flattering you? But look into my eyes . . . look. . . . Do I look like a liar? You see, I am the only one who can appreciate you; I am the only one who tells you the truth, my precious, wonderful darling. . . . Are you coming? Yes? You won't abandon me? . . .

TRIGORIN. I have no will of my own . . . I have never had a will of my own. . . . Flabby, feeble, always submissive—how can a woman care for such a man? Take me, carry me off, but don't let me move a step away from you. . . .

MADAME ARKADIN (*to herself*). Now he is mine! (*In an easy tone as though nothing had happened*) But, of course, if you like, you can stay. I'll go by myself and you can come afterwards, a week later. After all, why should you be in a hurry?

TRIGORIN. No, we may as well go together.

MADAME ARKADIN. As you please. Let us go together then (*a pause*).

(TRIGORIN *makes a note.*)

MADAME ARKADIN. What are you writing?

TRIGORIN. I heard a good name this morning, "The Maiden's Forest." It may be of use (*stretches*). So we are to go then? Again there will be railway carriages, stations, refreshment bars, mutton chops, conversations. . . .

SHAMRAEV (*enters*). I have the honour to announce, with regret, that the horses are ready. It's time, honoured lady, to set off for the station; the train comes in at five minutes past two. So please do me a favour, Irina Nikolayevna, do not forget to inquire what has become of the actor Suzdaltsev. Is he alive and well? We used to drink together at one time. . . . In "The Plundered Mail" he used to play incomparably . . . I remember the tragedian Izmaïlov, also a remarkable personality, acted with him in Elisavetograd. . . . Don't be in a hurry, honoured lady, you need not start for five minutes. Once they were acting conspirators in a melodrama and when they were suddenly discovered Izmaïlov had to say, "We are caught in a trap," but he said, "We are caught in a tap!" (*Laughs*) A tap!

(*While he is speaking* YAKOV *is busy looking after the luggage. The maid brings* MADAME ARKADIN *her hat, her coat, her umbrella and her gloves; they all help* MADAME ARKADIN *to put on her things. The man-cook looks in at the door on left and after some hesitation comes in. Enter* POLINA ANDREYEVNA, *then* SORIN *and* MEDVEDENKO.)

POLINA (*with a basket*). Here are some plums for the journey. . . . Very sweet ones. You may be glad to have something nice. . . .

MADAME ARKADIN. You are very kind, Polina Andreyevna.

POLINA. Good-bye, my dear! If anything has not been to your liking, forgive it (*weeps*).

MADAME ARKADIN (*embraces her*). Everything has been nice, everything! But you mustn't cry.

POLINA. The time flies so fast!

MADAME ARKADIN. There's no help for it.

SORIN (*in a great-coat with a cape to it, with his hat on and a stick in his hand, enters from door on left, crossing the stage*). Sister, it's time to start, or you may be too late after all. I am going to get into the carriage (*goes out*).

MEDVEDENKO. And I shall walk to the station . . . to see you off. I'll be there in no time . . . (*goes out*).

MADAME ARKADIN. Good-bye, dear friends. . . . If we are all alive and well, we shall meet again next summer. (*The maid, the cook and* YAKOV *kiss her hand.*) Don't forget me. (*Gives the cook a rouble*) Here's a rouble for the three of you.

THE COOK. We humbly thank you, madam! Good journey to you! We are very grateful for your kindness!

YAKOV. May God give you good luck!

SHAMRAEV. You might rejoice our hearts with a letter! Good-bye, Boris Alexeyevitch!

MADAME ARKADIN. Where is Konstantin? Tell him that I am starting; I must say good-bye. Well, don't remember evil against me. (*To* YAKOV) I gave the cook a rouble. It's for the three of you.

(*All go out on right. The stage is empty. Behind the scenes the noise that is usual when people are being seen off. The maid comes back to fetch the basket of plums from the table and goes out again.*)

TRIGORIN (*coming back*). I have forgotten my stick. I believe it is out there, on the verandah (*goes and, at door on left meets* NINA *who is coming in*). Is that you? We are going. . . .

NINA. I felt that we should see each other once more. (*Excitedly*) Boris Alexeyevitch, I have come to a decision, the die is cast, I am going on the stage. I shall be gone from here to-morrow; I am leaving my father, I am abandoning everything, I am beginning a new life. Like you, I am going . . . to Moscow. We shall meet there.

TRIGORIN (*looking round*). Stay at the "Slavyansky Bazaar" . . . Let me

know at once . . . Molchanovka, Groholsky House. . . . I am in a hurry
. . (*a pause*).

NINA. One minute more. . . .

TRIGORIN (*in an undertone*). You are so lovely. . . . Oh, what happiness
to think that we shall see each other soon! (*She sinks on his breast.*) I shall
see again those wonderful eyes, that inexpressibly beautiful tender smile . . .
those soft features, the expression of angelic purity. . . . My darling . . .
(*a prolonged kiss*).

CURTAIN.

(*Between the Third and Fourth Acts there is an interval of two years.*)

ACT IV

One of the drawing-rooms in SORIN'S *house, which has been turned into a
study for* KONSTANTIN TREPLEV. *On the right and left, doors leading to
inner apartments. In the middle, glass door leading on to the verandah.
Besides the usual drawing-room furniture there is, in corner on right, a
writing table, near door on left, a sofa, a bookcase and books in windows
and on the chairs. Evening. There is a single lamp alight with a shade on
it. It is half dark. There is the sound of the trees rustling, and the wind
howling in the chimney. A watchman is tapping. Enter* MEDVEDENKO
and MASHA.

MASHA (*calling*). Konstantin Gavrilitch! Konstantin Gavrilitch! (*Looking
round*) No, there is no one here. The old man keeps asking every minute,
where is Kostya, where is Kostya? He cannot live without him. . . .

MEDVEDENKO. He is afraid of being alone. (*Listening*) What awful weather!
This is the second day of it.

MASHA (*turns up the lamp*). There are waves on the lake. Great big ones.

MEDVEDENKO. How dark it is in the garden! We ought to have told them to
break up that stage in the garden. It stands as bare and ugly as a skeleton, and
the curtain flaps in the wind. When I passed it yesterday evening, it seemed as
though someone were crying in it.

MASHA. What next . . . . (*a pause*).

MEDVEDENKO. Let us go home, Masha.

MASHA (*shakes her head*). I shall stay here for the night.

MEDVEDENKO (*in an imploring voice*). Masha, do come! Our baby must be
hungry.

MASHA. Nonsense. Matryona will feed him (*a pause*).

MEDVEDENKO. I am sorry for him. He has been three nights now without
his mother.

MASHA. You are a bore. In old days you used at least to discuss general subjects, but now it is only home, baby, home, baby—that's all one can get out of you.

MEDVEDENKO. Come along, Masha!

MASHA. Go by yourself.

MEDVEDENKO. Your father won't let me have a horse.

MASHA. Yes, he will. You ask, and he will.

MEDVEDENKO. Very well, I'll ask. Then you will come to-morrow?

MASHA (*taking a pinch of snuff*). Very well, to-morrow. How you pester me.

(*Enter* TREPLEV *and* POLINA ANDREYEVNA; TREPLEV *brings in pillows and a quilt, and* POLINA ANDREYEVNA *sheets and pillow-cases; they lay them on the sofa, then* TREPLEV *goes to his table and sits down.*)

MASHA. What's this for, mother?

POLINA. Pyotr Nikolayevitch asked us to make a bed for him in Kostya's room.

MASHA. Let me do it (*makes the bed*).

POLINA (*sighing*). Old people are like children (*goes up to the writing table, and leaning on her elbow, looks at the manuscript; a pause*).

MEDVEDENKO. Well, I am going then. Good-bye, Masha (*kisses his wife's hand*). Good-bye, mother (*tries to kiss his mother-in-law's hand*).

POLINA (*with vexation*). Come, if you are going, go.

MEDVEDENKO. Good-bye, Konstantin Gavrilitch.

(TREPLEV *gives him his hand without speaking;* MEDVEDENKO *goes out.*)

POLINA (*looking at the MS.*). No one would have guessed or thought that you would have become a real author, Kostya. And now, thank God, they send you money from the magazines. (*Passes her hand over his hair*) And you have grown good-looking too. . . . Dear, good Kostya, do be a little kinder to my Mashenka!

MASHA (*as she makes the bed*). Leave him alone, mother.

POLINA (*to* TREPLEV). She is a nice little thing (*a pause*). A woman wants nothing, you know, Kostya, so long as you give her a kind look. I know from myself.

(TREPLEV *gets up from the table and walks away without speaking.*)

MASHA. Now you have made him angry. What induced you to pester him?

POLINA. I feel so sorry for you, Mashenka.

MASHA. Much use that is!

POLINA. My heart aches for you. I see it all, you know, I understand it all.

MASHA. It's all foolishness. There is no such thing as hopeless love except in novels. It's of no consequence. The only thing is one mustn't let oneself go and keep expecting something, waiting for the tide to turn. . . . When love gets into the heart there is nothing to be done but to clear it out. Here they promised to transfer my husband to another district. As soon as I am there, I shall forget it all. . . . I shall tear it out of my heart.

(*Two rooms away a melancholy waltz is played.*)

POLINA. That's Kostya playing. He must be depressed.

MASHA (*noiselessly dances a few waltz steps*). The great thing, mother, is not to have him before one's eyes. If they only give my Semyon his transfer, trust me, I shall get over it in a month. It's all nonsense.

(*Door on left opens.* DORN *and* MEDVEDENKO *wheel in* SORIN *in his chair.*)

MEDVEDENKO. I have six of them at home now. And flour is two kopeks per pound.

DORN. You've got to look sharp to make both ends meet.

MEDVEDENKO. It's all very well for you to laugh. You've got more money than you know what to do with.

DORN. Money? After thirty years of practice, my boy, troublesome work during which I could not call my soul my own by day or by night, I only succeeded in saving two thousand roubles, and that I spent not long ago abroad. I have nothing.

MASHA (*to her husband*). You have not gone?

MEDVEDENKO (*guiltily*). Well, how can I when they won't let me have a horse?

MASHA (*with bitter vexation in an undertone*). I can't bear the sight of you.

(*The wheel-chair remains in the left half of the room;* POLINA ANDRE-YEVNA, MASHA *and* DORN *sit down beside it,* MEDVEDENKO *moves mournfully to one side.*)

DORN. What changes there have been here! The drawing-room has been turned into a study.

MASHA. It is more convenient for Konstantin Gavrilitch to work here. Whenever he likes, he can walk out into the garden and think there.

(*A watchman taps.*)

SORIN. Where is my sister?

DORN. She has gone to the station to meet Trigorin. She will be back directly.

SORIN. Since you thought it necessary to send for my sister, I must be dangerously ill. (*After a silence*) It's a queer thing, I am dangerously ill and here they don't give me any medicines.

DORN. Well, what would you like to have? Valerian drops? Soda? Quinine?

SORIN. Ah, he is at his moralising again! What an infliction it is! (*With a motion of his head towards the sofa*) Is that bed for me?

POLINA. Yes, it's for you, Pyotr Nikolayevitch.

SORIN. Thank you.

DORN (*hums*). "The moon is floating in the midnight sky."

SORIN. I want to give Kostya a subject for a story. It ought to be called "The Man who Wished"—*L'homme qui a voulu*. In my youth I wanted to become a literary man—and didn't; I wanted to speak well—and I spoke horribly badly, (*mimicking himself*) "and all the rest of it, and all that, and so on, and so forth" . . . and I would go plodding on and on, trying to sum up till I was in a regular perspiration; I wanted to get married—and I didn't; I always wanted to live in town and here I am ending my life in the country —and so on.

DORN. I wanted to become an actual civil councillor—and I have.

SORIN (*laughs*). That I had no hankerings after. That happened of itself.

DORN. To be expressing dissatisfaction with life at sixty-two is really ungracious, you know.

SORIN. What a persistent fellow he is! You might understand that one wants to live!

DORN. That's just frivolity. It's the law of nature that every life must have an end.

SORIN. You argue like a man who has had enough. You are satisfied and so you are indifferent to life, nothing matters to you. But even you will be afraid to die.

DORN. The dread of death is an animal fear. One must overcome it. A rational fear of death is only possible for those who believe in eternal life and are conscious of their sins. And you, in the first place, don't believe, and, in the second, what sins have you to worry about? You have served in the courts of justice for twenty-five years—that's all.

SORIN (*laughs*). Twenty-eight. . . .

(TREPLEV *comes in and sits down on a stool at* SORIN's *feet.* MASHA *never takes her eyes off him.*)

DORN. We are hindering Konstantin Gavrilitch from working.

TREPLEV. Oh no, it doesn't matter (*a pause*).

MEDVEDENKO. Allow me to ask you, doctor, what town did you like best abroad?

DORN. Genoa.

TREPLEV. Why Genoa?

DORN. The life in the streets is so wonderful there. When you go out of the hotel in the evening, the whole street is packed with people. You wander aimlessly zigzagging about among the crowd, backwards and forwards; you live with it, are psychologically at one with it and begin almost to believe that a world-soul is really possible, such as was acted by Nina Zaretchny in your play. And, by the way, where is she now? How is she getting on?

TREPLEV. I expect she is quite well.

DORN. I was told that she was leading a rather peculiar life. How was that?

TREPLEV. That's a long story, doctor.

DORN. Well, tell it us shortly (*a pause*).

TREPLEV. She ran away from home and had an affair with Trigorin. You know that?

DORN. I know.

TREPLEV. She had a child. The child died. Trigorin got tired of her and went back to his old ties, as might have been expected. Though, indeed, he had never abandoned them, but in his weak-willed way contrived to keep both going. As far as I can make out from what I have heard, Nina's private life was a complete failure.

DORN. And the stage?

TREPLEV. I fancy that was worse still. She made her début at some holiday place near Moscow, then went to the provinces. All that time I did not lose sight of her, and wherever she went I followed her. She always took big parts, but she acted crudely, without taste, screamingly, with violent gestures. There were moments when she uttered a cry successfully or died successfully, but they were only moments.

DORN. Then she really has some talent?

TREPLEV. It was difficult to make it out. I suppose she has. I saw her but she would not see me, and the servants would not admit me at the hotel. I understood her state of mind and did not insist on seeing her (*a pause*). What more can I tell you? Afterwards, when I was back at home, I had some letters from her—warm, intelligent, interesting letters. She did not complain, but I felt that she was profoundly unhappy; every line betrayed sick overstrained nerves. And her imagination is a little unhinged. She signed herself the Sea-gull. In Pushkin's "Mermaid" the miller says that he is a raven, and in the same way in her letters she kept repeating that she was a sea-gull. Now she is here.

DORN. Here? How do you mean?

TREPLEV. In the town, staying at an inn. She has been there for five days. I did go to see her, and Marya Ilyinishna here went too, but she won't see anyone. Semyon Semyonitch declares he saw her yesterday afternoon in the fields a mile and a half from here.

MEDVEDENKO. Yes, I saw her. She went in that direction, towards the town. I bowed to her and asked her why she did not come to see us. She said she would come.

TREPLEV. She won't come (*a pause*). Her father and stepmother refuse to recognise her. They have put watchmen about so that she may not even go near the house (*walks away with the doctor towards the writing table*). How easy it is to be a philosopher on paper, doctor, and how difficult it is in life!

SORIN. She was a charming girl.

DORN. What?

SORIN. She was a charming girl, I say. Actual Civil Councillor Sorin was positively in love with her for a time.

DORN. The old Lovelace.

(SHAMRAEV'S *laugh is heard.*)

POLINA. I fancy our people have come back from the station. . . .

TREPLEV. Yes, I hear mother.

(*Enter* MADAME ARKADIN, TRIGORIN *and with them* SHAMRAEV.)

SHAMRAEV (*as he enters*). We all grow old and dilapidated under the influence of the elements, while you, honoured lady, are still young . . . a light blouse, sprightliness, grace. . . .

MADAME ARKADIN. You want to bring me ill-luck again, you tiresome man!

TRIGORIN. How do you do, Pyotr Nikolayevitch! So you are still poorly? That's bad! (*Seeing* MASHA, *joyfully*) Marya Ilyinishna!

MASHA. You know me, do you? (*shakes hands*).

TRIGORIN. Married?

MASHA. Long ago.

TRIGORIN. Are you happy? (*Bows to* DORN *and* MEDVEDENKO, *then hesitatingly approaches* TREPLEV) Irina Nikolayevna has told me that you have forgotten the past and are no longer angry.

(TREPLEV *holds out his hand.*)

MADAME ARKADIN (*to her son*). Boris Alexeyevitch has brought the magazine with your new story in it.

TREPLEV (*taking the magizine, to* TRIGORIN). Thank you, you are very kind. (*They sit down.*)

TRIGORIN. Your admirers send their greetings to you. . . . In Petersburg and Moscow there is great interest in your work and I am continually being asked questions about you. People ask what you are like, how old you are, whether you are dark or fair. Everyone imagines, for some reason, that you are no longer young. And no one knows your real name, as you always publish under a pseudonym. You are as mysterious as the Iron Mask.

TREPLEV. Will you be able to make a long stay?

TRIGORIN. No, I think I must go back to Moscow to-morrow. I am obliged to. I am in a hurry to finish my novel, and besides, I have promised something for a collection of tales that is being published. It's the old story, in fact.

(*While they are talking* MADAME ARKADIN *and* POLINA ANDREYEVNA *put a card-table in the middle of the room and open it out.* SHAMRAEV *lights candles and sets chairs. A game of lotto is brought out of the cupboard.*)

TRIGORIN. The weather has not given me a friendly welcome. There is a cruel wind. If it has dropped by to-morrow morning I shall go to the lake to fish. And I must have a look at the garden and that place where—you remember?—your play was acted. I've got a subject for a story, I only want to revive my recollections of the scene in which it is laid.

MASHA (*to her father*). Father, let my husband have a horse! He must get home.

SHAMRAEV (*mimicking*). Must get home—a horse! (*Sternly*) You can see for yourself: they have just been to the station. I can't send them out again.

MASHA. But there are other horses. (*Seeing that her father says nothing, waves her hand*) There's no doing anything with you.

MEDVEDENKO. I can walk, Masha. Really. . . .

POLINA (*with a sigh*). Walk in such weather . . . (*sits down to the card-table*). Come, friends.

MEDVEDENKO. It is only four miles. Good-bye (*kisses his wife's hand*).

Good-bye, mother. (*His mother-in-law reluctantly holds out her hand for him to kiss.*) I wouldn't trouble anyone, but the baby . . . (*bows to the company*). Good-bye . . . (*goes out with a guilty step*).

SHAMRAEV. He can walk right enough. He's not a general.

POLINA (*tapping on the table*). Come, friends. Don't let us waste time, we shall soon be called to supper.

(SHAMRAEV, MASHA *and* DORN *sit down at the table.*)

MADAME ARKADIN (*to* TRIGORIN). When the long autumn evenings come on, they play lotto here. Look, it's the same old lotto that we had when our mother used to play with us, when we were children. Won't you have a game before supper? (*sits down to the table with* TRIGORIN). It's a dull game, but it is not so bad when you are used to it (*deals three cards to everyone*).

TREPLEV (*turning the pages of the magazine*). He has read his own story, but he has not even cut mine (*puts the magazine down on the writing table, then goes towards door on left; as he passes his mother he kisses her on the head*).

MADAME ARKADIN. And you, Kostya?

TREPLEV. Excuse me, I would rather not . . . I am going out (*goes out*).

MADAME ARKADIN. The stake is ten kopeks. Put it down for me, doctor, will you?

DORN. Right.

MASHA. Has everyone put down their stakes? I begin . . . Twenty-two.

MADAME ARKADIN. Yes.

MASHA. Three!

DORN. Right!

MASHA. Did you play three? Eight! Eighty-one! Ten!

SHAMRAEV. Don't be in a hurry!

MADAME ARKADIN. What a reception I had in Harkov! My goodness! I feel dizzy with it still.

MASHA. Thirty-four!

(*A melancholy waltz is played behind the scenes.*)

MADAME ARKADIN. The students gave me an ovation. . . Three baskets of flowers . . . two wreaths and this, see (*unfastens a brooch on her throat and lays it on the table*).

SHAMRAEV. Yes, that is a thing. . . .

MASHA. Fifty!

DORN. Exactly fifty?

MADAME ARKADIN. I had a wonderful dress. . . . Whatever I don't know, I do know how to dress.

POLINA. Kostya is playing the piano; he is depressed, poor fellow.

SHAMRAEV. He is awfully abused in the newspapers.

MASHA. Seventy-seven!

MADAME ARKADIN. As though that mattered!

TRIGORIN. He never quite comes off. He has not yet hit upon his own medium. There is always something queer and vague, at times almost like delirium. Not a single living character.

MASHA. Eleven!

MADAME ARKADIN (*looking round at* SORIN). Petrusha, are you bored? (*a pause*). He is asleep.

DORN. The actual civil councillor is asleep.

MASHA. Seven! Ninety!

TRIGORIN. If I lived in such a place, beside a lake, do you suppose I should write? I should overcome this passion and should do nothing but fish.

MASHA. Twenty-eight!

TRIGORIN. Catching perch is so delightful!

DORN. Well, I believe in Konstantin Gavrilitch. There is something in him! There is something in him! He thinks in images; his stories are vivid, full of colour and they affect me strongly. The only pity is that he has not got definite aims. He produces an impression and that's all, but you can't get far with nothing but an impression. Irina Nikolayevna, are you glad that your son is a writer?

MADAME ARKADIN. Only fancy, I have not read anything of his yet. I never have time.

MASHA. Twenty-six!

(TREPLEV *comes in quietly and sits down at his table.*)

SHAMRAEV (*to* TRIGORIN). We have still got something here belonging to you, Boris Alexeyevitch.

TRIGORIN. What's that?

SHAMRAEV. Konstantin Gavrilitch shot a sea-gull and you asked me to get it stuffed for you.

TRIGORIN. I don't remember! (*Pondering*) I don't remember!

MASHA. Sixty-six! One!

TREPLEV (*flinging open the window, listens*). How dark it is! I don't know why I feel so uneasy.

MADAME ARKADIN. Kostya, shut the window, there's a draught.

(TREPLEV *shuts the window.*)

MASHA. Eighty-eight!

TRIGORIN. The game is mine!

MADAME ARKADIN (*gaily*). Bravo, bravo!

SHAMRAEV. Bravo!

MADAME ARKADIN. That man always has luck in everything (*gets up*). And now let us go and have something to eat. Our great man has not dined to-day. We will go on again after supper. (*To her son*) Kostya, leave your manuscripts and come to supper.

TREPLEV. I don't want any, mother, I am not hungry.

MADAME ARKADIN. As you like. (*Wakes* SORIN) Petrusha, supper! (*Takes* SHAMRAEV'S *arm*) I'll tell you about my reception in Harkov.

(POLINA ANDREYEVNA *puts out the candles on the table. Then she and* DORN *wheel the chair. All go out by door on left; only* TREPLEV, *sitting at the writing table, is left on the stage.*)

TREPLEV (*settling himself to write; runs through what he has written already*). I have talked so much about new forms and now I feel that little by little I am falling into a convention myself. (*Reads*) "The placard on the wall proclaimed. . . . The pale face in its setting of dark hair." Proclaimed, setting. That's stupid (*scratches out*). I will begin where the hero is awakened by the patter of the rain, and throw out all the rest. The description of the moonlight evening is long and overelaborate. Trigorin has worked out methods for himself, it's easy for him now. . . . With him the broken bottle neck glitters on the dam and the mill-wheel casts a black shadow—and there you have the moonlight night, while I have the tremulous light, and the soft twinkling of the stars, and the far-away strains of the piano dying away in the still fragrant air. . . . It's agonising (*a pause*). I come more and more to the conviction that it is not a question of new and old forms, but that what matters is that a man should write without thinking about forms at all, write because it springs freely from his soul. (*There is a tap at the window nearest to the table*) What is that? (*looks out of window*). There is nothing to be seen . . . (*opens the glass door and looks out into the garden*). Someone ran down the steps. (*Calls*) Who is there? (*Goes out and can be heard walking rapidly along the verandah; returns half a minute later with* NINA ZARETCHNY). Nina, Nina!

(NINA *lays her head on his breast and weeps with subdued sobs.*)

TREPLEV (*moved*). Nina! Nina! It's you . . . you. . . . It's as though I had foreseen it, all day long my heart has been aching and restless (*takes off her hat and cape*). Oh, my sweet, my precious, she has come at last. Don't let us cry, don't let us!

NINA. There is someone here.

TREPLEV. No one.

NINA. Lock the doors, someone may come in.

TREPLEV. No one will come in.

NINA. I know Irina Nikolayevna is here. Lock the doors.

TREPLEV (*locks the door on right, goes to door on left*). There is no lock on this one. I'll put a chair against it (*puts an armchair against the door*). Don't be afraid, no one will come.

NINA (*looking intently into his face*). Let me look at you. (*Looking round*) It's warm, it's nice. . . In old days this was the drawing-room. Am I very much changed?

TREPLEV. Yes . . . You are thinner and your eyes are bigger. Nina, how strange it is that I should be seeing you. Why would not you let me see you? Why haven't you come all this time? I know you have been here almost a week. . . . I have been to you several times every day; I stood under your window like a beggar.

NINA. I was afraid that you might hate me. I dream every night that you look at me and don't know me. If only you knew! Ever since I came I have been walking here . . . by the lake. I have been near your house many times and could not bring myself to enter it. Let us sit down. (*They sit down.*) Let us sit down and talk and talk. It's nice here, it's warm and snug. Do you hear the wind? There's a passage in Turgenev, "Well for the man on such a night who sits under the shelter of home, who has a warm corner in safety." I am a sea-gull. . . . No, that's not it (*rubs her forehead*). What was I saying? Yes . . . Turgenev . . . "And the Lord help all homeless wanderers!" . . . It doesn't matter (*sobs*).

TREPLEV. Nina, you are crying again. . . . Nina!

NINA. Never mind, it does me good . . . I haven't cried for two years. Yesterday, late in the evening, I came into the garden to see whether our stage was still there. It is still standing. I cried for the first time after two years and it eased the weight on my heart and made it lighter. You see, I am not crying now (*takes him by the hand*). And so now you are an author. . . You are an author; I am an actress. . . . We too have been drawn into the whirlpool. I lived joyously like a child—I woke up singing in the morning; I loved you and dreamed of fame, and now? Early to-morrow morning I must go to Yelets third-class . . . with peasants, and at Yelets the cultured tradesmen will pester me with attentions. Life is a coarse business!

TREPLEV. Why to Yelets?

NINA. I have taken an engagement for the whole winter. It is time to go.

TREPLEV. Nina, I cursed you, I hated you, I tore up your letters and photographs, but I was conscious every minute that my soul is bound to yours for ever. It's not in my power to leave off loving you, Nina. Ever since I lost you and began to get my work published my life has been unbearable—I am wretched. . . . My youth was, as it were, torn away all at once and it seems to me as though I have lived for ninety years already. I call upon you, I kiss the earth on which you have walked; wherever I look I see your face, that tender smile that lighted up the best days of my life. . . .

NINA (*distractedly*). Why does he talk like this, why does he talk like this?

TREPLEV. I am alone in the world, warmed by no affection. I am as cold as though I were in a cellar, and everything I write is dry, hard and gloomy. Stay here, Nina, I entreat you, or let me go with you!

(NINA *rapidly puts on her hat and cape.*)

TREPLEV. Nina, why is this? For God's sake, Nina! (*Looks at her as she puts her things on; a pause.*)

NINA. My horses are waiting at the gate. Don't see me off, I'll go alone. . . . (*Through her tears*) Give me some water. . . .

TREPLEV (*gives her some water*). Where are you going now?

NINA. To the town (*a pause*). Is Irina Nikolayevna here?

TREPLEV. Yes. . . . Uncle was taken worse on Thursday and we telegraphed for her.

NINA. Why do you say that you kissed the earth on which I walked? I ought to be killed. (*Bends over table*) I am so tired! If I could rest . . . if I could rest! (*Raising her head*) I am a sea-gull. . . . No, that's not it. I am an actress. Oh, well! (*Hearing* MADAME ARKADIN *and* TRIGORIN *laughing, she listens, then runs to door on left and looks through the keyhole.*) He is here too. . . . (*Turning back to* TREPLEV) Oh, well . . . it doesn't matter . . . no. . . . He did not believe in the stage, he always laughed at my dreams and little by little I left off believing in it too, and lost heart. . . . And then I was fretted by love and jealousy, and continually anxious over my little one. . . . I grew petty and trivial, I acted stupidly. . . . I did not know what to do with my arms, I did not know how to stand on the stage, could not control my voice. You can't understand what it feels like when one knows one is acting disgracefully. I am a sea-gull. No, that's not it. . . . Do you remember you shot a sea-gull? A man came by chance, saw it and, just to pass the time, destroyed it. . . . A subject for a short story. . . . That's not it, though (*rubs her forehead*). What was I saying? . . . I am talking of the stage. Now I am not like that. I am a real actress, I act with enjoyment, with enthusiasm, I am intoxicated when I am on the stage and feel that I am splendid. And since I have been here, I keep walking about and thinking, thinking and feeling that my soul is getting stronger every day. Now I know, I understand, Kostya, that in our work—in acting or writing—what matters is not fame, not glory, not what I dreamed of, but knowing how to be patient. To bear one's cross and have faith. I have faith and it all doesn't hurt so much, and when I think of my vocation I am not afraid of life.

TREPLEV (*mournfully*). You have found your path, you know which way you are going, but I am still floating in a chaos of dreams and images, not knowing what use it is to anyone. I have no faith and don't know what my vocation is.

NINA (*listening*). 'Sh-sh . . . I am going. Good-bye. When I become a great actress, come and look at me. Will you promise? But now . . . (*presses his hand*) it's late. I can hardly stand on my feet. . . . I am worn out and hungry. . . .

TREPLEV. Stay, I'll give you some supper.

NINA. No, no. . . . Don't see me off, I will go by myself. My horses are close by. . . . So she brought him with her? Well, it doesn't matter. When you see Trigorin, don't say anything to him. . . . I love him! I love him even more than before. . . . A subject for a short story . . . I love him, I love him passionately, I love him to despair. It was nice in old days, Kostya! Do you remember? How clear, warm, joyous and pure life was, what feelings we had— feelings like tender, exquisite flowers. . . . Do you remember? (*Recites*) "Men, lions, eagles, and partridges, horned deer, geese, spiders, silent fish that dwell in the water, star-fishes, and creatures which cannot be seen by the eye— all living things, all living things, all living things, have completed their cycle of sorrow, are extinct. . . . For thousands of years the earth has borne no living creature on its surface, and this poor moon lights its lamp in vain. On the meadow the cranes no longer waken with a cry and there is no sound of the

May beetles in the lime trees . . ." (*impulsively embraces* TREPLEV *and runs out of the glass door*).

TREPLEV (*after a pause*). It will be a pity if someone meets her in the garden and tells mother. It may upset mother. . . .

    (*He spends two minutes in tearing up all his manuscripts and throwing them under the table; then unlocks the door on right and goes out.*)

DORN (*trying to open the door on left*). Strange. The door seems to be locked . . . (*comes in and puts the armchair in its place*). An obstacle race.

    (*Enter* MADAME ARKADIN *and* POLINA ANDREYEVNA, *behind them* YAKOV *carrying a tray with bottles;* MASHA; *then* SHAMRAEV *and* TRIGORIN.)

MADAME ARKADIN. Put the claret and the beer for Boris Alexeyevitch here on the table. We will play as we drink it. Let us sit down, friends.

POLINA (*to* YAKOV). Bring tea too at the same time (*lights the candles and sits down to the card-table*).

SHAMRAEV (*leads* TRIGORIN *to the cupboard*). Here's the thing I was speaking about just now (*takes the stuffed sea-gull from the cupboard*). This is what you ordered.

TRIGORIN (*looking at the sea-gull*). I don't remember it. (*Musing*) I don't remember.

    (*The sound of a shot coming from right of stage; everyone starts.*)

MADAME ARKADIN (*frightened*). What's that?

DORN. That's nothing. It must be something in my medicine-chest that has gone off. Don't be anxious (*goes out at door on right, comes back in half a minute*). That's what it is. A bottle of ether has exploded. (*Hums*) "I stand before thee enchanted again. . . ."

MADAME ARKADIN (*sitting down to the table*). Ough, how frightened I was. It reminded me of how . . . (*hides her face in her hands*). It made me quite dizzy. . . .

DORN (*turning over the leaves of the magazine, to* TRIGORIN). There was an article in this two months ago—a letter from America—and I wanted to ask you, among other things (*puts his arm round* TRIGORIN'S *waist and leads him to the footlights*) as I am very much interested in the question. . . . (*In a lower tone, dropping his voice*) Get Irina Nikolayevna away somehow. The fact is, Konstantin Gavrilitch has shot himself. . . .

CURTAIN.

THE CHERRY ORCHARD

A Comedy in Four Acts

*First performed at Moscow,
January 17, 1904*

CHARACTERS IN THE PLAY

MADAME RANEVSKY (LYUBOV ANDREYEVNA) (*the owner of the Cherry Orchard*).
ANYA (*her daughter, aged* 17).
VARYA (*her adopted daughter, aged* 24).
GAEV (LEONID ANDREYEVITCH) (*brother of Madame Ranevsky*).
LOPAHIN (YERMOLAY ALEXEYEVITCH) (*a Merchant*).
TROFIMOV (PYOTR SERGEYEVITCH) (*a Student*).
SEMYONOV-PISHTCHIK (*a Landowner*).
CHARLOTTA IVANOVNA (*a Governess*).
EPIHODOV (SEMYON PANTALEYEVITCH) (*a Clerk*).
DUNYASHA (*a Maid*).
FIRS (*an old Valet, aged* 87).
YASHA (*a young Valet*).
A VAGRANT.
THE STATION MASTER.
A POST-OFFICE CLERK.
VISITORS, SERVANTS.

The action takes place on the estate of
MADAME RANEVSKY.

ACT I

A room, which has always been called the nursery. One of the doors leads into ANYA'S *room. Dawn, sun rises during the scene. May, the cherry trees in flower, but it is cold in the garden with the frost of early morning. Windows closed.*

Enter DUNYASHA *with a candle and* LOPAHIN *with a book in his hand.*

LOPAHIN. The train's in, thank God. What time is it?

DUNYASHA. Nearly two o'clock (*puts out the candle*). It's daylight already.

LOPAHIN. The train's late! Two hours, at least (*yawns and stretches*). I'm a pretty one; what a fool I've been. Came here on purpose to meet them at the station and dropped asleep. . . . Dozed off as I sat in the chair. It's annoying. . . . You might have waked me.

DUNYASHA. I thought you had gone (*listens*). There, I do believe they're coming!

LOPAHIN (*listens*). No, what with the luggage and one thing and another (*a pause*). Lyubov Andreyevna has been abroad five years; I don't know what she is like now. . . . She's a splendid woman. A good-natured, kind-hearted woman. I remember when I was a lad of fifteen, my poor father—he used to keep a little shop here in the village in those days—gave me a punch in the face with his fist and made my nose bleed. We were in the yard here, I forget what we'd come about—he had had a drop. Lyubov Andreyevna—I can see her now—she was a slim young girl then—took me to wash my face, and then brought me into this very room, into the nursery. "Don't cry, little peasant," says she, "it will be well in time for your wedding day" . . . (*a pause*). Little peasant. . . . My father was a peasant, it's true, but here am I in a white waistcoat and brown shoes, like a pig in a bun shop. Yes, I'm a rich man, but for all my money, come to think, a peasant I was, and a peasant I am (*turns over the pages of the book*). I've been reading this book and I can't make head or tail of it. I fell asleep over it (*a pause*).

DUNYASHA. The dogs have been awake all night, they feel that the mistress is coming.

LOPAHIN. Why, what's the matter with you, Dunyasha?

DUNYASHA. My hands are all of a tremble. I feel as though I should faint.

LOPAHIN. You're a spoilt soft creature, Dunyasha. And dressed like a lady

57

too, and your hair done up. That's not the thing. One must know one's place.

(*Enter* EPIHODOV *with a nosegay; he wears a pea-jacket and highly polished creaking topboots; he drops the nosegay as he comes in.*)

EPIHODOV (*picking up the nosegay*). Here! the gardener's sent this, says you're to put it in the dining-room (*gives* DUNYASHA *the nosegay*).

LOPAHIN. And bring me some kvass.

DUNYASHA. I will (*goes out*).

EPIHODOV. It's chilly this morning, three degrees of frost, though the cherries are all in flower. I can't say much for our climate (*sighs*). I can't. Our climate is not often propitious to the occasion. Yermolay Alexeyevitch, permit me to call your attention to the fact that I purchased myself a pair of boots the day before yesterday, and they creak, I venture to assure you, so that there's no tolerating them. What ought I to grease them with?

LOPAHIN. Oh, shut up! Don't bother me.

EPIHODOV. Every day some misfortune befalls me. I don't complain, I'm used to it, and I wear a smiling face.

(DUNYASHA *comes in, hands* LOPAHIN *the kvass.*)

EPIHODOV. I am going (*stumbles against a chair, which falls over*). There! (*as though triumphant*). There you see now, excuse the expression, an accident like that among others. . . . It's positively remarkable (*goes out*).

DUNYASHA. Do you know, Yermolay Alexeyevitch, I must confess, Epihodov has made me a proposal.

LOPAHIN. Ah!

DUNYASHA. I'm sure I don't know. . . . He's a harmless fellow, but sometimes when he begins talking, there's no making anything of it. It's all very fine and expressive, only there's no understanding it. I've a sort of liking for him too. He loves me to distraction. He's an unfortunate man; every day there's something. They tease him about it—two and twenty misfortunes they call him.

LOPAHIN (*listening*). There! I do believe they're coming.

DUNYASHA. They are coming! What's the matter with me? . . . I'm cold all over.

LOPAHIN. They really are coming. Let's go and meet them. Will she know me? It's five years since I saw her.

DUNYASHA (*in a flutter*). I shall drop this very minute. . . . Ah, I shall drop.

(*There is a sound of two carriages driving up to the house.* LOPAHIN *and* DUNYASHA *go out quickly. The stage is left empty. A noise is heard in the adjoining rooms.* FIRS, *who has driven to meet* MADAME RANEVSKY, *crosses the stage hurriedly leaning on a stick. He is wearing old-fashioned livery and a high hat. He says something to himself, but not a word can be distinguished. The noise behind the scenes goes on increasing. A voice: "Come, let's go in here." Enter* LYUBOV ANDREYEVNA, ANYA, *and* CHARLOTTA IVANOVNA *with a pet dog on a chain, all in travelling dresses.* VARYA *in an out-door coat with a kerchief over her head,* GAEV, SEMYONOV-PISHTCHIK, LOPAHIN, DUNYASHA *with bag and parasol, servants with other articles. All walk across the room.*)

ANYA. Let's come in here. Do you remember what room this is, mamma?

LYUBOV (*joyfully, through her tears*). The nursery!

VARYA. How cold it is, my hands are numb. (*To* LYUBOV ANDREYEVNA) Your rooms, the white room and the lavender one, are just the same as ever, mamma.

LYUBOV. My nursery, dear delightful room. . . . I used to sleep here when I was little . . . (*cries*). And here I am, like a little child . . . (*kisses her brother and* VARYA, *and then her brother again*). Varya's just the same as ever, like a nun. And I knew Dunyasha (*kisses* DUNYASHA).

GAEV. The train was two hours late. What do you think of that? Is that the way to do things?

CHARLOTTA (*to* PISHTCHIK). My dog eats nuts, too.

PISHTCHIK (*wonderingly*). Fancy that!

(*They all go out except* ANYA *and* DUNYASHA.)

DUNYASHA. We've been expecting you so long (*takes* ANYA's *hat and coat*).

ANYA. I haven't slept for four nights on the journey. I feel dreadfully cold.

DUNYASHA. You set out in Lent, there was snow and frost, and now? My darling! (*laughs and kisses her*). I have missed you, my precious, my joy. I must tell you . . . I can't put it off a minute. . . .

ANYA (*wearily*). What now?

DUNYASHA. Epihodov, the clerk, made me a proposal just after Easter.

ANYA. It's always the same thing with you . . . (*straightening her hair*). I've lost all my hairpins . . (*she is staggering from exhaustion*).

DUNYASHA. I don't know what to think, really. He does love me, he does love me so!

ANYA (*looking towards her door, tenderly*). My own room, my windows just as though I had never gone away. I'm home! To-morrow morning I shall get up and run into the garden. . . . Oh, if I could get to sleep! I haven't slept all the journey, I was so anxious and worried.

DUNYASHA. Pyotr Sergeyevitch came the day before yesterday.

ANYA (*joyfully*). Petya!

DUNYASHA. He's asleep in the bath house, he has settled in there. I'm afraid of being in their way, says he. (*Glancing at her watch*) I was to have waked him, but Varvara Mihalovna told me not to. Don't you wake him, says she.

(*Enter* VARYA *with a bunch of keys at her waist.*)

VARYA. Dunyasha, coffee and make haste. . . . Mamma's asking for coffee.

DUNYASHA. This very minute (*goes out*).

VARYA. Well, thank God, you've come. You're home again (*petting her*). My little darling has come back! My precious beauty has come back again!

ANYA. I have had a time of it!

VARYA. I can fancy.

ANYA. We set off in Holy Week—it was so cold then, and all the way Charlotta would talk and show off her tricks. What did you want to burden me with Charlotta for?

VARYA. You couldn't have travelled all alone, darling. At seventeen!

ANYA. We got to Paris at last, it was cold there—snow. I speak French shockingly. Mamma lives on the fifth floor, I went up to her and there were a lot of French people, ladies, an old priest with a book. The place smelt of tobacco and so comfortless. I felt sorry, oh! so sorry for mamma all at once, I put my arms round her neck, and hugged her and wouldn't let her go. Mamma was as kind as she could be, and she cried. . . .

VARYA (through her tears). Don't speak of it, don't speak of it!

ANYA. She had sold her villa at Mentone, she had nothing left, nothing. I hadn't a farthing left either, we only just had enough to get here. And mamma doesn't understand! When we had dinner at the stations, she always ordered the most expensive things and gave the waiters a whole rouble. Charlotta's just the same. Yasha too must have the same as we do; it's simply awful. You know Yasha is mamma's valet now, we brought him here with us.

VARYA. Yes, I've seen the young rascal.

ANYA. Well, tell me—have you paid the arrears on the mortgage?

VARYA. How could we get the money?

ANYA. Oh, dear! Oh, dear!

VARYA. In August the place will be sold.

ANYA. My goodness!

LOPAHIN (peeps in at the door and moos like a cow). Moo! (disappears).

VARYA (weeping). There, that's what I could do to him (shakes her fist).

ANYA (embracing VARYA, softly). Varya, has he made you an offer? (VARYA shakes her head.) Why, but he loves you. Why is it you don't come to an understanding? What are you waiting for?

VARYA. I believe that there never will be anything between us. He has a lot to do, he has no time for me . . . and takes no notice of me. Bless the man, it makes me miserable to see him. . . . Everyone's talking of our being married, everyone's congratulating me, and all the while there's really nothing in it; it's all like a dream. (In another tone) You have a new brooch like a bee.

ANYA (mournfully). Mamma bought it. (Goes into her own room and in a light-hearted childish tone) And you know, in Paris I went up in a balloon!

VARYA. My darling's home again! My pretty is home again!

(DUNYASHA returns with the coffee-pot and is making the coffee.)

VARYA (standing at the door). All day long, darling, as I go about looking after the house, I keep dreaming all the time. If only we could marry you to a rich man, then I should feel more at rest. Then I would go off by myself on a pilgrimage to Kiev, to Moscow . . . and so I would spend my life going from one holy place to another. . . . I would go on and on. . . . What bliss!

ANYA. The birds are singing in the garden. What time is it?

VARYA. It must be nearly three. It's time you were asleep, darling (*going into* ANYA's *room*). What bliss!

(YASHA *enters with a rug and a travelling bag.*)

YASHA (*crosses the stage, mincingly*). May one come in here, pray?

DUNYASHA. I shouldn't have known you, Yasha. How you have changed abroad.

YASHA. H'm! . . . And who are you?

DUNYASHA. When you went away, I was that high (*shows distance from floor*). Dunyasha, Fyodor's daughter. . . . You don't remember me!

YASHA. H'm! . . . You're a peach! (*Looks round and embraces her: she shrieks and drops a saucer.* YASHA *goes out hastily.*)

VARYA (*in the doorway, in a tone of vexation*). What now?

DUNYASHA (*through her tears*). I have broken a saucer.

VARYA. Well, that brings good luck.

ANYA (*coming out of her room*). We ought to prepare mamma: Petya is here.

VARYA. I told them not to wake him.

ANYA (*dreamily*). It's six years since father died. Then only a month later little brother Grisha was drowned in the river, such a pretty boy he was, only seven. It was more than mamma could bear, so she went away, went away without looking back (*shuddering*). . . . How well I understand her, if only she knew! (*a pause*) And Petya Trofimov was Grisha's tutor, he may remind her.

(*Enter* FIRS: *he is wearing a pea-jacket and a white waistcoat.*)

FIRS (*goes up to the coffee-pot, anxiously*). The mistress will be served here (*puts on white gloves*). Is the coffee ready? (*Sternly to* DUNYASHA) Girl! Where's the cream?

DUNYASHA. Ah, mercy on us! (*goes out quickly*).

FIRS (*fussing round the coffee-pot*). Ech! you good-for-nothing! (*Muttering to himself*) Come back from Paris. And the old master used to go to Paris too . . . horses all the way (*laughs*).

VARYA. What is it, Firs?

FIRS. What is your pleasure? (*Gleefully*) My lady has come home! I have lived to see her again! Now I can die (*weeps with joy*).

(*Enter* LYUBOV ANDREYEVNA, LOPAHIN, GAEV *and* SEMYONOV-PISHTCHIK; *the latter is in a short-waisted full coat of fine cloth, and full trousers.* GAEV, *as he comes in, makes a gesture with his arms and his whole body, as though he were playing billiards.*)

LYUBOV. How does it go? Let me remember. Cannon off the red!

GAEV. That's it—in off the white! Why, once, sister, we used to sleep together in this very room, and now I'm fifty-one, strange as it seems.

LOPAHIN. Yes, time flies.

GAEV. What do you say?

LOPAHIN. Time, I say, flies.

GAEV. What a smell of patchouli!

ANYA. I'm going to bed. Good-night, mamma (*kisses her mother*).

LYUBOV. My precious darling (*kisses her hands*). Are you glad to be home? I can't believe it.

ANYA. Good-night, uncle.

GAEV (*kissing her face and hands*). God bless you! How like you are to your mother! (*To his sister*) At her age you were just the same, Lyuba.

(ANYA *shakes hands with* LOPAHIN *and* PISHTCHIK, *then goes out, shutting the door after her.*)

LYUBOV. She's quite worn out.

PISHTCHIK. Aye, it's a long journey, to be sure.

VARYA (*to* LOPAHIN *and* PISHTCHIK). Well, gentlemen? It's three o'clock and time to say good-bye.

LYUBOV (*laughs*). You're just the same as ever, Varya (*draws her to her and kisses her*). I'll just drink my coffee and then we will go and rest. (FIRS *puts a cushion under her feet.*) Thanks, friend. I am so fond of coffee, I drink it day and night. Thanks, dear old man (*kisses* FIRS).

VARYA. I'll just see whether all the things have been brought in (*goes out*).

LYUBOV. Can it really be me sitting here? (*laughs*). I want to dance about and clap my hands. (*Covers her face with her hands*) And I could drop asleep in a moment! God knows I love my country, I love it tenderly; I couldn't look out of the window in the train, I kept crying so. (*Through her tears*) But I must drink my coffee, though. Thank you, Firs, thanks, dear old man. I'm so glad to find you still alive.

FIRS. The day before yesterday.

GAEV. He's rather deaf.

LOPAHIN. I have to set off for Harkov directly, at five o'clock. . . . It is annoying! I wanted to have a look at you, and a little talk. . . . You are just as splendid as ever.

PISHTCHIK (*breathing heavily*). Handsomer, indeed. . . . Dressed in Parisian style . . . completely bowled me over.

LOPAHIN. Your brother, Leonid Andreyevitch here, is always saying that I'm a low-born knave, that I'm a money-grubber, but I don't care one straw for that. Let him talk. Only I do want you to believe in me as you used to. I do want your wonderful tender eyes to look at me as they used to in the old days. Merciful God! My father was a serf of your father and of your grandfather, but you—you—did so much for me once, that I've forgotten all that; I love you as though you were my kin . . . more than my kin.

LYUBOV. I can't sit still, I simply can't . . . (*jumps up and walks about in violent agitation*). This happiness is too much for me. . . . You may laugh at me, I know I'm silly. . . . My own bookcase (*kisses the bookcase*). My little table.

GAEV. Nurse died while you were away.

LYUBOV (*sits down and drinks coffee*). Yes, the Kingdom of Heaven be hers! You wrote me of her death.

GAEV. And Anastasy is dead. Squinting Petruchka has left me and is in service now with the police captain in the town (*takes a box of caramels out of his pocket and sucks one*).

PISHTCHIK. My daughter, Dashenka, wishes to be remembered to you.

LOPAHIN. I want to tell you something very pleasant and cheering (*glancing at his watch*). I'm going directly . . . there's no time to say much . . . well, I can say it in a couple of words. I needn't tell you your cherry orchard is to be sold to pay your debts; the 22nd of August is the date fixed for the sale; but don't you worry, dearest lady, you may sleep in peace, there is a way of saving it. . . . This is what I propose. I beg your attention! Your estate is not twenty miles from the town, the railway runs close by it, and if the cherry orchard and the land along the river bank were cut up into building plots and then let on lease for summer villas, you would make an income of at least 25,000 roubles a year out of it.

GAEV. That's all rot, if you'll excuse me.

LYUBOV. I don't quite understand you, Yermolay Alexeyevitch.

LOPAHIN. You will get a rent of at least 25 roubles a year for a three-acre plot from summer visitors, and if you say the word now, I'll bet you what you like there won't be one square foot of ground vacant by the autumn, all the plots will be taken up. I congratulate you; in fact, you are saved. It's a perfect situation with that deep river. Only, of course, it must be cleared—all the old buildings, for example, must be removed, this house too, which is really good for nothing and the old cherry orchard must be cut down.

LYUBOV. Cut down? My dear fellow, forgive me, but you don't know what you are talking about. If there is one thing interesting—remarkable indeed—in the whole province, it's just our cherry orchard.

LOPAHIN. The only thing remarkable about the orchard is that it's a very large one. There's a crop of cherries every alternate year, and then there's nothing to be done with them, no one buys them.

GAEV. This orchard is mentioned in the "Encyclopædia."

LOPAHIN (*glancing at his watch*). If we don't decide on something and don't take some steps, on the 22nd of August the cherry orchard and the whole estate too will be sold by auction. Make up your minds! There is no other way of saving it, I'll take my oath on that. No, no!

FIRS. In old days, forty or fifty years ago, they used to dry the cherries, soak them, pickle them, make jam too, and they used——

GAEV. Be quiet, Firs.

FIRS. And they used to send the preserved cherries to Moscow and to Harkov by the waggon-load. That brought the money in! And the preserved cherries in those days were soft and juicy, sweet and fragrant. . . . They knew the way to do them then. . . .

LYUBOV. And where is the recipe now?

FIRS. It's forgotten. Nobody remembers it.

PISHTCHIK (*to* LYUBOV ANDREYEVNA). What's it like in Paris? Did you eat frogs there?

LYUBOV. Oh, I ate crocodiles.

PISHTCHIK. Fancy that now!

LOPAHIN. There used to be only the gentlefolks and the peasants in the country, but now there are these summer visitors. All the towns, even the small ones, are surrounded nowadays by these summer villas. And one may say for sure, that in another twenty years there'll be many more of these people and that they'll be everywhere. At present the summer visitor only drinks tea in his verandah, but maybe he'll take to working his bit of land too, and then your cherry orchard would become happy, rich and prosperous. . . .

GAEV (*indignant*). What rot!

(*Enter* VARYA *and* YASHA.)

VARYA. There are two telegrams for you, mamma (*takes out keys and opens an old-fashioned bookcase with a loud crack*). Here they are.

LYUBOV. From Paris (*tears the telegrams, without reading them*). I have done with Paris.

GAEV. Do you know, Lyuba, how old that bookcase is? Last week I pulled out the bottom drawer and there I found the date branded on it. The bookcase was made just a hundred years ago. What do you say to that? We might have celebrated its jubilee. Though it's an inanimate object, still it is a *bookcase*.

PISHTCHIK (*amazed*). A hundred years! Fancy that now.

GAEV. Yes. . . . It is a thing . . . (*feeling the bookcase*). Dear, honoured bookcase! Hail to thee who for more than a hundred years hast served the pure ideals of good and justice; thy silent call to fruitful labour has never flagged in those hundred years, maintaining (*in tears*) in the generations of man, courage and faith in a brighter future and fostering in us ideals of good and social consciousness (*a pause*).

LOPAHIN. Yes. . . .

LYUBOV. You are just the same as ever, Leonid.

GAEV (*a little embarrassed*). Cannon off the right into the pocket!

LOPAHIN (*looking at his watch*). Well, it's time I was off.

YASHA (*handing* LYUBOV ANDREYEVNA *medicine*). Perhaps you will take your pills now.

PISHTCHIK. You shouldn't take medicines, my dear madam . . . they do no harm and no good. Give them here . . . honoured lady (*takes the pill-box, pours the pills into the hollow of his hand, blows on them, puts them in his mouth and drinks off some kvass*). There!

LYUBOV (*in alarm*). Why, you must be out of your mind!

PISHTCHIK. I have taken all the pills.

LOPAHIN. What a glutton! (*All laugh*).

FIRS. His honour stayed with us in Easter week, ate a gallon and a half of cucumbers . . . (*mutters*).

LYUBOV. What is he saying?

VARYA. He has taken to muttering like that for the last three years. We are used to it.

YASHA. His declining years!

(CHARLOTTA IVANOVNA, *a very thin, lanky figure in a white dress with a lorgnette in her belt, walks across the stage.*)

LOPAHIN. I beg your pardon, Charlotta Ivanovna, I have not had time to greet you (*tries to kiss her hand*).

CHARLOTTA (*pulling away her hand*). If I let you kiss my hand, you'll be wanting to kiss my elbow, and then my shoulder.

LOPAHIN. I've no luck to-day! (*all laugh.*) Charlotta Ivanovna, show us some tricks!

LYUBOV. Charlotta, do show us some tricks!

CHARLOTTA. I don't want to. I'm sleepy (*goes out*).

LOPAHIN. In three weeks' time we shall meet again (*kisses LYUBOV AN-DREYEVNA'S hand*). Good-bye till then—I must go. (*To GAEV*) Good-bye. (*Kisses PISHTCHIK*) Good-bye. (*Gives his hand to VARYA, then to FIRS and YASHA*) I don't want to go. (*To LYUBOV ANDREYEVNA*) If you think over my plan for the villas and make up your mind, then let me know; I will lend you 50,000 roubles. Think of it seriously.

VARYA (*angrily*). Well, do go, for goodness sake.

LOPAHIN. I'm going, I'm going (*goes out*).

GAEV. Low-born knave! I beg pardon, though . . . Varya is going to marry him, he's Varya's fiancé.

VARYA. Don't talk nonsense, uncle.

LYUBOV. Well, Varya, I shall be delighted. He's a good man.

PISHTCHIK. He is, one must acknowledge, a most worthy man. And my Dashenka . . . says too that . . . she says . . . various things (*snores, but at once wakes up*). But all the same, honoured lady, could you oblige me . . . with a loan of 240 roubles . . . to pay the interest on my mortgage to-morrow?

VARYA (*dismayed*). No, no.

LYUBOV. I really haven't any money.

PISHTCHIK. It will turn up (*laughs*). I never lose hope. I thought every-thing was over, I was a ruined man, and lo and behold—the railway passed through my land and . . . they paid me for it. And something else will turn up again, if not to-day, then to-morrow . . . Dashenka'll win two hundred thousand . . . she's got a lottery ticket.

LYUBOV. Well, we've finished our coffee, we can go to bed.

FIRS (*brushes GAEV, reprovingly*). You have got on the wrong trousers again! What am I to do with you?

VARYA (*softly*). Anya's asleep. (*Softly opens the window*) Now the sun's risen, it's not a bit cold. Look, mamma, what exquisite trees! My goodness! And the air! The starlings are singing!

GAEV (*opens another window*). The orchard is all white. You've not forgotten it, Lyuba? That long avenue that runs straight, straight as an arrow, how it shines on a moonlight night. You remember? You've not forgotten?

LYUBOV (*looking out of the window into the garden*). Oh, my childhood, my innocence! It was in this nursery I used to sleep, from here I looked out into the orchard, happiness waked with me every morning and in those days the orchard was just the same, nothing has changed (*laughs with delight*). All, all white! Oh, my orchard! After the dark gloomy autumn, and the cold winter; you are young again, and full of happiness, the heavenly angels have never left you. . . . If I could cast off the burden that weighs on my heart, if I could forget the past!

GAEV. H'm! and the orchard will be sold to pay our debts; it seems strange. . . .

LYUBOV. See, our mother walking . . . all in white, down the avenue! (*Laughs with delight.*) It is she!

GAEV. Where?

VARYA. Oh, don't, mamma!

LYUBOV. There is no one. It was my fancy. On the right there, by the path to the arbour, there is a white tree bending like a woman. . . .

(*Enter* TROFIMOV *wearing a shabby student's uniform and spectacles.*)

LYUBOV. What a ravishing orchard! White masses of blossom, blue sky. . . .

TROFIMOV. Lyubov Andreyevna! (*She looks round at him.*) I will just pay my respects to you and then leave you at once (*kisses her hand warmly*). I was told to wait until morning, but I hadn't the patience to wait any longer. . . .

(LYUBOV ANDREYEVNA *looks at him in perplexity.*)

VARYA (*through her tears*). This is Petya Trofimov.

TROFIMOV. Petya Trofimov, who was your Grisha's tutor. . . . Can I have changed so much?

(LYUBOV ANDREYEVNA *embraces him and weeps quietly.*)

GAEV (*in confusion*). There, there, Lyuba.

VARYA (*crying*). I told you, Petya, to wait till to-morrow.

LYUBOV. My Grisha . . . my boy . . . Grisha . . . my son!

VARYA. We can't help it, mamma, it is God's will.

TROFIMOV (*softly through his tears*). There . . . there.

LYUBOV (*weeping quietly*). My boy was lost . . . drowned. Why? Oh, why, dear Petya? (*More quietly*) Anya is asleep in there, and I'm talking loudly . . . making this noise. . . . But, Petya? Why have you grown so ugly? Why do you look so old?

TROFIMOV. A peasant-woman in the train called me a mangy-looking gentleman.

LYUBOV. You were quite a boy then, a pretty little student, and now your hair's thin—and spectacles. Are you really a student still? (*Goes towards the door.*)

TROFIMOV. I seem likely to be a perpetual student.

LYUBOV (*kisses her brother, then* VARYA). Well, go to bed. . . . You are older too, Leonid.

PISHTCHIK (*follows her*). I suppose it's time we were asleep. . . . Ugh! my gout! I'm staying the night! Lyubov Andreyevna, my dear soul, if you could . . . to-morrow morning . . . 240 roubles.

GAEV. That's always his story.

PISHTCHIK. 240 roubles . . . to pay the interest on my mortgage.

LYUBOV. My dear man, I have no money.

PISHTCHIK. I'll pay it back, my dear . . . a trifling sum.

LYUBOV. Oh, well, Leonid will give it you. . . . You give him the money, Leonid.

GAEV. Me give it him! Let him wait till he gets it!

LYUBOV. It can't be helped, give it him. He needs it. He'll pay it back.

(LYUBOV ANDREYEVNA, TROFIMOV, PISHTCHIK *and* FIRS *go out.* GAEV, VARYA *and* YASHA *remain.*)

GAEV. Sister hasn't got out of the habit of flinging away her money. (*To* YASHA) Get away, my good fellow, you smell of the hen-house.

YASHA (*with a grin*). And you, Leonid Andreyevitch, are just the same as ever.

GAEV. What's that? (*To* VARYA) What did he say?

VARYA (*to* YASHA). Your mother has come from the village; she has been sitting in the servants' room since yesterday, waiting to see you.

YASHA. Oh, bother her!

VARYA. For shame!

YASHA. What's the hurry? She might just as well have come to-morrow (*goes out*).

VARYA. Mamma's just the same as ever, she hasn't changed a bit. If she had her own way, she'd give away everything.

GAEV. Yes (*a pause*). If a great many remedies are suggested for some disease, it means that the disease is incurable. I keep thinking and racking my brains; I have many schemes, a great many, and that really means none. If we could only come in for a legacy from somebody, or marry our Anya to a very rich man, or we might go to Yaroslavl and try our luck with our old aunt, the Countess. She's very, very rich, you know.

VARYA (*weeps*). If God would help us.

GAEV. Don't blubber. Aunt's very rich, but she doesn't like us. First, sister married a lawyer instead of a nobleman. . . .

(ANYA *appears in the doorway.*)

GAEV. And then her conduct, one can't call it virtuous. She is good, and kind, and nice, and I love her, but, however one allows for extenuating circumstances, there's no denying that she's an immoral woman. One feels it in her slightest gesture.

VARYA (*in a whisper*). Anya's in the doorway.

GAEV. What do you say? (*a pause*). It's queer, there seems to be something wrong with my right eye. I don't see as well as I did. And on Thursday when I was in the district Court . . .

(*Enter* ANYA.)

VARYA. Why aren't you asleep, Anya?

ANYA. I can't get to sleep.

GAEV. My pet (*kisses* ANYA's *face and hands*). My child (*weeps*). You are not my niece, you are my angel, you are everything to me. Believe me, believe . . .

ANYA. I believe you, uncle. Everyone loves you and respects you . . . but, uncle dear, you must be silent . . . simply be silent. What were you saying just now about my mother, about your own sister? What made you say that?

GAEV. Yes, yes . . . (*puts his hand over his face*). Really, that was awful! My God, save me! And to-day I made a speech to the bookcase . . so stupid! And only when I had finished, I saw how stupid it was.

VARYA. It's true, uncle, you ought to keep quiet. Don't talk, that's all.

ANYA. If you could keep from talking, it would make things easier for you, too.

GAEV. I won't speak (*kisses* ANYA's *and* VARYA's *hands*). I'll be silent. Only this is about business. On Thursday I was in the district Court; well, there was a large party of us there and we began talking of one thing and another, and this and that, and do you know, I believe that it will be possible to raise a loan on an I.O.U. to pay the arrears on the mortgage.

VARYA. If the Lord would help us!

GAEV. I'm going on Tuesday; I'll talk of it again. (*To* VARYA) Don't blubber. (*To* ANYA) Your mamma will talk to Lopahin; of course, he won't refuse her. And as soon as you're rested you shall go to Yaroslavl to the Countess, your great-aunt. So we shall all set to work in three directions at once, and the business is done. We shall pay off arrears, I'm convinced of it (*puts a caramel in his mouth*). I swear on my honour, I swear by anything you like, the estate shan't be sold (*excitedly*). By my own happiness, I swear it! Here's my hand on it, call me the basest, vilest of men, if I let it come to an auction! Upon my soul I swear it!

ANYA (*her equanimity has returned, she is quite happy*). How good you are, uncle, and how clever! (*Embraces her uncle.*) I'm at peace now! Quite at peace! I'm happy!

(*Enter* FIRS.)

FIRS (*reproachfully*). Leonid Andreyevitch, have you no fear of God? When are you going to bed?

GAEV. Directly, directly. You can go, Firs. I'll . . . yes, I will undress myself. Come, children, bye-bye. We'll go into details to-morrow, but now go to bed (*kisses* ANYA *and* VARYA). I'm a man of the 'eighties. They run down that period, but still I can say I have had to suffer not a little for my convictions in my life. It's not for nothing that the peasant loves me. One must know the peasant! One must know how . . .

ANYA. At it again, uncle!

VARYA. Uncle dear, you'd better be quiet!

FIRS (*angrily*). Leonid Andreyevitch!

GAEV. I'm coming. I'm coming. Go to bed. Potted the shot—there's a shot for you! A beauty! (*Goes out. FIRS hobbling after him.*)

ANYA. My mind's at rest now. I don't want to go to Yaroslavl, I don't like my great-aunt, but still my mind's at rest. Thanks to uncle (*sits down*).

VARYA. We must go to bed. I'm going. Something unpleasant happened while you were away. In the old servants' quarters there are only the old servants, as you know—Efimyushka, Polya and Yevstigney—and Karp too. They began letting stray people in to spend the night—I said nothing. But all at once I heard they had been spreading a report that I gave them nothing but pease pudding to eat. Out of stinginess, you know. . . . And it was all Yevstigney's doing. . . . Very well, I said to myself. . . . If that's how it is, I thought, wait a bit. I sent for Yevstigney . . . (*yawns*). He comes. . . . "How's this, Yevstigney," I said, "you could be such a fool as to? . . ." (*Looking at* ANYA) Anitchka! (*a pause*). She's asleep (*puts her arm round* ANYA). Come to bed . . . come along! (*leads her*). My darling has fallen asleep! Come . . . (*They go.*)

(*Far away beyond the orchard a shepherd plays on a pipe.* TROFIMOV *crosses the stage and, seeing* VARYA *and* ANYA, *stands still.*)

VARYA. 'Sh! asleep, asleep. Come, my own.

ANYA (*softly, half asleep*). I'm so tired. Still those bells. Uncle . . . dear . . . mamma and uncle. . . .

VARYA. Come, my own, come along.

(*They go into* ANYA'S *room.*)

TROFIMOV (*tenderly*). My sunshine! My spring.

CURTAIN.

ACT II

The open country. An old shrine, long abandoned and fallen out of the perpendicular; near it a well, large stones that have apparently once been tombstones, and an old garden seat. The road to GAEV's house is seen. On one side rise dark poplars; and there the cherry orchard begins. In the distance a row of telegraph poles and far, far away on the horizon there is faintly outlined a great town, only visible in very fine clear weather. It is near sunset. CHARLOTTA, YASHA and DUNYASHA are sitting on the seat. EPIHODOV is standing near, playing something mournful on a guitar. All sit plunged in thought. CHARLOTTA wears an old forage cap; she has taken a gun from her shoulder and is tightening the buckle on the strap.

CHARLOTTA (*musingly*). I haven't a real passport of my own, and I don't know how old I am, and I always feel that I'm a young thing. When I was a little girl, my father and mother used to travel about to fairs and give performances—very good ones. And I used to dance *salto-mortale* and all sorts of things. And when papa and mamma died, a German lady took me and had me educated. And so I grew up and became a governess. But where I came from, and who I am, I don't know. . . . Who my parents were, very likely they weren't married . . . I don't know (*takes a cucumber out of her pocket and eats*). I know nothing at all (*a pause*). One wants to talk and has no one to talk to . . . I have nobody.

EPIHODOV (*plays on the guitar and sings*). "What care I for the noisy world! What care I for friends or foes!" How agreeable it is to play on the mandoline!

DUNYASHA. That's a guitar, not a mandoline (*looks in a hand-mirror and powders herself*).

EPIHODOV. To a man mad with love, it's a mandoline. (*Sings*) "Were her heart but aglow with love's mutual flame." (YASHA *joins in.*)

CHARLOTTA. How shockingly these people sing! Foo! Like jackals!

DUNYASHA (*to* YASHA). What happiness, though, to visit foreign lands.

YASHA. Ah, yes! I rather agree with you there (*yawns, then lights a cigar*).

EPIHODOV. That's comprehensible. In foreign lands everything has long since reached full complexion.

YASHA. That's so, of course.

EPIHODOV. I'm a cultivated man, I read remarkable books of all sorts, but I can never make out the tendency I am myself precisely inclined for, whether to live or to shoot myself, speaking precisely, but nevertheless I always carry a revolver. Here it is . . . (*shows revolver*).

CHARLOTTA. I've had enough, and now I'm going (*puts on the gun*). Epihodov, you're a very clever fellow, and a very terrible one too, all the women must be wild about you. Br-r-r! (*goes*) These clever fellows are all so stupid; there's not a creature for me to speak to. . . . Always alone, alone, nobody belonging to me . . . and who I am, and why I'm on earth, I don't know (*walks away slowly*).

EPIHODOV. Speaking precisely, not touching upon other subjects, I'm bound to admit about myself, that destiny behaves mercilessly to me, as a storm to a little boat. If, let us suppose, I am mistaken, then why did I wake up this morning, to quote an example, and look round, and there on my chest was a spider of fearful magnitude . . . like this (*shows with both hands*). And then I take up a jug of kvass, to quench my thirst, and in it there is something in the highest degree unseemly of the nature of a cockroach (*a pause*). Have you read Buckle? (*a pause*). I am desirous of troubling you, Dunyasha, with a couple of words.

DUNYASHA. Well, speak.

EPIHODOV. I should be desirous to speak with you alone (*sighs*).

DUNYASHA (*embarrassed*). Well—only bring me my mantle first. It's by the cupboard. It's rather damp here.

EPIHODOV. Certainly. I will fetch it. Now I know what I must do with my revolver (*takes guitar and goes off playing on it*).

YASHA. Two and twenty misfortunes! Between ourselves, he's a fool (*yawns*).

DUNYASHA. God grant he doesn't shoot himself! (*a pause*) I am so nervous, I'm always in a flutter. I was a little girl when I was taken into our lady's house, and now I have quite grown out of peasant ways, and my hands are white, as white as a lady's. I'm such a delicate, sensitive creature, I'm afraid of everything. I'm so frightened. And if you deceive me, Yasha, I don't know what will become of my nerves.

YASHA (*kisses her*). You're a peach! Of course a girl must never forget herself; what I dislike more than anything is a girl being flighty in her behaviour.

DUNYASHA. I'm passionately in love with you, Yasha; you are a man of culture—you can give your opinion about anything (*a pause*).

YASHA (*yawns*). Yes, that's so. My opinion is this: if a girl loves anyone, that means that she has no principles (*a pause*). It's pleasant smoking a cigar in the open air (*listens*). Someone's coming this way . . . it's the gentlefolk (DUNYASHA *embraces him impulsively*). Go home, as though you had been to the river to bathe; go by that path, or else they'll meet you and suppose I have made an appointment with you here. That I can't endure.

DUNYASHA (*coughing softly*). The cigar has made my head ache . . . (*goes off*).

(YASHA *remains sitting near the shrine. Enter* LYUBOV ANDREYEVNA, GAEV *and* LOPAHIN.)

LOPAHIN. You must make up your mind once for all—there's no time to lose. It's quite a simple question, you know. Will you consent to letting the land for building or not? One word in answer: Yes or no? Only one word!

LYUBOV. Who is smoking such horrible cigars here? (*sits down*).

GAEV. Now the railway line has been brought near, it's made things very convenient (*sits down*). Here we have been over and lunched in town. Cannon off the white! I should like to go home and have a game.

LYUBOV. You have plenty of time.

LOPAHIN. Only one word! (*Beseechingly*). Give me an answer!

GAEV (*yawning*). What do you say?

LYUBOV (*looks in her purse*). I had quite a lot of money here yesterday, and there's scarcely any left to-day. My poor Varya feeds us all on milk soup for the sake of economy; the old folks in the kitchen get nothing but pease pudding, while I waste my money in a senseless way (*drops purse, scattering gold pieces*). There, they have all fallen out! (*annoyed*).

YASHA. Allow me, I'll soon pick them up (*collects the coins*).

LYUBOV. Pray do, Yasha. And what did I go off to the town to lunch for?

Your restaurant's a wretched place with its music and the tablecloth smelling of soap. . . . Why drink so much, Leonid? And eat so much? And talk so much? To-day you talked a great deal again in the restaurant, and all so inappropriately. About the era of the 'seventies, about the decadents. And to whom? Talking to waiters about decadents!

LOPAHIN. Yes.

GAEV (*waving his hand*). I'm incorrigible; that's evident. (*Irritably to* YASHA) Why is it you keep fidgeting about in front of us!

YASHA (*laughs*). I can't help laughing when I hear your voice.

GAEV (*to his sister*). Either I or he . . .

LYUBOV. Get along! Go away, Yasha.

YASHA (*gives* LYUBOV ANDREYEVNA *her purse*). Directly (*hardly able to suppress his laughter*). This minute . . . (*goes off*).

LOPAHIN. Deriganov, the millionaire, means to buy your estate. They say he is coming to the sale himself.

LYUBOV. Where did you hear that?

LOPAHIN. That's what they say in town.

GAEV. Our aunt in Yaroslavl has promised to send help; but when, and how much she will send, we don't know.

LOPAHIN. How much will she send? A hundred thousand? Two hundred?

LYUBOV. Oh, well! . . . Ten or fifteen thousand, and we must be thankful to get that.

LOPAHIN. Forgive me, but such reckless people as you are—such queer, unbusiness-like people—I never met in my life. One tells you in plain Russian your estate is going to be sold, and you seem not to understand it.

LYUBOV. What are we to do? Tell us what to do.

LOPAHIN. I do tell you every day. Every day I say the same thing. You absolutely must let the cherry orchard and the land on building leases; and do it at once, as quick as may be—the auction's close upon us! Do understand! Once make up your mind to build villas, and you can raise as much money as you like, and then you are saved.

LYUBOV. Villas and summer visitors—forgive me saying so—it's so vulgar.

GAEV. There I perfectly agree with you.

LOPAHIN. I shall sob, or scream, or fall into a fit. I can't stand it! You drive me mad! (*To* GAEV) You're an old woman!

GAEV. What do you say?

LOPAHIN. An old woman! (*Gets up to go.*)

LYUBOV (*in dismay*). No, don't go! Do stay, my dear friend! Perhaps we shall think of something.

LOPAHIN. What is there to think of?

LYUBOV. Don't go, I entreat you! With you here it's more cheerful, anyway (*a pause*). I keep expecting something, as though the house were going to fall about our ears.

GAEV (*in profound dejection*). Potted the white! It fails—a kiss.

LYUBOV. We have been great sinners. . . .

LOPAHIN. You have no sins to repent of.

GAEV (*puts a caramel in his mouth*). They say I've eaten up my property in caramels (*laughs*).

LYUBOV. Oh, my sins! I've always thrown my money away recklessly like a lunatic. I married a man who made nothing but debts. My husband died of champagne—he drank dreadfully. To my misery I loved another man, and immediately—it was my first punishment—the blow fell upon me, here, in the river . . . my boy was drowned and I went abroad—went away for ever, never to return, not to see that river again . . . I shut my eyes, and fled, distracted, and *he* after me . . . pitilessly, brutally. I bought a villa at Mentone, for *he* fell ill there, and for three years I had no rest day or night. His illness wore me out, my soul was dried up. And last year, when my villa was sold to pay my debts, I went to Paris and there he robbed me of everything and abandoned me for another woman; and I tried to poison myself. . . . So stupid, so shameful! . . . And suddenly I felt a yearning for Russia, for my country, for my little girl . . . (*dries her tears*). Lord, Lord, be merciful! Forgive my sins! Do not chastise me more! (*Takes a telegram out of her pocket*) I got this to-day from Paris. He implores forgiveness, entreats me to return (*tears up the telegram*). I fancy there is music somewhere (*listens*).

GAEV. That's our famous Jewish orchestra. You remember, four violins, a flute and a double bass.

LYUBOV. That still in existence? We ought to send for them one evening, and give a dance.

LOPAHIN (*listens*). I can't hear. . . . (*Hums softly*) "For money the Germans will turn a Russian into a Frenchman." (*Laughs*) I did see such a piece at the theatre yesterday! It was funny!

LYUBOV. And most likely there was nothing funny in it. You shouldn't look at plays, you should look at yourselves a little oftener. How grey your lives are! How much nonsense you talk.

LOPAHIN. That's true. One may say honestly, we live a fool's life (*pause*). My father was a peasant, an idiot; he knew nothing and taught me nothing, only beat me when he was drunk, and always with his stick. In reality I am just such another blockhead and idiot. I've learnt nothing properly. I write a wretched hand. I write so that I feel ashamed before folks, like a pig.

LYUBOV. You ought to get married, my dear fellow.

LOPAHIN. Yes . . . that's true.

LYUBOV. You should marry our Varya, she's a good girl.

LOPAHIN. Yes.

LYUBOV. She's a good-natured girl, she's busy all day long, and what's more, she loves you. And you have liked her for ever so long.

LOPAHIN. Well? I'm not against it. . . . She's a good girl (*pause*).

GAEV. I've been offered a place in the bank: 6,000 roubles a year. Did you know?

LYUBOV. You would never do for that! You must stay as you are.

(*Enter* FIRS *with overcoat.*)

FIRS. Put it on, sir, it's damp.

GAEV (*putting it on*). You bother me, old fellow.

FIRS. You can't go on like this. You went away in the morning without leaving word (*looks him over*).

LYUBOV. You look older, Firs!

FIRS. What is your pleasure?

LOPAHIN. You look older, she said.

FIRS. I've had a long life. They were arranging my wedding before your
papa was born . . . (*laughs*). I was the head footman before the emancipation came. I wouldn't consent to be set free then; I stayed on with the old
master . . . (*a pause*). I remember what rejoicings they made and didn't
know themselves what they were rejoicing over.

LOPAHIN. Those were fine old times. There was flogging anyway.

FIRS (*not hearing*). To be sure! The peasants knew their place, and the
masters knew theirs; but now they're all at sixes and sevens, there's no making
it out.

GAEV. Hold your tongue, Firs. I must go to town to-morrow. I have been
promised an introduction to a general, who might let us have a loan.

LOPAHIN. You won't bring that off. And you won't pay your arrears, you
may rest assured of that.

LYUBOV. That's all his nonsense. There is no such general.

(*Enter* TROFIMOV, ANYA *and* VARYA.)

GAEV. Here come our girls.

ANYA. There's mamma on the seat.

LYUBOV (*tenderly*). Come here, come along. My darlings! (*Embraces* ANYA
and VARYA.) If you only knew how I love you both. Sit beside me, there, like
that. (*All sit down.*)

LOPAHIN. Our perpetual student is always with the young ladies.

TROFIMOV. That's not your business.

LOPAHIN. He'll soon be fifty, and he's still a student.

TROFIMOV. Drop your idiotic jokes.

LOPAHIN. Why are you so cross, you queer fish?

TROFIMOV. Oh, don't persist!

LOPAHIN (*laughs*). Allow me to ask you what's your idea of me?

TROFIMOV. I'll tell you my idea of you, Yermolay Alexeyevitch: you are
a rich man, you'll soon be a millionaire. Well, just as in the economy of nature
a wild beast is of use, who devours everything that comes in his way, so you
too have your use.

(*All laugh.*)

VARYA. Better tell us something about the planets, Petya.

LYUBOV. No, let us go on with the conversation we had yesterday.

TROFIMOV. What was it about?

GAEV. About pride.

TROFIMOV. We had a long conversation yesterday, but we came to no con-clusion. In pride, in your sense of it, there is something mystical. Perhaps you are right from your point of view; but if one looks at it simply, without subtlety, what sort of pride can there be, what sense is there in it, if man in his physiological formation is very imperfect, if in the immense majority of cases he is coarse, dull-witted, profoundly unhappy? One must give up glori-fication of self. One should work, and nothing else.

GAEV. One must die in any case.

TROFIMOV. Who knows? And what does it mean—dying? Perhaps man has a hundred senses, and only the five we know are lost at death, while the other ninety-five remain alive.

LYUBOV. How clever you are, Petya!

LOPAHIN (ironically). Fearfully clever!

TROFIMOV. Humanity progresses, perfecting its powers. Everything that is beyond its ken now will one day become familiar and comprehensible; only we must work, we must with all our powers aid the seeker after truth. Here among us in Russia the workers are few in number as yet. The vast majority of the intellectual people I know, seek nothing, do nothing, are not fit as yet for work of any kind. They call themselves intellectual, but they treat their servants as inferiors, behave to the peasants as though they were animals, learn little, read nothing seriously, do practically nothing, only talk about science and know very little about art. They are all serious people, they all have severe faces, they all talk of weighty matters and air their theories, and yet the vast majority of us—ninety-nine per cent.—live like savages, at the least thing fly to blows and abuse, eat piggishly, sleep in filth and stuffiness, bugs every-where, stench and damp and moral impurity. And it's clear all our fine talk is only to divert our attention and other people's. Show me where to find the crèches there's so much talk about, and the reading-rooms? They only exist in novels: in real life there are none of them. There is nothing but filth and vulgarity and Asiatic apathy. I fear and dislike very serious faces. I'm afraid of serious conversations. We should do better to be silent.

LOPAHIN. You know, I get up at five o'clock in the morning, and I work from morning to night; and I've money, my own and other people's, always passing through my hands, and I see what people are made of all round me. One has only to begin to do anything to see how few honest, decent people there are. Sometimes when I lie awake at night, I think: "Oh! Lord, thou hast given us immense forests, boundless plains, the widest horizons, and living here we ourselves ought really to be giants."

LYUBOV. You ask for giants! They are no good except in story-books; in real life they frighten us.

(EPIHODOV advances in the background, playing on the guitar.)

LYUBOV (dreamily). There goes Epihodov.

ANYA (dreamily). There goes Epihodov.

GAEV. The sun has set, my friends.

TROFIMOV. Yes.

GAEV (*not loudly, but, as it were, declaiming*). O nature, divine nature, thou art bright with eternal lustre, beautiful and indifferent! Thou, whom we call mother, thou dost unite within thee life and death! Thou dost give life and dost destroy!

VARYA (*in a tone of supplication*). Uncle!

ANYA. Uncle, you are at it again!

TROFIMOV. You'd much better be cannoning off the red!

GAEV. I'll hold my tongue, I will.

(*All sit plunged in thought. Perfect stillness. The only thing audible is the muttering of* FIRS. *Suddenly there is a sound in the distance, as it were from the sky—the sound of a breaking harp-string, mournfully dying away.*)

LYUBOV. What is that?

LOPAHIN. I don't know. Somewhere far away a bucket fallen and broken in the pits. But somewhere very far away.

GAEV. It might be a bird of some sort—such as a heron.

TROFIMOV. Or an owl.

LYUBOV (*shudders*). I don't know why, but it's horrid (*a pause*).

FIRS. It was the same before the calamity—the owl hooted and the samovar hissed all the time.

GAEV. Before what calamity?

FIRS. Before the emancipation (*a pause*).

LYUBOV. Come, my friends, let us be going; evening is falling. (*To* ANYA) There are tears in your eyes. What is it, darling? (*Embraces her.*)

ANYA. Nothing, mamma; it's nothing.

TROFIMOV. There is somebody coming.

(*The wayfarer appears in a shabby white forage cap and an overcoat; he is slightly drunk.*)

WAYFARER. Allow me to inquire, can I get to the station this way?

GAEV. Yes. Go along that road.

WAYFARER. I thank you most feelingly (*coughing*). The weather is superb. (*Declaims*) My brother, my suffering brother! . . . Come out to the Volga! Whose groan do you hear? . . . (*To* VARYA) Mademoiselle, vouchsafe a hungry Russian thirty kopeks.

(VARYA *utters a shriek of alarm.*)

LOPAHIN (*angrily*). There's a right and a wrong way of doing everything!

LYUBOV (*hurriedly*). Here, take this (*looks in her purse*). I've no silver. No matter—here's gold for you.

WAYFARER. I thank you most feelingly! (*goes off*).

(*Laughter.*)

VARYA (*frightened*). I'm going home—I'm going . . . Oh, mamma, the servants have nothing to eat, and you gave him gold!

LYUBOV. There's no doing anything with me. I'm so silly! When we get home, I'll give you all I possess. Yermolay Alexeyevitch, you will lend me some more . . . !

LOPAHIN. I will.

LYUBOV. Come, friends, it's time to be going. And Varya, we have made a match of it for you. I congratulate you.

VARYA (*through her tears*). Mamma, that's not a joking matter.

LOPAHIN. "Ophelia, get thee to a nunnery!"

GAEV. My hands are trembling; it's a long while since I had a game of billiards.

LOPAHIN. "Ophelia! Nymph, in thy orisons be all my sins remember'd."

LYUBOV. Come, it will soon be supper-time.

VARYA. How he frightened me! My heart's simply throbbing.

LOPAHIN. Let me remind you, ladies and gentlemen: on the 22nd of August the cherry orchard will be sold. Think about that! Think about it!

(*All go off, except* TROFIMOV *and* ANYA.)

ANYA (*laughing*). I'm grateful to the wayfarer! He frightened Varya and we are left alone.

TROFIMOV. Varya's afraid we shall fall in love with each other, and for days together she won't leave us. With her narrow brain she can't grasp that we are above love. To eliminate the petty and transitory which hinders us from being free and happy—that is the aim and meaning of our life. Forward! We go forward irresistibly towards the bright star that shines yonder in the distance. Forward! Do not lag behind, friends.

ANYA (*claps her hands*). How well you speak! (*a pause*). It is divine here to-day.

TROFIMOV. Yes, it's glorious weather.

ANYA. Somehow, Petya, you've made me so that I don't love the cherry orchard as I used to. I used to love it so dearly. I used to think that there was no spot on earth like our garden.

TROFIMOV. All Russia is our garden. The earth is great and beautiful—there are many beautiful places in it (*a pause*). Think only, Anya, your grandfather, and great-grandfather, and all your ancestors were slave-owners—the owners of living souls—and from every cherry in the orchard, from every leaf, from every trunk there are human creatures looking at you. Cannot you hear their voices? Oh, it is awful! Your orchard is a fearful thing, and when in the evening or at night one walks about the orchard, the old bark on the trees glimmers dimly in the dusk, and the old cherry trees seem to be dreaming of centuries gone by and tortured by fearful visions. Yes! We are at least two hundred years behind, we have really gained nothing yet, we have no definite attitude to the past, we do nothing but theorise or complain of depression or drink vodka. It is clear that to begin to live in the present we must first expiate our past, we must break with it; and we can expiate it only by suffering, by extraordinary unceasing labour. Understand that, Anya.

ANYA. The house we live in has long ceased to be our own, and I shall leave it, I give you my word.

TROFIMOV. If you have the house keys, fling them into the well and go away. Be free as the wind.

ANYA (*in ecstasy*). How beautifully you said that!

TROFIMOV. Believe me, Anya, believe me! I am not thirty yet, I am young, I am still a student, but I have gone through so much already! As soon as winter comes I am hungry, sick, careworn, poor as a beggar, and what ups and downs of fortune have I not known! And my soul was always, every minute day and night, full of inexplicable forebodings. I have a foreboding of happiness, Anya. I see glimpses of it already.

ANYA (*pensively*). The moon is rising.

(EPIHODOV *is heard playing still the same mournful song on the guitar. The moon rises. Somewhere near the poplars* VARYA *is looking for* ANYA *and calling* "Anya! where are you?")

TROFIMOV. Yes, the moon is rising (*a pause*). Here is happiness—here it comes! It is coming nearer and nearer; already I can hear its footsteps. And if we never see it—if we may never know it—what does it matter? Others will see it after us.

VARYA'S VOICE. Anya! Where are you?

TROFIMOV. That Varya again! (*Angrily*) It's revolting!

ANYA. Well, let's go down to the river. It's lovely there.

TROFIMOV. Yes, let's go. (*They go.*)

VARYA'S VOICE. Anya! Anya!

CURTAIN.

ACT III

A drawing-room divided by an arch from a larger drawing-room. A chandelier burning. The Jewish orchestra, the same that was mentioned in Act II, is heard playing in the ante-room. It is evening. In the larger drawing-room they are dancing the grand chain. The voice of SEMYONOV-PISHTCHIK "Promenade à une paire!" *Then enter the drawing-room in couples first* PISHTCHIK *and* CHARLOTTA IVANOVNA, *then* TROFIMOV *and* LYUBOV ANDREYEVNA, *thirdly* ANYA *with the Post-Office Clerk, fourthly* VARYA *with the Station Master, and other guests.* VARYA *is quietly weeping and wiping away her tears as she dances. In the last couple is* DUNYASHA. *They move across the drawing-room.* PISHTCHIK *shouts:* "Grand rond, balancez!" *and* "Les Cavaliers à genou et remerciez vos dames."

FIRS *in a swallow-tail coat brings in seltzer water on a tray.* PISHTCHIK *and* TROFIMOV *enter the drawing-room.*

PISHTCHIK. I am a full-blooded man; I have already had two strokes. Dancing's hard work for me, but as they say, if you're in the pack, you must bark with the rest. I'm as strong, I may say, as a horse. My parent, who would have his joke—may the Kingdom of Heaven be his!—used to say about our origin that the ancient stock of the Semyonov-Pishtchiks was derived from the very horse that Caligula made a member of the senate (*sits down*). But I've no money, that's where the mischief is. A hungry dog believes in nothing but meat . . . (*snores, but at once wakes up*). That's like me . . . I can think of nothing but money.

TROFIMOV. There really is something horsy about your appearance.

PISHTCHIK. Well . . . a horse is a fine beast . . . a horse can be sold.

(*There is the sound of billiards being played in an adjoining room. VARYA appears in the arch leading to the larger drawing-room.*)

TROFIMOV (*teasing*). Madame Lopahin! Madame Lopahin!

VARYA (*angrily*). Mangy-looking gentleman!

TROFIMOV. Yes, I am a mangy-looking gentleman, and I'm proud of it!

VARYA (*pondering bitterly*). Here we have hired musicians and nothing to pay them! (*Goes out.*)

TROFIMOV (*to PISHTCHIK*). If the energy you have wasted during your lifetime in trying to find the money to pay your interest, had gone to something else, you might in the end have turned the world upside down.

PISHTCHIK. Nietzsche, the philosopher, a very great and celebrated man . . . of enormous intellect . . . says in his works, that one can make forged bank-notes.

TROFIMOV. Why, have you read Nietzsche?

PISHTCHIK. What next . . . Dashenka told me. . . . And now I am in such a position, I might just as well forge bank-notes. The day after to-morrow I must pay 310 roubles—130 I have procured (*feels in his pockets, in alarm*). The money's gone! I have lost my money! (*Through his tears*) Where's the money? (*Gleefully*) Why, here it is behind the lining. . . . It has made me hot all over.

(*Enter LYUBOV ANDREYEVNA and CHARLOTTA IVANOVNA.*)

LYUBOV (*hums the Lezginka*). Why is Leonid so long? What can he be doing in town? (*To DUNYASHA*) Offer the musicians some tea.

TROFIMOV. The sale hasn't taken place, most likely.

LYUBOV. It's the wrong time to have the orchestra, and the wrong time to give a dance. Well, never mind (*sits down and hums softly*).

CHARLOTTA (*gives PISHTCHIK a pack of cards*). Here's a pack of cards, Think of any card you like.

PISHTCHIK. I've thought of one.

CHARLOTTA. Shuffle the pack now. That's right. Give it here, my dear Mr. Pishtchik. Ein, zwei, drei—now look, it's in your breast pocket.

PISHTCHIK (*taking a card out of his breast pocket*). The eight of spades! Perfectly right! (*Wonderingly*) Fancy that now!

CHARLOTTA (*holding pack of cards in her hands, to* TROFIMOV). Tell me quickly which is the top card.

TROFIMOV. Well, the queen of spades.

CHARLOTTA. It is! (*To* PISHTCHIK) Well, which card is uppermost?

PISHTCHIK. The ace of hearts.

CHARLOTTA. It is! (*claps her hands, pack of cards disappears*). Ah! what lovely weather it is to-day!

    (*A mysterious feminine voice which seems coming out of the floor answers her.* "Oh, yes, it's magnificent weather, madam.")

CHARLOTTA. You are my perfect ideal.

VOICE. And I greatly admire you too, madam.

STATION MASTER (*applauding*). The lady ventriloquist—bravo!

PISHTCHIK (*wonderingly*). Fancy that now! Most enchanting Charlotta Ivanovna. I'm simply in love with you.

CHARLOTTA. In love? (*Shrugging shoulders*) What do you know of love, guter Mensch, aber schlechter Musikant?

TROFIMOV (*pats* PISHTCHIK *on the shoulder*). You dear old horse. . . .

CHARLOTTA. Attention, please! Another trick! (*takes a travelling rug from a chair*). Here's a very good rug; I want to sell it (*shaking it out*). Doesn't anyone want to buy it?

PISHTCHIK (*wonderingly*). Fancy that!

CHARLOTTA. Ein, zwei, drei! (*quickly picks up rug she has dropped; behind the rug stands* ANYA; *she makes a curtsey, runs to her mother, embraces her and runs back into the larger drawing-room amidst general enthusiasm.*)

LYUBOV (*applauds*). Bravo! Bravo!

CHARLOTTA. Now again! Ein, zwei, drei! (*lifts up the rug; behind the rug stands* VARYA, *bowing*).

PISHTCHIK (*wonderingly*). Fancy that now!

CHARLOTTA. That's the end (*throws the rug at* PISHTCHIK, *makes a curtsey, runs into the larger drawing-room*).

PISHTCHIK (*hurries after her*). Mischievous creature! Fancy! (*Goes out.*)

LYUBOV. And still Leonid doesn't come. I can't understand what he's doing in the town so long! Why, everything must be over by now. The estate is sold, or the sale has not taken place. Why keep us so long in suspense?

VARYA (*trying to console her*). Uncle's bought it. I feel sure of that.

TROFIMOV (*ironically*). Oh, yes!

VARYA. Great-aunt sent him an authorisation to buy it in her name, and transfer the debt. She's doing it for Anya's sake, and I'm sure God will be merciful. Uncle will buy it.

LYUBOV. My aunt in Yaroslavl sent fifteen thousand to buy the estate in her name, she doesn't trust us—but that's not enough even to pay the arrears (*hides her face in her hands*). My fate is being sealed to-day, my fate . . .

TROFIMOV (*teasing* VARYA). Madame Lopahin.

VARYA (*angrily*). Perpetual student! Twice already you've been sent down from the University.

LYUBOV. Why are you angry, Varya? He's teasing you about Lopahin. Well, what of that? Marry Lopahin if you like, he's a good man, and interesting; if you don't want to, don't! Nobody compels you, darling.

VARYA. I must tell you plainly, mamma, I look at the matter seriously; he's a good man, I like him.

LYUBOV. Well, marry him. I can't see what you're waiting for.

VARYA. Mamma. I can't make him an offer myself. For the last two years, everyone's been talking to me about him. Everyone talks; but he says nothing or else makes a joke. I see what it means. He's growing rich, he's absorbed in business, he has no thoughts for me. If I had money, were it ever so little, if I had only a hundred roubles, I'd throw everything up and go far away. I would go into a nunnery.

TROFIMOV. What bliss!

VARYA (*to* TROFIMOV). A student ought to have sense! (*In a soft tone with tears*) How ugly you've grown, Petya! How old you look! (*To* LYUBOV ANDREYEVNA, *no longer crying*) But I can't do without work, mamma; I must have something to do every minute.

(*Enter* YASHA.)

YASHA (*hardly restraining his laughter*). Epihodov has broken a billiard cue! (*Goes out.*)

VARYA. What is Epihodov doing here? Who gave him leave to play billiards? I can't make these people out (*goes out*).

LYUBOV. Don't tease her, Petya. You see she has grief enough without that.

TROFIMOV. She is so very officious, meddling in what's not her business. All the summer she's given Anya and me no peace. She's afraid of a love affair between us. What's it to do with her? Besides, I have given no grounds for it. Such triviality is not in my line. We are above love!

LYUBOV. And I suppose I am beneath love. (*Very uneasily*) Why is it Leonid's not here? If only I could know whether the estate is sold or not! It seems such an incredible calamity that I really don't know what to think. I am distracted . . . I shall scream in a minute . . . I shall do something stupid. Save me, Petya, tell me something, talk to me!

TROFIMOV. What does it matter whether the estate is sold to-day or not? That's all done with long ago. There's no turning back, the path is overgrown. Don't worry yourself, dear Lyubov Andreyevna. You mustn't deceive yourself; for once in your life you must face the truth!

LYUBOV. What truth? You see where the truth lies, but I seem to have lost my sight, I see nothing. You settle every great problem so boldly, but tell me, my dear boy, isn't it because you're young—because you haven't yet understood one of your problems through suffering? You look forward boldly, and isn't it that you don't see and don't expect anything dreadful because life is still hidden from your young eyes? You're bolder, more honest, deeper than we are, but think, be just a little magnanimous, have pity on me. I was born here, you know, my father and mother lived here, my grandfather lived here, I love this house. I can't conceive of life without the cherry orchard, and if it really must be sold, then sell me with the orchard (*embraces* TROFIMOV, *kisses him on the forehead*). My boy was drowned here (*weeps*). Pity me, my dear kind fellow.

TROFIMOV. You know I feel for you with all my heart.

LYUBOV. But that should have been said differently, so differently (*takes out her handkerchief, telegram falls on the floor*). My heart is so heavy to-day. It's so noisy here, my soul is quivering at every sound, I'm shuddering all over, but I can't go away; I'm afraid to be quiet and alone. Don't be hard on me, Petya . . . I love you as though you were one of ourselves. I would gladly let you marry Anya—I swear I would—only, my dear boy, you must take your degree, you do nothing—you're simply tossed by fate from place to place. That's so strange. It is, isn't it? And you must do something with your beard to make it grow somehow (*laughs*). You look so funny!

TROFIMOV (*picks up the telegram*). I've no wish to be a beauty.

LYUBOV. That's a telegram from Paris. I get one every day. One yesterday and one to-day. That savage creature is ill again, he's in trouble again. He begs forgiveness, beseeches me to go, and really I ought to go to Paris to see him. You look shocked, Petya. What am I to do, my dear boy, what am I to do? He is ill, he is alone and unhappy, and who'll look after him, who'll keep him from doing the wrong thing, who'll give him his medicine at the right time? And why hide it or be silent? I love him, that's clear. I love him! I love him! He's a millstone about my neck, I'm going to the bottom with him, but I love that stone and can't live without it (*presses* TROFIMOV's *hand*). Don't think ill of me, Petya, don't tell me anything, don't tell me . . .

TROFIMOV (*through his tears*). For God's sake forgive my frankness: why, he robbed you!

LYUBOV. No! No! No! You mustn't speak like that (*covers her ears*).

TROFIMOV. He is a wretch! You're the only person that doesn't know it! He's a worthless creature! A despicable wretch!

LYUBOV (*getting angry, but speaking with restraint*). You're twenty-six or twenty-seven years old, but you're still a schoolboy.

TROFIMOV. Possibly.

LYUBOV. You should be a man at your age! You should understand what love means! And you ought to be in love yourself. You ought to fall in love! (*Angrily*) Yes, yes, and it's not purity in you, you're simply a prude, a comic fool, a freak.

TROFIMOV (*in horror*). The things she's saying!

LYUBOV. I am above love! You're not above love, but simply as our Firs here says, "You are a good-for-nothing." At your age not to have a mistress!

TROFIMOV (*in horror*). This is awful! The things she is saying! (*goes rapidly into the larger drawing-room clutching his head*). This is awful! I can't stand it! I'm going. (*Goes off, but at once returns.*) All is over between us! (*Goes off into the ante-room.*)

LYUBOV (*shouts after him*). Petya! Wait a minute! You funny creature! I was joking! Petya! (*There is a sound of somebody running quickly downstairs and suddenly falling with a crash. ANYA and VARYA scream, but there is a sound of laughter at once*).

LYUBOV. What has happened?

(ANYA *runs in.*)

ANYA (*laughing*). Petya's fallen downstairs! (*Runs out.*)

LYUBOV. What a queer fellow that Petya is!

(*The Station Master stands in the middle of the larger room and reads "The Magdalene," by Alexey Tolstoy. They listen to him, but before he has recited many lines strains of a waltz are heard from the ante-room and the reading is broken off. All dance. TROFIMOV, ANYA, VARYA and LYUBOV ANDREYEVNA come in from the ante-room.*)

LYUBOV. Come, Petya—come, pure heart! I beg your pardon. Let's have a dance! (*dances with PETYA*).

(ANYA *and* VARYA *dance.* FIRS *comes in, puts his stick down near the side door.* YASHA *also comes into the drawing-room and looks on at the dancing.*)

YASHA. What is it, old man?

FIRS. I don't feel well. In old days we used to have generals, barons and admirals dancing at our balls, and now we send for the post-office clerk and the station master and even they're not overanxious to come. I am getting feeble. The old master, the grandfather, used to give sealing-wax for all complaints. I have been taking sealing-wax for twenty years or more. Perhaps that's what's kept me alive.

YASHA. You bore me, old man! (*yawns*). It's time you were done with.

FIRS. Ach, you're a good-for-nothing! (*mutters*).

(TROFIMOV *and* LYUBOV ANDREYEVNA *dance in larger room and then on to the stage*).

LYUBOV. *Merci.* I'll sit down a little (*sits down*). I'm tired.

(*Enter* ANYA.)

ANYA (*excitedly*). There's a man in the kitchen has been saying that the cherry orchard's been sold to-day.

LYUBOV. Sold to whom?

ANYA. He didn't say to whom. He's gone away.

(*She dances with* TROFIMOV, *and they go off into the larger room.*)

YASHA. There was an old man gossiping there, a stranger.

FIRS. Leonid Andreyevitch isn't here yet, he hasn't come back. He has his light overcoat on, *demi-saison*, he'll catch cold for sure. Ach! Foolish young things!

LYUBOV. I feel as though I should die. Go, Yasha, find out to whom it has been sold.

YASHA. But he went away long ago, the old chap (*laughs*).

LYUBOV (*with slight vexation*). What are you laughing at? What are you pleased at?

YASHA. Epihodov is so funny. He's a silly fellow, two and twenty misfortunes.

LYUBOV. Firs, if the estate is sold, where will you go?

FIRS. Where you bid me, there I'll go.

LYUBOV. Why do you look like that? Are you ill? You ought to be in bed.

FIRS. Yes (*ironically*). Me go to bed and who's to wait here? Who's to see to things without me? I'm the only one in all the house.

YASHA (*to* LYUBOV ANDREYEVNA). Lyubov Andreyevna, permit me to make a request of you; if you go back to Paris again, be so kind as to take me with you. It's positively impossible for me to stay here (*looking about him; in an undertone*). There's no need to say it, you see for yourself—an uncivilised country, the people have no morals, and then the dullness! The food in the kitchen's abominable, and then Firs runs after one muttering all sorts of unsuitable words. Take me with you, please do!

(*Enter* PISHTCHIK.)

PISHTCHIK. Allow me to ask you for a waltz, my dear lady. (LYUBOV ANDREYEVNA *goes with him.*) Enchanting lady, I really must borrow of you just 180 roubles (*dances*), only 180 roubles. (*They pass into the larger room.*)

YASHA (*hums softly*). "Knowest thou my soul's emotion."

(*In the larger drawing-room, a figure in a grey top hat and in check trousers is gesticulating and jumping about. Shouts of "Bravo, Charlotta Ivanovna."*)

DUNYASHA (*she has stopped to powder herself*). My young lady tells me to dance. There are plenty of gentlemen, and too few ladies, but dancing makes me giddy and makes my heart beat. Firs, the post-office clerk said something to me just now that quite took my breath away.

(*Music becomes more subdued.*)

FIRS. What did he say to you?

DUNYASHA. He said I was like a flower.

YASHA (*yawns*). What ignorance! (*Goes out.*)

DUNYASHA. Like a flower. I am a girl of such delicate feelings, I am awfully fond of soft speeches.

FIRS. Your head's being turned.

(*Enter* EPIHODOV.)

EPIHODOV. You have no desire to see me, Dunyasha. I might be an insect (*sighs*). Ah! life!

DUNYASHA. What is it you want?

EPIHODOV. Undoubtedly you may be right (*sighs*). But of course, if one looks at it from that point of view, if I may so express myself, you have, excuse my plain speaking, reduced me to a complete state of mind. I know my destiny. Every day some misfortune befalls me and I have long ago grown accustomed to it, so that I look upon my fate with a smile. You gave me your word, and though I——

DUNYASHA. Let us have a talk later, I entreat you, but now leave me in peace, for I am lost in reverie (*plays with her fan*).

EPIHODOV. I have a misfortune every day, and if I may venture to express myself, I merely smile at it, I even laugh.

(VARYA *enters from the larger drawing-room.*)

VARYA. You still have not gone, Epihodov. What a disrespectful creature you are, really! (*To* DUNYASHA) Go along, Dunyasha! (*To* EPIHODOV) First you play billiards and break the cue, then you go wandering about the drawing-room like a visitor!

EPIHODOV. You really cannot, if I may so express myself, call me to account like this.

VARYA. I'm not calling you to account, I'm speaking to you. You do nothing but wander from place to place and don't do your work. We keep you as a counting-house clerk, but what use you are I can't say.

EPIHODOV (*offended*). Whether I work or whether I walk, whether I eat or whether I play billiards, is a matter to be judged by persons of understanding and my elders.

VARYA. You dare to tell me that! (*Firing up*) You dare! You mean to say I've no understanding. Begone from here! This minute!

EPIHODOV (*intimidated*). I beg you to express yourself with delicacy.

VARYA (*beside herself with anger*). This moment! get out! away! (*He goes towards the door, she following him.*) Two and twenty misfortunes! Take yourself off! Don't let me set eyes on you! (EPIHODOV *has gone out, behind the door his voice,* "I shall lodge a complaint against you.") What! You're coming back? (*Snatches up the stick* FIRS *has put down near the door.*) Come! Come! Come! I'll show you! What! you're coming? Then take that! (*She swings the stick, at the very moment that* LOPAHIN *comes in.*)

LOPAHIN. Very much obliged to you!

VARYA (*angrily and ironically*). I beg your pardon!

LOPAHIN. Not at all! I humbly thank you for your kind reception!

VARYA. No need of thanks for it. (*Moves away, then looks round and asks softly*) I haven't hurt you?

LOPAHIN. Oh, no! Not at all! There's an immense bump coming up, though!

VOICES FROM LARGER ROOM. Lopahin has come! Yermolay Alexeyevitch!

PISHTCHIK. What do I see and hear? (*Kisses* LOPAHIN.) There's a whiff of cognac about you, my dear soul, and we're making merry here too!

(*Enter* LYUBOV ANDREYEVNA.)

LYUBOV. Is it you, Yermolay Alexeyevitch? Why have you been so long? Where's Leonid?

LOPAHIN. Leonid Andreyevitch arrived with me. He is coming.

LYUBOV (*in agitation*). Well! Well! Was there a sale? Speak!

LOPAHIN (*embarrassed, afraid of betraying his joy*). The sale was over at four o'clock. We missed our train—had to wait till half-past nine. (*Sighing heavily*) Ugh! I feel a little giddy.

(*Enter* GAEV. *In his right hand he has purchases, with his left hand he is wiping away his tears.*)

LYUBOV. Well, Leonid? What news? (*Impatiently, with tears*) Make haste, for God's sake!

GAEV (*makes her no answer, simply waves his hand. To* FIRS, *weeping*) Here, take them; there's anchovies, Kertch herrings. I have eaten nothing all day. What I have been through! (*Door into the billiard room is open. There is heard a knocking of balls and the voice of* YASHA *saying* "Eighty-seven." GAEV'S *expression changes, he leaves off weeping*). I am fearfully tired. Firs, come and help me change my things (*goes to his own room across the larger drawing-room*).

PISHTCHIK. How about the sale? Tell us, do!

LYUBOV. Is the cherry orchard sold?

LOPAHIN. It is sold.

LYUBOV. Who has bought it?

LOPAHIN. I have bought it. (*A pause.* LYUBOV *is crushed; she would fall down if she were not standing near a chair and table.*)

(VARYA *takes keys from her waist-band, flings them on the floor in middle of drawing-room and goes out.*)

LOPAHIN. I have bought it! Wait a bit, ladies and gentlemen, pray. My head's a bit muddled, I can't speak (*laughs*). We came to the auction. Deriganov was there already. Leonid Andreyevitch only had 15,000 and Deriganov bid 30,000, besides the arrears, straight off. I saw how the land lay. I bid against him. I bid 40,000, he bid 45,000, I said 55, and so he went on, adding 5 thousands and I adding 10. Well . . . So it ended. I bid 90, and it was knocked down to me. Now the cherry orchard's mine! Mine! (*chuckles*) My God, the cherry orchard's mine! Tell me that I'm drunk, that I'm out of my mind, that it's all a dream (*stamps with his feet*). Don't laugh at me! If my father and my grandfather could rise from their graves and see all that has happened! How their Yermolay, ignorant, beaten Yermolay, who used to run about barefoot in winter, how that very Yermolay has bought the finest estate in the world! I have bought the estate where my father and grandfather were slaves, where they weren't even admitted into the kitchen. I am asleep, I am dreaming! It is all fancy, it is the work of your imagination plunged in the darkness of ignorance (*picks up keys, smiling fondly*). She threw away the keys; she means to show she's not the housewife now (*jingles the keys*). Well, no matter. (*The orchestra is heard tuning up.*) Hey, musicians! Play! I want to hear you. Come, all of you, and look how Yermolay Lopahin will take the axe to the cherry orchard, how the trees will fall to the ground! We will build houses on it and our grandsons and great-grandsons will see a new life springing up there. Music! Play up!

(*Music begins to play.* LYUBOV ANDREYEVNA *has sunk into a chair and is weeping bitterly.*)

LOPAHIN (*reproachfully*). Why, why didn't you listen to me? My poor friend! Dear lady, there's no turning back now. (*With tears*) Oh, if all this could be over, oh, if our miserable disjointed life could somehow soon be changed!

PISHTCHIK (*takes him by the arm, in an undertone*). She's weeping, let us go and leave her alone. Come (*takes him by the arm and leads him into the larger drawing-room*).

LOPAHIN. What's that? Musicians, play up! All must be as I wish it. (*With irony*) Here comes the new master, the owner of the cherry orchard! (*Accidentally tips over a little table, almost upsetting the candelabra.*) I can pay for everything! (*Goes out with* PISHTCHIK. *No one remains on the stage or in the larger drawing-room except* LYUBOV, *who sits huddled up, weeping bitterly. The music plays softly.* ANYA *and* TROFIMOV *come in quickly.* ANYA *goes up to her mother and falls on her knees before her.* TROFIMOV *stands at the entrance to the larger drawing-room.*)

ANYA. Mamma! Mamma, you're crying, dear, kind, good mamma! My precious! I love you! I bless you! The cherry orchard is sold, it is gone, that's true, that's true! But don't weep, mamma! Life is still before you, you have still your good, pure heart! Let us go, let us go, darling, away from here! We will make a new garden, more splendid than this one; you will see it, you will understand. And joy, quiet, deep joy, will sink into your soul like the sun at evening! And you will smile, mamma! Come, darling, let us go!

CURTAIN.

ACT IV

SCENE: *Same as in First Act. There are neither curtains on the windows nor pictures on the walls: only a little furniture remains piled up in a corner as if for sale. There is a sense of desolation; near the outer door and in the background of the scene are packed trunks, travelling bags, etc. On the left the door is open, and from here the voices of* VARYA *and* ANYA *are audible.* LOPAHIN *is standing waiting.* YASHA *is holding a tray with glasses full of champagne. In front of the stage* EPIHODOV *is tying up a box. In the background behind the scene a hum of talk from the peasants who have come to say good-bye. The voice of* GAEV: "Thanks, brothers, thanks!"*

YASHA. The peasants have come to say good-bye. In my opinion, Yermolay Alexeyevitch, the peasants are good-natured, but they don't know much about things.

(The hum of talk dies away. Enter across front of stage LYUBOV AN-
DREYEVNA *and* GAEV. *She is not weeping, but is pale; her face is
quivering—she cannot speak.)*

GAEV. You gave them your purse, Lyuba. That won't do—that won't do!

LYUBOV. I couldn't help it! I couldn't help it!

(Both go out.)

LOPAHIN *(in the doorway, calls after them)*. You will take a glass at parting? Please do. I didn't think to bring any from the town, and at the station I
could only get one bottle. Please take a glass *(a pause)*. What? You don't care
for any? *(Comes away from the door)* If I'd known, I wouldn't have bought
it. Well, and I'm not going to drink it. (YASHA *carefully sets the tray down
on a chair.*) You have a glass, Yasha, anyway.

YASHA. Good luck to the travellers, and luck to those that stay behind!
(drinks) This champagne isn't the real thing, I can assure you.

LOPAHIN. It cost eight roubles the bottle *(a pause)*. It's devilish cold here.

YASHA. They haven't heated the stove to-day—it's all the same since we're
going *(laughs)*.

LOPAHIN. What are you laughing for?

YASHA. For pleasure.

LOPAHIN. Though it's October, it's as still and sunny as though it were
summer. It's just right for building! *(Looks at his watch; says in doorway)*
Take note, ladies and gentlemen, the train goes in forty-seven minutes; so you
ought to start for the station in twenty minutes. You must hurry up!

*(*TROFIMOV *comes in from out of doors wearing a greatcoat.)*

TROFIMOV. I think it must be time to start, the horses are ready. The devil
only knows what's become of my goloshes; they're lost. *(In the doorway)*
Anya! My goloshes aren't here. I can't find them.

LOPAHIN. And I'm getting off to Harkov. I am going in the same train with
you. I'm spending all the winter at Harkov. I've been wasting all my time
gossiping with you and fretting with no work to do. I can't get on without
work. I don't know what to do with my hands, they flap about so queerly, as
if they didn't belong to me.

TROFIMOV. Well, we're just going away, and you will take up your profit-
able labours again.

LOPAHIN. Do take a glass.

TROFIMOV. No, thanks.

LOPAHIN. Then you're going to Moscow now?

TROFIMOV. Yes. I shall see them as far as the town, and to-morrow I shall
go on to Moscow.

LOPAHIN. Yes, I daresay, the professors aren't giving any lectures, they're
waiting for your arrival.

TROFIMOV. That's not your business.

LOPAHIN. How many years have you been at the University?

TROFIMOV. Do think of something newer than that—that's stale and flat (*hunts for goloshes*). You know we shall most likely never see each other again, so let me give you one piece of advice at parting: don't wave your arms about—get out of the habit. And another thing, building villas, reckoning up that the summer visitors will in time become independent farmers—reckoning like that, that's not the thing to do either. After all, I am fond of you: you have fine delicate fingers like an artist, you've a fine delicate soul.

LOPAHIN (*embraces him*). Good-bye, my dear fellow. Thanks for everything. Let me give you money for the journey, if you need it.

TROFIMOV. What for? I don't need it.

LOPAHIN. Why, you haven't got a halfpenny.

TROFIMOV. Yes, I have, thank you. I got some money for a translation. Here it is in my pocket, (*anxiously*) but where can my goloshes be!

VARYA (*from the next room*). Take the nasty things! (*Flings a pair of goloshes on to the stage.*)

TROFIMOV. Why are you so cross, Varya? h'm! . . . but those aren't my goloshes.

LOPAHIN. I sowed three thousand acres with poppies in the spring, and now I have cleared forty thousand profit. And when my poppies were in flower, wasn't it a picture! So here, as I say, I made forty thousand, and I'm offering you a loan because I can afford to. Why turn up your nose? I am a peasant—I speak bluntly.

TROFIMOV. Your father was a peasant, mine was a chemist—and that proves absolutely nothing whatever. (LOPAHIN *takes out his pocket-book.*) Stop that—stop that. If you were to offer me two hundred thousand I wouldn't take it. I am an independent man, and everything that all of you, rich and poor alike, prize so highly and hold so dear, hasn't the slightest power over me—it's like so much fluff fluttering in the air. I can get on without you. I can pass by you. I am strong and proud. Humanity is advancing towards the highest truth, the highest happiness, which is possible on earth, and I am in the front ranks.

LOPAHIN. Will you get there?

TROFIMOV. I shall get there (*a pause*). I shall get there, or I shall show others the way to get there.

(*In the distance is heard the stroke of an axe on a tree.*)

LOPAHIN. Good-bye, my dear fellow; it's time to be off. We turn up our noses at one another, but life is passing all the while. When I am working hard without resting, then my mind is more at ease, and it seems to me as though I too know what I exist for; but how many people there are in Russia, my dear boy, who exist, one doesn't know what for. Well, it doesn't matter. That's not what keeps things spinning. They tell me Leonid Andreyevitch has taken a situation. He is going to be a clerk at the bank—6,000 roubles a year. Only, of course, he won't stick to it—he's too lazy.

ANYA (*in the doorway*). Mamma begs you not to let them chop down the orchard until she's gone.

TROFIMOV. Yes, really, you might have the tact (*walks out across the front of the stage*).

LOPAHIN. I'll see to it! I'll see to it! Stupid fellows! (*Goes out after him.*)

ANYA. Has Firs been taken to the hospital?

YASHA. 1 told them this morning. No doubt they have taken him.

ANYA (*to* EPIHODOV, *who passes across the drawing-room*). Semyon Pantaleyevitch, inquire, please, if Firs has been taken to the hospital.

YASHA (*in a tone of offence*). I told Yegor this morning—why ask a dozen times?

EPIHODOV. Firs is advanced in years. It's my conclusive opinion no treatment would do him good; it's time he was gathered to his fathers. And I can only envy him (*puts a trunk down on a cardboard hat-box and crushes it*). There, now, of course—I knew it would be so.

YASHA (*jeeringly*). Two and twenty misfortunes!

VARYA (*through the door*). Has Firs been taken to the hospital?

ANYA. Yes.

VARYA. Why wasn't the note for the doctor taken too?

ANYA. Oh, then, we must send it after them (*goes out*).

VARYA (*from the adjoining room*). Where's Yasha? Tell him his mother's come to say good-bye to him.

YASHA (*waves his hand*). They put me out of all patience! (DUNYASHA *has all this time been busy about the luggage. Now, when* YASHA *is left alone, she goes up to him*).

DUNYASHA. You might just give me one look, Yasha. You're going away. You're leaving me (*weeps and throws herself on his neck*).

YASHA. What are you crying for? (*drinks the champagne*). In six days I shall be in Paris again. To-morrow we shall get into the express train and roll away in a flash. I can scarcely believe it! *Vive la France!* It doesn't suit me here—it's not the life for me; there's no doing anything. I have seen enough of the ignorance here. I have had enough of it (*drinks champagne*). What are you crying for? Behave yourself properly, and then you won't cry.

DUNYASHA (*powders her face, looking in a pocket-mirror*). Do send me a letter from Paris. You know how I loved you, Yasha—how I loved you! I am a tender creature, Yasha.

YASHA. Here they are coming!

(*Busies himself about the trunks, humming softly. Enter* LYUBOV AN-
    DREYEVNA, GAEV, ANYA *and* CHARLOTTA IVANOVNA.)

GAEV. We ought to be off. There's not much time now (*looking at* YASHA). What a smell of herrings!

LYUBOV. In ten minutes we must get into the carriage (*casts a look about the room*). Farewell, dear house, dear old home of our fathers! Winter will pass and spring will come, and then you will be no more; they will tear you down! How much those walls have seen! (*Kisses her daughter passionately.*) My treasure, how bright you look! Your eyes are sparkling like diamonds! Are you glad? Very glad?

ANYA. Very glad! A new life is beginning, mamma.

GAEV. Yes, really, everything is all right now. Before the cherry orchard was sold, we were all worried and wretched, but afterwards, when once the question was settled conclusively, irrevocably, we all felt calm and even cheerful. I am a bank clerk now—I am a financier—cannon off the red. And you, Lyuba, after all, you are looking better; there's no question of that.

LYUBOV. Yes. My nerves are better, that's true. (*Her hat and coat are handed to her.*) I'm sleeping well. Carry out my things, Yasha. It's time. (*To* ANYA) My darling, we shall soon see each other again. I am going to Paris. I can live there on the money your Yaroslavl auntie sent us to buy the estate with—hurrah for auntie!—but that money won't last long.

ANYA. You'll come back soon, mamma, won't you? I'll be working up for my examination in the high school, and when I have passed that, I shall set to work and be a help to you. We will read all sorts of things together, mamma, won't we? (*Kisses her mother's hands.*) We will read in the autumn evenings. We'll read lots of books, and a new wonderful world will open out before us (*dreamily*). Mamma, come soon.

LYUBOV. I shall come, my precious treasure (*embraces her*).

(*Enter* LOPAHIN. CHARLOTTA *softly hums a song.*)

GAEV. Charlotta's happy; she's singing!

CHARLOTTA (*picks up a bundle like a swaddled baby*). Bye, bye, my baby. (*A baby is heard crying: "Ooah! ooah!"*) Hush, hush, my pretty boy! (*Ooah! ooah!*) Poor little thing! (*Throws the bundle back.*) You must please find me a situation. I can't go on like this.

LOPAHIN. We'll find you one, Charlotta Ivanovna. Don't you worry yourself.

GAEV. Everyone's leaving us. Varya's going away. We have become of no use all at once.

CHARLOTTA. There's nowhere for me to be in the town. I must go away. (*Hums*) What care I . . .

(*Enter* PISHTCHIK.)

LOPAHIN. The freak of nature!

PISHTCHIK (*gasping*). Oh! . . . let me get my breath. . . . I'm worn out . . . my most honoured . . . Give me some water.

GAEV. Want some money, I suppose? Your humble servant! I'll go out of the way of temptation (*goes out*).

PISHTCHIK. It's a long while since I have been to see you . . . dearest lady. (*To* LOPAHIN) You are here . . . glad to see you . . . a man of immense intellect . . . take . . . here (*gives* LOPAHIN) 400 roubles. That leaves me owing 840.

LOPAHIN (*shrugging his shoulders in amazement*). It's like a dream. Where did you get it?

PISHTCHIK. Wait a bit . . . I'm hot . . . a most extraordinary occurrence! Some Englishmen came along and found in my land some sort of white clay. (*To* LYUBOV ANDREYEVNA) And 400 for you . . . most lovely . . . wonderful (*gives money*). The rest later (*sips water*). A young man in the train was telling me just now that a great philosopher advises jumping off a house-top. "Jump!" says he; "the whole gist of the problem lies in that." (*Wonderingly*) Fancy that, now! Water, please!

LOPAHIN. What Englishmen?

PISHTCHIK. I have made over to them the rights to dig the clay for twenty-four years . . . and now, excuse me . . . I can't stay . . . I must be trotting on. I'm going to Znoikovo . . . to Kardamanovo. . . . I'm in debt all round (*sips*). . . . To your very good health! . . . I'll come in on Thursday.

LYUBOV. We are just off to the town, and to-morrow I start for abroad.

PISHTCHIK. What! (*In agitation*) Why to the town? Oh, I see the furniture . . . the boxes. No matter . . . (*through his tears*) . . . no matter . . . men of enormous intellect . . . these Englishmen. . . . Never mind . . . be happy. God will succour you . . . no matter . . . everything in this world must have an end (*kisses* LYUBOV ANDREYEVNA'S *hand*). If the rumour reaches you that my end has come, think of this . . . old horse, and say: "There once was such a man in the world . . . Semyonov-Pishtchik . . . the Kingdom of Heaven be his!" . . . most extraordinary weather . . . yes. (*Goes out in violent agitation, but at once returns and says in the doorway*) Dashenka wishes to be remembered to you (*goes out*).

LYUBOV. Now we can start. I leave with two cares in my heart. The first is leaving Firs ill. (*Looking at her watch*) We have still five minutes.

ANYA. Mamma, Firs has been taken to the hospital. Yasha sent him off this morning.

LYUBOV. My other anxiety is Varya. She is used to getting up early and working; and now, without work, she's like a fish out of water. She is thin and pale, and she's crying, poor dear! (*a pause*) You are well aware, Yermolay Alexeyevitch, I dreamed of marrying her to you, and everything seemed to show that you would get married (*whispers to* ANYA *and motions to* CHARLOTTA *and both go out*). She loves you—she suits you. And I don't know—I don't know why it is you seem, as it were, to avoid each other. I can't understand it!

LOPAHIN. I don't understand it myself, I confess. It's queer somehow, altogether. If there's still time, I'm ready now at once. Let's settle it straight off, and go ahead; but without you, I feel I shan't make her an offer.

LYUBOV. That's excellent. Why, a single moment's all that's necessary. I'll call her at once.

LOPAHIN. And there's champagne all ready too (*looking into the glasses*). Empty! Someone's emptied them already. (YASHA *coughs.*) I call that greedy.

LYUBOV (*eagerly*). Capital! We will go out. Yasha, *allez!* I'll call her in. (*At the door*) Varya, leave all that; come here. Come along! (*goes out with* YASHA).

LOPAHIN (*looking at his watch*). Yes.

(*A pause. Behind the door, smothered laughter and whispering, and, at last, enter* VARYA.)

VARYA (*looking a long while over the things*). It is strange, I can't find it anywhere.

LOPAHIN. What are you looking for?

VARYA. I packed it myself, and I can't remember (*a pause*).

LOPAHIN. Where are you going now, Varvara Mihailova?

VARYA. I? To the Ragulins. I have arranged to go to them to look after the house—as a housekeeper.

LOPAHIN. That's in Yashnovo? It'll be seventy miles away (*a pause*). So this is the end of life in this house!

VARYA (*looking among the things*). Where is it? Perhaps I put it in the trunk. Yes, life in this house is over—there will be no more of it.

LOPAHIN. And I'm just off to Harkov—by this next train. I've a lot of business there. I'm leaving Epihodov here, and I've taken him on.

VARYA. Really!

LOPAHIN. This time last year we had snow already, if you remember; but now it's so fine and sunny. Though it's cold, to be sure—three degrees of frost.

VARYA. I haven't looked (*a pause*). And besides, our thermometer's broken (*a pause*).

(*Voice at the door from the yard:* "Yermolay Alexeyevitch!")

LOPAHIN (*as though he had long been expecting this summons*). This minute!

(LOPAHIN *goes out quickly.* VARYA *sitting on the floor and laying her head on a bag full of clothes, sobs quietly. The door opens.* LYUBOV ANDREYEVNA *comes in cautiously.*)

LYUBOV. Well? (*a pause*) We must be going.

VARYA (*has wiped her eyes and is no longer crying*). Yes, mamma, it's time to start. I shall have time to get to the Ragulins to-day, if only you're not late for the train.

LYUBOV (*in the doorway*). Anya, put your things on.

(*Enter* ANYA, *then* GAEV *and* CHARLOTTA IVANOVNA. GAEV *has on a warm coat with a hood. Servants and cabmen come in.* EPIHODOV *bustles about the luggage.*)

LYUBOV. Now we can start on our travels.

ANYA (*joyfully*). On our travels!

GAEV. My friends—my dear, my precious friends! Leaving this house for ever, can I be silent? Can I refrain from giving utterance at leave-taking to those emotions which now flood all my being?

ANYA (*supplicatingly*). Uncle!

VARYA. Uncle, you mustn't!

GAEV (*dejectedly*). Cannon and into the pocket . . . I'll be quiet. . . .

(*Enter* TROFIMOV *and afterwards* LOPAHIN.)

TROFIMOV. Well, ladies and gentlemen, we must start.

LOPAHIN. Epihodov, my coat!

LYUBOV. I'll stay just one minute. It seems as though I have never seen before what the walls, what the ceilings in this house were like, and now I look at them with greediness, with such tender love.

GAEV. I remember when I was six years old sitting in that window on Trinity Day watching my father going to church.

LYUBOV. Have all the things been taken?

LOPAHIN. I think all. (*Putting on overcoat, to* EPIHODOV) You, Epihodov, mind you see everything is right.

EPIHODOV (*in a husky voice*). Don't you trouble, Yermolay Alexeyevitch.

LOPAHIN. Why, what's wrong with your voice?

EPIHODOV. I've just had a drink of water, and I choked over something.

YASHA (*contemptuously*). The ignorance!

LYUBOV. We are going—and not a soul will be left here.

LOPAHIN. Not till the spring.

VARYA (*pulls a parasol out of a bundle, as though about to hit someone with it.* LOPAHIN *makes a gesture as though alarmed*). What is it? I didn't mean anything.

TROFIMOV. Ladies and gentlemen, let us get into the carriage. It's time. The train will be in directly.

VARYA. Petya, here they are, your goloshes, by that box. (*With tears*) And what dirty old things they are!

TROFIMOV (*putting on his goloshes*). Let us go, friends!

GAEV (*greatly agitated, afraid of weeping*). The train—the station! Double baulk, ah!

LYUBOV. Let us go!

LOPAHIN. Are we all here? (*Locks the side-door on left.*) The things are all here. We must lock up. Let us go!

ANYA. Good-bye, home! Good-bye to the old life!

TROFIMOV. Welcome to the new life!

(TROFIMOV *goes out with* ANYA. VARYA *looks round the room and goes out slowly.* YASHA *and* CHARLOTTA IVANOVNA, *with her dog, go out.*)

LOPAHIN. Till the spring, then! Come, friends, till we meet! (*Goes out.*)

(LYUBOV ANDREYEVNA *and* GAEV *remain alone. As though they had been waiting for this, they throw themselves on each other's necks, and break into subdued smothered sobbing, afraid of being overheard.*)

GAEV (*in despair*). Sister, my sister!

LYUBOV. Oh, my orchard!—my sweet, beautiful orchard! My life, my youth, my happiness, good-bye! good-bye!

VOICE OF ANYA (*calling gaily*). Mamma!

VOICE OF TROFIMOV (*gaily, excitedly*). Aa—oo!

LYUBOV. One last look at the walls, at the windows. My dear mother loved to walk about this room.

GAEV. Sister, sister!

VOICE OF ANYA. Mamma!

VOICE OF TROFIMOV. Aa—oo!

LYUBOV. We are coming. (*They go out.*)

(*The stage is empty. There is the sound of the doors being locked up, then of the carriages driving away. There is silence. In the stillness there is the dull stroke of an axe in a tree, clanging with a mournful lonely sound. Footsteps are heard.* FIRS *appears in the doorway on the right. He is dressed as always—in a pea-jacket and white waistcoat, with slippers on his feet. He is ill.*)

FIRS (*goes up to the doors, and tries the handles*). Locked! They have gone . . . (*sits down on sofa*). They have forgotten me. . . . Never mind . . . I'll sit here a bit. . . . I'll be bound Leonid Andreyevitch hasn't put his fur coat on and has gone off in his thin overcoat (*sighs anxiously*). I didn't see after him. . . . These young people . . . (*mutters something that can't be distinguished*). Life has slipped by as though I hadn't lived. (*Lies down*) I'll lie down a bit. . . . There's no strength in you, nothing left you—all gone! Ech! I'm good for nothing (*lies motionless*).

(*A sound is heard that seems to come from the sky, like a breaking harp-string, dying away mournfully. All is still again, and there is heard nothing but the strokes of the axe far away in the orchard.*)

CURTAIN.

THREE SISTERS

First performed in 1901

CHARACTERS IN THE PLAY

ANDREY SERGEYEVITCH PROZOROV.

NATALYA IVANOVNA, *also called* NATASHA (*his fiancée, afterwards his wife*).

OLGA
MASHA } (*his sisters*).
IRINA

FYODOR ILYITCH KULIGIN (*a high-school teacher, husband of* MASHA).

LIEUTENANT-COLONEL ALEXANDR IGNATYEVITCH VERSHININ (*Battery-Commander*).

BARON NIKOLAY LVOVITCH TUSENBACH (*Lieutenant*).

VASSILY VASSILYEVITCH SOLYONY (*Captain*).

IVAN ROMANITCH TCHEBUTYKIN (*Army Doctor*).

ALEXEY PETROVITCH FEDOTIK (*Second Lieutenant*).

VLADIMIR KARLOVITCH RODDEY (*Second Lieutenant*).

FERAPONT (*an old Porter from the Rural Board*).

ANFISA (*the Nurse, an old woman of eighty*).

The action takes place in a provincial town.

ACT I

In the house of the PROZOROVS. *A drawing-room with columns beyond which a large room is visible. Mid-day; it is bright and sunny. The table in the farther room is being laid for lunch.*

OLGA, *in the dark blue uniform of a high-school teacher, is correcting exercise books, at times standing still and then walking up and down;* MASHA, *in a black dress, with her hat on her knee, is reading a book;* IRINA, *in a white dress, is standing plunged in thought.*

OLGA. Father died just a year ago, on this very day—the fifth of May, your name-day, Irina. It was very cold, snow was falling. I felt as though I should not live through it; you lay fainting as though you were dead. But now a year has passed and we can think of it calmly; you are already in a white dress, your face is radiant. (*The clock strikes twelve.*) The clock was striking then too (*a pause*). I remember the band playing and the firing at the cemetery as they carried the coffin. Though he was a general in command of a brigade, yet there weren't many people there. It was raining, though. Heavy rain and snow.

IRINA. Why recall it!

(BARON TUSENBACH, TCHEBUTYKIN *and* SOLYONY *appear near the table in the dining-room, beyond the columns.*)

OLGA. It is warm to-day, we can have the windows open, but the birches are not in leaf yet. Father was given his brigade and came here with us from Moscow eleven years ago and I remember distinctly that in Moscow at this time, at the beginning of May, everything was already in flower; it was warm, and everything was bathed in sunshine. It's eleven years ago, and yet I remember it all as though we had left it yesterday. Oh, dear! I woke up this morning, I saw a blaze of sunshine. I saw the spring, and joy stirred in my heart. I had a passionate longing to be back at home again!

TCHEBUTYKIN. The devil it is!

TUSENBACH. Of course, it's nonsense.

(MASHA, *brooding over a book, softly whistles a song.*)

OLGA. Don't whistle, Masha. How can you! (*a pause*) Being all day in school and then at my lessons till the evening gives me a perpetual headache and thoughts as gloomy as though I were old. And really these four years that

99

I have been at the high-school I have felt my strength and my youth oozing away from me every day. And only one yearning grows stronger and stronger. . . .

IRINA. To go back to Moscow. To sell the house, to make an end of everything here, and off to Moscow. . . .

OLGA. Yes! To Moscow, and quickly.

(TCHEBUTYKIN *and* TUSENBACH *laugh.*)

IRINA. Andrey will probably be a professor, he will not live here anyhow. The only difficulty is poor Masha.

OLGA. Masha will come and spend the whole summer in Moscow every year.

(MASHA *softly whistles a tune.*)

IRINA. Please God it will all be managed. (*Looking out of window*) How fine it is to-day. I don't know why I feel so light-hearted! I remembered this morning that it was my name-day and at once I felt joyful and thought of my childhood when mother was living. And I was thrilled by such wonderful thoughts, such thoughts!

OLGA. You are radiant to-day and looking lovelier than usual. And Masha is lovely too. Andrey would be nice-looking, but he has grown too fat and that does not suit him. And I have grown older and ever so much thinner. I suppose it's because I get so cross with the girls at school. To-day now I am free, I am at home, and my head doesn't ache, and I feel younger than yesterday. I am only twenty-eight. . . . It's all quite right, it's all from God, but it seems to me that if I were married and sitting at home all day, it would be better (*a pause*). I should be fond of my husband.

TUSENBACH (*to* SOLYONY). You talk such nonsense, I am tired of listening to you. (*Coming into the drawing-room*) I forgot to tell you, you will receive a visit to-day from Vershinin, the new commander of our battery (*sits down to the piano*).

OLGA. Well, I shall be delighted.

IRINA. Is he old?

TUSENBACH. No, nothing to speak of. Forty or forty-five at the most (*softly plays the piano*). He seems to be a nice fellow. He is not stupid, that's certain. Only he talks a lot.

IRINA. Is he interesting?

TUSENBACH. Yes, he is all right, only he has a wife, a mother-in-law and two little girls. And it's his second wife too. He is paying calls and telling everyone that he has a wife and two little girls. He'll tell you so too. His wife seems a bit crazy, with her hair in a long plait like a girl's, always talks in a high-flown style, makes philosophical reflections and frequently attempts to commit suicide, evidently to annoy her husband. I should have left a woman like that years ago, but he puts up with her and merely complains.

SOLYONY (*coming into the drawing-room with* TCHEBUTYKIN). With one hand I can only lift up half a hundredweight, but with both hands I can lift up a hundredweight and a half or even a hundredweight and three-quarters. From that I conclude that two men are not only twice but three times as strong as one man, or even more. . . .

TCHEBUTYKIN (*reading the newspaper as he comes in*). For hair falling out . . . two ounces of naphthaline in half a bottle of spirit . . . to be dissolved and used daily . . . (*puts it down in his note-book*). Let's make a note of it! No, I don't want it . . . (*scratches it out*). It doesn't matter.

IRINA. Ivan Romanitch, dear Ivan Romanitch!

TCHEBUTYKIN. What is it, my child, my joy?

IRINA. Tell me, why is it I am so happy to-day? As though I were sailing with the great blue sky above me and big white birds flying over it. Why is it? Why?

TCHEBUTYKIN (*kissing both her hands, tenderly*). My white bird. . . .

IRINA. When I woke up this morning, got up and washed, it suddenly seemed to me as though everything in the world was clear to me and that I knew how one ought to live. Dear Ivan Romanitch, I know all about it. A man ought to work, to toil in the sweat of his brow, whoever he may be, and all the purpose and meaning of his life, his happiness, his ecstasies lie in that alone. How delightful to be a workman who gets up before dawn and breaks stones on the road, or a shepherd, or a schoolmaster teaching children, or an engine-driver. . . . Oh, dear! to say nothing of human beings, it would be better to be an ox, better to be a humble horse and work, than a young woman who wakes at twelve o'clock, then has coffee in bed, then spends two hours dressing. . . . Oh, how awful that is! Just as one has a craving for water in hot weather I have a craving for work. And if I don't get up early and work, give me up as a friend, Ivan Romanitch.

TCHEBUTYKIN (*tenderly*). I'll give you up, I'll give you up. . . .

OLGA. Father trained us to get up at seven o'clock. Now Irina wakes at seven and lies in bed at least till nine thinking. And she looks so serious! (*Laughs*)

IRINA. You are used to thinking of me as a child and are surprised when I look serious. I am twenty!

TUSENBACH. The yearning for work, oh dear, how well I understand it! I have never worked in my life. I was born in cold, idle Petersburg, in a family that had known nothing of work or cares of any kind. I remember, when I came home from the school of cadets, a footman used to pull off my boots. I used to be troublesome, but my mother looked at me with reverential awe, and was surprised when other people did not do the same. I was guarded from work. But I doubt if they have succeeded in guarding me completely, I doubt it! The time is at hand, an avalanche is moving down upon us, a mighty clearing storm which is coming, is already near and will soon blow the laziness, the indifference, the distaste for work, the rotten boredom out of our society. I shall work, and in another twenty-five or thirty years every one will have to work. Every one!

TCHEBUTYKIN. I am not going to work.

TUSENBACH. You don't count.

SOLYONY. In another twenty-five years you won't be here, thank God. In two or three years you will kick the bucket, or I shall lose my temper and put a bullet through your head, my angel. (*Pulls a scent-bottle out of his pocket and sprinkles his chest and hands.*)

TCHEBUTYKIN (*laughs*). And I really have never done anything at all. I haven't done a stroke of work since I left the University, I have never read a book, I read nothing but newspapers . . . (*takes another newspaper out of his pocket*). Here . . . I know, for instance, from the newspapers that there was such a person as Dobrolyubov, but what he wrote, I can't say. . . . Goodness only knows. . . . (*A knock is heard on the floor from the storey below.*) There . . . they are calling me downstairs, someone has come for me. I'll be back directly. . . . Wait a minute . . . (*goes out hurriedly, combing his beard*).

IRINA. He's got something up his sleeve.

TUSENBACH. Yes, he went out with a solemn face, evidently he is just going to bring you a present.

IRINA. What a nuisance!

OLGA. Yes, it's awful. He is always doing something silly.

MASHA. By the sea-strand an oak-tree green . . . upon that oak a chain of gold . . . upon that oak a chain of gold (*gets up, humming softly*).

OLGA. You are not very cheerful to-day, Masha.

(MASHA, *humming, puts on her hat.*)

OLGA. Where are you going?

MASHA. Home.

IRINA. How queer! . . .

TUSENBACH. To go away from a name-day party!

MASHA. Never mind. . . . I'll come in the evening. Good-bye, my darling . . . (*kisses* IRINA). Once again I wish you, be well and happy. In old days, when father was alive, we always had thirty or forty officers here on name-days; it was noisy, but to-day there is only a man and a half, and it is as still as the desert. . . . I'll go. . . . I am in the blues to-day, I am feeling glum, so don't you mind what I say (*laughing through her tears*). We'll talk some other time, and so for now good-bye, darling, I am going. . . .

IRINA (*discontentedly*). Oh, how tiresome you are. . . .

OLGA (*with tears*). I understand you, Masha.

SOLYONY. If a man philosophises, there will be philosophy or sophistry, anyway, but if a woman philosophises, or two do it, then you may just snap your fingers!

MASHA. What do you mean to say by that, you terrible person?

SOLYONY. Nothing. He had not time to say "alack," before the bear was on his back (*a pause*).

MASHA (*to* OLGA, *angrily*). Don't blubber!

(*Enter* ANFISA *and* FERAPONT *carrying a cake.*)

ANFISA. This way, my good man. Come in, your boots are clean. (*To* IRINA) From the Rural Board, from Mihail Ivanitch Protopopov. . . . A cake.

IRINA. Thanks. Thank him (*takes the cake*).

FERAPONT. What?

IRINA (*more loudly*). Thank him from me!

OLGA. Nurse dear, give him some pie. Ferapont, go along, they will give you some pie.

FERAPONT. Eh?

ANFISA. Come along, Ferapont Spiridonitch, my good soul, come along . . . (*goes out with* FERAPONT).

MASHA. I don't like that Protopopov, that Mihail Potapitch or Ivanitch. He ought not to be invited.

IRINA. I did not invite him.

MASHA. That's a good thing.

(*Enter* TCHEBUTYKIN, *followed by an orderly with a silver samovar; a hum of surprise and displeasure.*)

OLGA (*putting her hands over her face*). A samovar! How awful! (*Goes out to the table in the dining-room.*)

IRINA. My dear Ivan Romanitch, what are you thinking about!

TUSENBACH (*laughs*). I warned you!

MASHA. Ivan Romanitch, you really have no conscience!

TCHEBUTYKIN. My dear girls, my darlings, you are all that I have, you are the most precious treasures I have on earth. I shall soon be sixty, I am an old man, alone in the world, a useless old man. . . There is nothing good in me, except my love for you, and if it were not for you, I should have been dead long ago. . . . (*To* IRINA) My dear, my little girl, I've known you from a baby . . . I've carried you in my arms. . . . I loved your dear mother. . . .

IRINA. But why such expensive presents?

TCHEBUTYKIN (*angry and tearful*). Expensive presents. . . . Get along with you! (*to the orderly*) Take the samovar in there . . . (*Mimicking*) Expensive presents . . . (*The orderly carries the samovar into the dining-room.*)

ANFISA (*crossing the room*). My dears, a colonel is here, a stranger. . . He has taken off his greatcoat, children, he is coming in here. Irinushka, you must be nice and polite, dear . . . (*As she goes out*) And it's time for lunch already . . . mercy on us. . . .

TUSENBACH. Vershinin, I suppose.

(*Enter* VERSHININ.)

TUSENBACH. Colonel Vershinin.

VERSHININ (*to* MASHA *and* IRINA). I have the honour to introduce myself, my name is Vershinin. I am very, very glad to be in your house at last. How you have grown up! Aie-aie!

IRINA. Please sit down. We are delighted to see you.

VERSHININ (*with animation*). How glad I am, how glad I am! But there are three of you sisters. I remember—three little girls. I don't remember your faces, but that your father, Colonel Prozorov, had three little girls I remember perfectly, and saw them with my own eyes. How time passes! Hey-ho, how it passes!

TUSENBACH. Alexandr lgnatyevitch has come from Moscow.

IRINA. From Moscow? You have come from Moscow?

VERSHININ. Yes. Your father was in command of a battery there, and I was an officer in the same brigade. (*To* MASHA) Your face, now, I seem to remember.

MASHA. I don't remember you.

IRINA. Olya! Olya! (*Calls into the dining-room*) Olya, come!

(OLGA *comes out of the dining-room into the drawing-room.*)

IRINA. Colonel Vershinin is from Moscow, it appears.

VERSHININ. So you are Olga Sergeyevna, the eldest. . . . And you are Marya. . . . And you are Irina, the youngest. . . .

OLGA. You come from Moscow?

VERSHININ. Yes. I studied in Moscow. I began my service there, I served there for years, and at last I have been given a battery here—I have come here as you see. I don't remember you exactly, I only remember you were three sisters. I remember your father. If I shut my eyes, I can see him as though he were living. I used to visit you in Moscow. . . .

OLGA. I thought I remembered everyone, and now all at once . . .

VERSHININ. My name is Alexandr Ignatyevitch.

IRINA. Alexandr Ignatyevitch, you have come from Moscow. . . . What a surprise!

OLGA. We are going to move there, you know.

IRINA. We are hoping to be there by the autumn. It's our native town, we were born there. . . . In Old Basmanny Street . . . (*both laugh with delight*).

MASHA. To see some one from our own town unexpectedly! (*Eagerly*) Now I remember! Do you remember, Olya, they used to talk of the "love-sick major"? You were a lieutenant at that time and were in love, and for some reason everyone called you "major" to tease you. . . .

VERSHININ (*laughs*). Yes, yes. . . . The love-sick major, that was it.

MASHA. You only had a moustache then. . . . Oh, how much older you look! (*through tears*) how much older!

VERSHININ. Yes, when I was called the love-sick major I was young, I was in love. Now it's very different.

OLGA. But you haven't a single grey hair. You have grown older but you are not old.

VERSHININ. I am in my forty-third year, though. Is it long since you left Moscow?

IRINA. Eleven years. But why are you crying, Masha, you queer girl? . . . (*through her tears*) I shall cry too. . . .

MASHA. I am all right. And in which street did you live?

VERSHININ. In Old Basmanny.

OLGA. And that's where we lived too. . . .

VERSHININ. At one time I lived in Nyemetsky Street. I used to go from there to the Red Barracks. There is a gloomy-looking bridge on the way, where the water makes a noise. It makes a lonely man feel melancholy (*a pause*). And here what a broad, splendid river! A marvellous river!

OLGA. Yes, but it is cold. It's cold here and there are gnats. . . .

VERSHININ. How can you! You've such a splendid healthy Russian climate here. Forest, river . . . and birches here too. Charming, modest birches, I love them better than any other trees. It's nice to live here. The only strange thing is that the railway station is fifteen miles away. . . . And no one knows why it is so.

SOLYONY. I know why it is. (*They all look at him.*) Because if the station had been near it would not have been so far, and if it is far, it's because it is not near.

(*An awkward silence.*)

TUSENBACH. He is fond of his joke, Vassily Vassilyevitch.

OLGA. Now I recall you, too. I remember.

VERSHININ. I knew your mother.

TCHEBUTYKIN. She was a fine woman, the Kingdom of Heaven be hers.

IRINA. Mother is buried in Moscow.

OLGA. In the Novo-Dyevitchy. . . .

MASHA. Would you believe it, I am already beginning to forget her face. So people will not remember us either . . . they will forget us.

VERSHININ. Yes. They will forget us. Such is our fate, there is no help for it. What seems to us serious, significant, very important, will one day be forgotten or will seem unimportant (*a pause*). And it's curious that we can't possibly tell what exactly will be considered great and important, and what will seem paltry and ridiculous. Did not the discoveries of Copernicus or Columbus, let us say, seem useless and ridiculous at first, while the nonsensical writings of some wiseacre seemed true? And it may be that our present life, which we accept so readily, will in time seem queer, uncomfortable, not sensible, not clean enough, perhaps even sinful. . . .

TUSENBACH. Who knows? Perhaps our age will be called a great one and remembered with respect. Now we have no torture-chamber, no executions, no invasions, but at the same time how much unhappiness there is!

SOLYONY (*in a high-pitched voice*). Chook, chook, chook. . . . It's bread and meat to the baron to talk about ideas.

TUSENBACH. Vassily Vassilyevitch, I ask you to let me alone . . . (*moves to another seat*). It gets boring, at last.

SOLYONY (*in a high-pitched voice*). Chook, chook, chook. . . .

TUSENBACH (*to* VERSHININ). The unhappiness which one observes now—there is so much of it—does indicate, however, that society has reached a certain moral level. . . .

VERSHININ. Yes, yes, of course.

TCHEBUTYKIN. You said just now, baron, that our age will be called great; but people are small all the same . . . (*gets up*). Look how small I am.

(*A violin is played behind the scenes.*)

MASHA. That's Andrey playing, our brother.

IRINA. He is the learned one of the family. We expect him to become a professor. Father was a military man, but his son has gone in for a learned career.

MASHA. It was father's wish.

OLGA. We have been teasing him to-day. We think he is a little in love.

IRINA. With a young lady living here. She will come in to-day most likely.

MASHA. Oh, how she dresses! It's not that her clothes are merely ugly or out of fashion, they are simply pitiful. A queer gaudy yellowish skirt with some sort of vulgar fringe and a red blouse. And her cheeks scrubbed till they shine! Andrey is not in love with her—I won't admit that, he has some taste anyway—it's simply for fun, he is teasing us, playing the fool. I heard yesterday that she is going to be married to Protopopov, the chairman of our Rural Board. And a very good thing too. . . . (*At the side door*) Andrey, come here, dear, for a minute!

(*Enter* ANDREY.)

OLGA. This is my brother, Andrey Sergeyevitch.

VERSHININ. My name is Vershinin.

ANDREY. And mine is Prozorov (*mops his perspiring face*). You are our new battery commander?

OLGA. Only fancy, Alexandr Ignatyevitch comes from Moscow.

ANDREY. Really? Well, then, I congratulate you. My sisters will let you have no peace.

VERSHININ. I have had time to bore your sisters already.

IRINA. See what a pretty picture-frame Andrey has given me to-day! (*Shows the frame*) He made it himself.

VERSHININ (*looking at the frame and not knowing what to say*). Yes . . . it is a thing. . . .

IRINA. And that frame above the piano, he made that too!

(ANDREY *waves his hand in despair and moves away.*)

OLGA. He is learned, and he plays the violin, and he makes all sorts of things with the fretsaw. In fact he is good all round. Andrey, don't go! That's a way he has—he always tries to make off! Come here!

(MASHA *and* IRINA *take him by the arms and, laughing, lead him back.*)

MASHA. Come, come!

ANDREY. Leave me alone, please!

MASHA. How absurd he is! Alexandr Ignatyevitch used to be called the love-sick major at one time, and he was not a bit offended.

VERSHININ. Not in the least!

MASHA. And I should like to call you the love-sick violinist!

IRINA. Or the love-sick professor!

OLGA. He is in love! Andryusha is in love!

IRINA (*claps her hands*). Bravo, bravo! Encore! Andryusha is in love!

TCHEBUTYKIN (*comes up behind* ANDREY *and puts both arms round his waist*). Nature our hearts for love created! (*Laughs, then sits down and reads the newspaper which he takes out of his pocket.*)

ANDREY. Come, that's enough, that's enough . . . (*mops his face*). I haven't slept all night and this morning I don't feel quite myself, as they say. I read till four o'clock and then went to bed, but it was no use. I thought of one thing and another, and then it gets light so early; the sun simply pours into my bedroom. I want while I am here during the summer to translate a book from the English. . . .

VERSHININ. You read English then?

ANDREY. Yes. Our father, the Kingdom of Heaven be his, oppressed us with education. It's absurd and silly, but it must be confessed I began to get fatter after his death, and I have grown too fat in one year, as though a weight had been taken off my body. Thanks to our father we all know English, French and German, and Irina knows Italian too. But what it cost us!

MASHA. In this town to know three languages is an unnecessary luxury! Not even a luxury, but an unnecessary encumbrance, like a sixth finger. We know a great deal that is unnecessary.

VERSHININ. What next! (*laughs*) You know a great deal that is unnecessary! I don't think there can be a town so dull and dismal that intelligent and educated people are unnecessary in it. Let us suppose that of the hundred thousand people living in this town, which is, of course, uncultured and behind the times, there are only three of your sort. It goes without saying that you cannot conquer the mass of darkness round you; little by little, as you go on living, you will be lost in the crowd. You will have to give in to it. Life will get the better of you, but still you will not disappear without a trace. After you there may appear perhaps six like you, then twelve and so on until such as you form a majority. In two or three hundred years life on earth will be unimaginably beautiful, marvellous. Man needs such a life and, though he hasn't it yet, he must have a presentiment of it, expect it, dream of it, prepare for it; for that he must see and know more than his father and grandfather (*laughs*). And you complain of knowing a great deal that's unnecessary.

MASHA (*takes off her hat*). I'll stay to lunch.

IRINA (*with a sigh*). All that really ought to be written down. . . .

(ANDREY *has slipped away unobserved.*)

TUSENBACH. You say that after many years life on earth will be beautiful and marvellous. That's true. But in order to have any share, however far off, in it now one must be preparing for it, one must be working. . . .

VERSHININ (*gets up*). Yes. What a lot of flowers you have! (*Looking round*) And delightful rooms. I envy you! I've been knocking about all my life from one wretched lodging to another, always with two chairs and a sofa and stoves which smoke. What I have been lacking all my life is just such flowers . . . (*rubs his hands*). But there, it's no use thinking about it!

TUSENBACH. Yes, we must work. I'll be bound you think the German is getting sentimental. But on my honour I am Russian and I can't even speak German. My father belonged to the Orthodox Church . . . (*a pause*).

VERSHININ (*walks about the stage*). I often think, what if one were to begin life over again, knowing what one is about! If one life, which has been already lived, were only a rough sketch so to say, and the second were the fair copy! Then, I fancy, every one of us would try before everything not to repeat himself, anyway he would create a different setting for his life; would have a house like this with plenty of light and masses of flowers. . . . I have a wife and two little girls, my wife is in delicate health and so on and so on, but if I were to begin life over again I would not marry. . . . No, no!

(*Enter* KULIGIN *in the uniform of a school-master.*)

KULIGIN (*goes up to* IRINA). Dear sister, allow me to congratulate you on your name-day and with all my heart to wish you good health and everything else that one can desire for a girl of your age. And to offer you as a gift this little book (*gives her a book*). The history of our high-school for fifty years, written by myself. An insignificant little book, written because I had nothing better to do, but still you can read it. Good morning, friends. (*To* VERSHININ) My name is Kuligin, teacher in the high-school here. (*To* IRINA) In that book you will find a list of all who have finished their studies in our high-school during the last fifty years. *Feci quod potui, facidnt meliora potentes* (*kisses* MASHA).

IRINA. Why, but you gave me a copy of this book at Easter.

KULIGIN (*laughs*). Impossible! If that's so, give it me back, or better still, give it to the Colonel. Please accept it, Colonel. Some day when you are bored you can read it.

VERSHININ. Thank you (*is about to take leave*). I am extremely glad to have made your acquaintance. . . .

OLGA. You are going? No, no!

IRINA. You must stay to lunch with us. Please do.

OLGA. Pray do!

VERSHININ (*bows*). I believe I have chanced on a name-day. Forgive me, I did not know and have not congratulated you . . . (*Walks away with* OLGA *into the dining-room.*)

KULIGIN. To-day, gentlemen, is Sunday, a day of rest. Let us all rest and enjoy ourselves each in accordance with our age and our position. The carpets should be taken up for the summer and put away till the winter. . . Persian powder or naphthaline. . . . The Romans were healthy because they knew how to work and they knew how to rest, they had *mens sana in corpore sano*. Their life was moulded into a certain framework. Our headmaster says that the most important thing in every life is its framework. . . . What loses its framework, comes to an end—and it's the same in our everyday life. (*Puts his arm round* MASHA's *waist, laughing.*) Masha loves me. My wife loves me. And the window curtains, too, ought to be put away together with the carpets.

. . . To-day I feel cheerful and in the best of spirits. Masha, at four o'clock this afternoon we have to be at the headmaster's. An excursion has been arranged for the teachers and their families.

MASHA. I am not going.

KULIGIN (*grieved*). Dear Masha, why not?

MASHA. We'll talk about it afterwards . . . (*Angrily*) Very well, I will go, only let me alone, please . . . (*walks away*).

KULIGIN. And then we shall spend the evening at the headmaster's. In spite of the delicate state of his health, that man tries before all things to be sociable. He is an excellent, noble personality. A splendid man. Yesterday, after the meeting, he said to me, "I am tired, Fyodor Ilyitch, I am tired." (*Looks at the clock, then at his watch*) Your clock is seven minutes fast. "Yes," he said, "I am tired."

(*Sounds of a violin behind the scenes.*)

OLGA. Come to lunch, please. There's a pie!

KULIGIN. Ah, Olga, my dear Olga! Yesterday I was working from early morning till eleven o'clock at night and was tired out, and to-day I feel happy (*goes up to the table in the dining-room*). My dear. . . .

TCHEBUTYKIN (*puts the newspaper in his pocket and combs his beard*). Pie? Splendid!

MASHA (*to* TCHEBUTYKIN, *sternly*). Only mind you don't drink to-day! Do you hear? It's bad for you to drink.

TCHEBUTYKIN. Oh, come, that's a thing of the past. It's two years since I got drunk. (*Impatiently*) But there, my good girl, what does it matter!

MASHA. Anyway, don't you dare to drink. Don't dare. (*Angrily, but so as not to be heard by her husband*) Again, damnation take it, I am to be bored a whole evening at the headmaster's!

TUSENBACH. I wouldn't go if I were you. . . . It's very simple.

TCHEBUTYKIN. Don't go, my love.

MASHA. Oh, yes, don't go! . . . It's a damnable life, insufferable . . . (*goes to the dining-room*).

TCHEBUTYKIN (*following her*). Come, come. . . .

SOLYONY (*going to the dining-room*). Chook, chook, chook. . . .

TUSENBACH. Enough, Vassily Vassilyevitch! Leave off!

SOLYONY. Chook, chook, chook. . . .

KULIGIN (*gaily*). Your health, Colonel! I am a school-master and one of the family here, Masha's husband. . . . She is very kind, really, very kind. . . .

VERSHININ. I'll have some of this dark-coloured vodka . . . (*drinks*). To your health! (*To* OLGA.) I feel so happy with all of you!

(*No one is left in the drawing-room but* IRINA *and* TUSENBACH.)

IRINA. Masha is in low spirits to-day. She was married at eighteen, when she thought him the cleverest of men. But now it's not the same. He is the kindest of men, but he is not the cleverest.

OLGA (*impatiently*). Andrey, do come!

ANDREY (*behind the scenes*). I am coming (*comes in and goes to the table*).
TUSENBACH. What are you thinking about?
IRINA. Nothing. I don't like that Solyony of yours, I am afraid of him. He
keeps on saying such stupid things. . . .
TUSENBACH. He is a queer man. I am sorry for him and annoyed by him,
but more sorry. I think he is shy. . . . When one is alone with him he is very
intelligent and friendly, but in company he is rude, a bully. Don't go yet, let
them sit down to the table. Let me be by you. What are you thinking of?
(*a pause*) You are twenty, I am not yet thirty. How many years have we
got before us, a long, long chain of days full of my love for you. . . .
IRINA. Nikolay Lvovitch, don't talk to me about love.
TUSENBACH (*not listening*). I have a passionate craving for life, for struggle, for work, and that craving is mingled in my soul with my love for you,
Irina, and just because you are beautiful it seems to me that life too is beautiful! What are you thinking of?
IRINA. You say life is beautiful. . . . Yes, but what if it only seems so! Life
for us three sisters has not been beautiful yet, we have been stifled by it as
plants are choked by weeds. . . . I am shedding tears. . . . I mustn't do that
(*hurriedly wipes her eyes and smiles*). I must work, I must work. The reason
we are depressed and take such a gloomy view of life is that we know nothing
of work. We come of people who despised work. . . .
   (*Enter* NATALYA IVANOVNA; *she is wearing a pink dress with a green sash.*)
NATASHA. They are sitting down to lunch already. . . . I am late . . .
(*Steals a glance at herself in the glass and sets herself to rights*) I think my
hair is all right. (*Seeing* IRINA) Dear Irina Sergeyevna, I congratulate you!
(*Gives her a vigorous and prolonged kiss.*) You have a lot of visitors, I really
feel shy. . . . Good day, Baron!
OLGA (*coming into the drawing-room*). Well, here is Natalya Ivanovna!
How are you, my dear? (*Kisses her.*)
NATASHA. Congratulations on the name-day. You have such a big party and
I feel awfully shy. . . .
OLGA. Nonsense, we have only our own people. (*In an undertone, in alarm*)
You've got on a green sash! My dear, that's not nice!
NATASHA. Why, is that a bad omen?
OLGA. No, it's only that it doesn't go with your dress . . . and it looks
queer. . . .
NATASHA (*in a tearful voice*). Really? But you know it's not green exactly,
it's more a dead colour (*follows* OLGA *into the dining-room*).
   (*In the dining-room they are all sitting down to lunch; there is no one in
     the drawing-room.*)
KULIGIN. I wish you a good husband, Irina. It's time for you to think of
getting married.
TCHEBUTYKIN. Natalya Ivanovna, I hope we may hear of your engagement,
too.

KULIGIN. Natalya Ivanovna has got a suitor already.

MASHA (*strikes her plate with her fork*). Ladies and gentlemen, I want to make a speech!

KULIGIN. You deserve three bad marks for conduct.

VERSHININ. How nice this cordial is! What is it made of?

SOLYONY. Beetles.

IRINA (*in a tearful voice*). Ugh, ugh! How disgusting.

OLGA. We are going to have roast turkey and apple pie for supper. Thank God I am at home all day and shall be at home in the evening. . . . Friends, won't you come this evening?

VERSHININ. Allow me to come too.

IRINA. Please do.

NATASHA. They don't stand on ceremony.

TCHEBUTYKIN. Nature our hearts for love created! (*Laughs*)

ANDREY (*angrily*). Do leave off, I wonder you are not tired of it!

(FEDOTIK *and* RODDEY *come in with a big basket of flowers.*)

FEDOTIK. I say, they are at lunch already.

RODDEY (*speaking loudly, with a lisp*). At lunch? Yes, they are at lunch already. . . .

FEDOTIK. Wait a minute (*takes a snapshot*). One! Wait another minute . . . (*takes another snapshot*). Two! Now it's ready. (*They take the basket and walk into the dining-room, where they are greeted noisily*).

RODDEY (*loudly*). My congratulations! I wish you everything, everything! The weather is delightful, perfectly magnificent. I've been out all the morning for a walk with the high-school boys. I teach them gymnastics.

FEDOTIK. You may move, Irina Sergeyevna, you may move (*taking a photograph*). You look charming to-day (*taking a top out of his pocket*). Here is a top, by the way. . . . It has a wonderful note. . . .

IRINA. How lovely!

MASHA. By the sea-shore an oak-tree green. . . . Upon that oak a chain of gold . . . (*Complainingly*) Why do I keep saying that? That phrase has been haunting me all day. . . .

KULIGIN. Thirteen at table!

RODDEY (*loudly*). Surely you do not attach importance to such superstitions? (*Laughter*)

KULIGIN. If there are thirteen at table, it means that someone present is in love. It's not you, Ivan Romanovitch, by any chance? (*Laughter*)

TCHEBUTYKIN. I am an old sinner, but why Natalya Ivanovna is overcome, I can't imagine . . .

(*Loud laughter;* NATASHA *runs out from the dining-room into the drawing-room followed by* ANDREY.)

ANDREY. Come, don't take any notice! Wait a minute . . . stop, I entreat you. . . .

NATASHA. I am ashamed. . . . I don't know what's the matter with me and they make fun of me. I know it's improper for me to leave the table like this, but I can't help it. . . . I can't . . . (*covers her face with her hands*).

ANDREY. My dear girl, I entreat you, I implore you, don't be upset. I assure you they are only joking, they do it in all kindness. My dear, my sweet, they are all kind, warm-hearted people and they are fond of me and of you. Come here to the window, here they can't see us . . . (*looks round*).

NATASHA. I am so unaccustomed to society! . . .

ANDREY. Oh youth, lovely, marvellous youth! My dear, my sweet, don't be so distressed! Believe me, believe me. . . . I feel so happy, my soul is full of love and rapture. . . . Oh, they can't see us, they can't see us! Why, why, I love you, when I first loved you—oh, I don't know. My dear, my sweet, pure one, be my wife! I love you, I love you . . . as I have never loved anyone . . . (*a kiss*).

(*Two officers come in and, seeing the pair kissing, stop in amazement.*)

CURTAIN.

ACT II

The same scene as in the First Act. Eight o'clock in the evening. Behind the scenes in the street there is the faintly audible sound of a concertina. There is no light. NATALYA IVANOVNA enters in a dressing-gown, carrying a candle; she comes in and stops at the door leading to ANDREY's room.

NATASHA. What are you doing, Andryusha? Reading? Never mind, I only just asked . . . (*goes and opens another door and, peeping into it, shuts it again.*) Is there a light?

ANDREY (*enters with a book in his hand*). What is it, Natasha?

NATASHA. I was looking to see whether there was a light. . . . It's Carnival, the servants are not themselves; one has always to be on the lookout for fear something goes wrong. Last night at twelve o'clock I passed through the dining-room, and there was a candle left burning. I couldn't find out who had lighted it (*puts down the candle*). What's the time?

ANDREY (*looking at his watch*). A quarter past eight.

NATASHA. And Olga and Irina aren't in yet. They haven't come in. Still at work, poor dears! Olga is at the teachers' council and Irina at the telegraph office . . . (*sighs*). I was saying to your sister this morning, "Take care of yourself, Irina darling," said I. But she won't listen. A quarter past eight, you say? I am afraid our Bobik is not at all well. Why is he so cold? Yesterday he was feverish and to-day he is cold all over. . . . I am so anxious!

ANDREY. It's all right, Natasha. The boy is quite well.

NATASHA. We had better be careful about his food, anyway. I am anxious. And I am told that the mummers are going to be here for the Carnival at nine o'clock this evening. It would be better for them not to come, Andryusha.

ANDREY. I really don't know. They've been invited, you know.

NATASHA. Baby woke up this morning, looked at me, and all at once he gave a smile; so he knew me. "Good morning, Bobik!" said I. "Good morning, darling!" And he laughed. Children understand; they understand very well. So I shall tell them, Andryusha, not to let the carnival party come in.

ANDREY (*irresolutely*). That's for my sisters to say. It's for them to give orders.

NATASHA. Yes, for them too; I will speak to them. They are so kind . . . (*is going*). I've ordered junket for supper. The doctor says you must eat nothing but junket, or you will never get thinner (*stops*). Bobik is cold. I am afraid his room is chilly, perhaps. We ought to put him in a different room till the warm weather comes, anyway. Irina's room, for instance, is just right for a nursery: it's dry and the sun shines there all day. I must tell her; she might share Olga's room for the time. . . . She is never at home, anyway, except for the night . . . (*a pause*). Andryushantchik, why don't you speak?

ANDREY. Nothing. I was thinking. . . . Besides, I have nothing to say.

NATASHA. Yes . . . what was it I meant to tell you? . . . Oh, yes; Ferapont has come from the Rural Board, and is asking for you.

ANDREY (*yawns*). Send him in.

(NATASHA *goes out;* ANDREY, *bending down to the candle which she has left behind, reads. Enter* FERAPONT; *he wears an old shabby overcoat, with the collar turned up, and has a scarf over his ears.*)

ANDREY. Good evening, my good man. What is it?

FERAPONT. The Chairman has sent a book and a paper of some sort here . . . (*gives the book and an envelope*).

ANDREY. Thanks. Very good. But why have you come so late? It is past eight.

FERAPONT. Eh?

ANDREY (*louder*). I say, you have come late. It is eight o'clock.

FERAPONT. Just so. I came before it was dark, but they wouldn't let me see you. The master is busy, they told me. Well, of course, if you are busy, I am in no hurry (*thinking that* ANDREY *has asked him a question*). Eh?

ANDREY. Nothing (*examines the book*). To-morrow is Friday. We haven't a sitting, but I'll come all the same . . . and do my work. It's dull at home . . . (*a pause*). Dear old man, how strangely life changes and deceives one! To-day I was so bored and had nothing to do, so I picked up this book—old university lectures—and I laughed. . . . Good heavens! I am the secretary of the Rural Board of which Protopopov is the chairman. I am the secretary, and the most I can hope for is to become a member of the Board! Me, a member of the local Rural Board, while I dream every night I am professor of the University of Moscow—a distinguished man, of whom all Russia is proud!

FERAPONT. I can't say, sir. . . . I don't hear well. . . .

ANDREY. If you did hear well, perhaps I should not talk to you. I must talk to somebody, and my wife does not understand me. My sisters I am somehow afraid of—I'm afraid they will laugh at me and make me ashamed. . . . I don't drink, I am not fond of restaurants, but how I should enjoy sitting at Tyestov's in Moscow at this moment, dear old chap!

FERAPONT. A contractor was saying at the Board the other day that there were some merchants in Moscow eating pancakes; one who ate forty, it seems, died. It was either forty or fifty, I don't remember.

ANDREY. In Moscow you sit in a huge room at a restaurant; you know no one and no one knows you, and at the same time you don't feel a stranger. . . . But here you know everyone and everyone knows you, and yet you are a stranger—a stranger. . . . A stranger, and lonely. . . .

FERAPONT. Eh? (a pause) And the same contractor says—maybe it's not true—that there's a rope stretched right across Moscow.

ANDREY. What for?

FERAPONT. I can't say, sir. The contractor said so.

ANDREY. Nonsense (reads). Have you ever been in Moscow?

FERAPONT (after a pause). No, never. It was not God's will I should (a pause). Am I to go?

ANDREY. You can go. Good-bye. (FERAPONT goes out.) Good-bye (reading). Come to-morrow morning and take some papers here. . . . Go. . . . (a pause). He has gone (a ring). Yes, it is a business . . . (stretches and goes slowly into his own room).

(Behind the scenes a Nurse is singing, rocking a baby to sleep. Enter MASHA and VERSHININ. While they are talking a maidservant is lighting a lamp and candles in the dining-room).

MASHA. I don't know (a pause). I don't know. Of course habit does a great deal. After father's death, for instance, it was a long time before we could get used to having no orderlies in the house. But apart from habit, I think it's a feeling of justice makes me say so. Perhaps it is not so in other places, but in our town the most decent, honourable, and well-bred people are all in the army.

VERSHININ. I am thirsty. I should like some tea.

MASHA (glancing at the clock). They will soon be bringing it. I was married when I was eighteen, and I was afraid of my husband because he was a teacher, and I had only just left school. In those days I thought him an awfully learned, clever, and important person. And now it is not the same, unfortunately. . . .

VERSHININ. Yes. . . . I see. . . .

MASHA. I am not speaking of my husband—I am used to him; but among civilians generally there are so many rude, ill-mannered, badly-brought-up people. Rudeness upsets and distresses me: I am unhappy when I see that a man is not refined, not gentle, not polite enough. When I have to be among the teachers, my husband's colleagues, it makes me quite miserable.

VERSHININ. Yes. . . . But, to my mind, it makes no difference whether they are civilians or military men—they are equally uninteresting, in this town anyway. It's all the same! If one listens to a man of the educated class here, civilian or military, he is worried to death by his wife, worried to death by his house, worried to death by his estate, worried to death by his horses. . . . A Russian is peculiarly given to exalted ideas, but why is it he always falls so short in life? Why?

MASHA. Why?

VERSHININ. Why is he worried to death by his children and by his wife? And why are his wife and children worried to death by him?

MASHA. You are rather depressed this evening.

VERSHININ. Perhaps. . . . I've had no dinner to-day, and had nothing to eat since the morning. My daughter is not quite well, and when my little girls are ill I am consumed by anxiety; my conscience reproaches me for having given them such a mother. Oh, if you had seen her to-day! She is a wretched creature! We began quarrelling at seven o'clock in the morning, and at nine I slammed the door and went away (a pause). I never talk about it. Strange, it's only to you I complain (kisses her hand). Don't be angry with me. . . . Except for you I have no one—no one . . . (a pause).

MASHA. What a noise in the stove! Before father died there was howling in the chimney. There, just like that.

VERSHININ. Are you superstitious?

MASHA. Yes.

VERSHININ. That's strange (kisses her hand). You are a splendid, wonderful woman. Splendid! Wonderful! It's dark, but I see the light in your eyes.

MASHA (moves to another chair). It's lighter here.

VERSHININ. I love you—love, love. . . . I love your eyes, your movements, I see them in my dreams. . . . Splendid, wonderful woman!

MASHA (laughing softly). When you talk to me like that, for some reason I laugh, though I am frightened. . . . Please don't do it again . . . (In an undertone) You may say it, though; I don't mind . . . (covers her face with her hands). I don't mind. . . . Someone is coming. Talk of something else.

(IRINA and TUSENBACH come in through the dining-room.)

TUSENBACH. I've got a three-barrelled name. My name is Baron Tusenbach-Krone-Altschauer, but I belong to the Orthodox Church and am just as Russian as you. There is very little of the German left in me—nothing, perhaps, but the patience and perseverance with which I bore you. I see you home every evening.

IRINA. How tired I am!

TUSENBACH. And every day I will come to the telegraph office and see you home. I'll do it for ten years, for twenty years, till you drive me away . . . (Seeing MASHA and VERSHININ, delightedly) Oh, it's you! How are you?

IRINA. Well, I am home at last. (To MASHA) A lady came just now to telegraph to her brother in Saratov that her son died to-day, and she could not think of the address. So she sent it without an address—simply to Saratov.

She was crying. And I was rude to her for no sort of reason. Told her I had no time to waste. It was so stupid. Are the Carnival people coming to-night?

MASHA. Yes.

IRINA (*sits down in an arm-chair*). I must rest. I am tired.

TUSENBACH (*with a smile*). When you come from the office you seem so young, so forlorn . . . (*a pause*).

IRINA. I am tired. No, I don't like telegraph work, I don't like it.

MASHA. You've grown thinner . . . (*whistles*). And you look younger, rather like a boy in the face.

TUSENBACH. That's the way she does her hair.

IRINA. I must find some other job, this does not suit me. What I so longed for, what I dreamed of is the very thing that it's lacking in. . . . It is work without poetry, without meaning. . . . (*a knock on the floor*). There's the doctor knocking. . . . (*To* TUSENBACH) Do knock, dear. . . . I can't. . . . I am tired.

(TUSENBACH *knocks on the floor.*)

IRINA. He will come directly. We ought to do something about it. The doctor and our Andrey were at the Club yesterday and they lost again. I am told Andrey lost two hundred roubles.

MASHA (*indifferently*). Well, it can't be helped now.

IRINA. A fortnight ago he lost money, in December he lost money. I wish he'd make haste and lose everything, then perhaps we should go away from this town. My God, every night I dream of Moscow, it's perfect madness (*laughs*). We'll move there in June and there is still left February, March, April, May . . . almost half a year.

MASHA. The only thing is Natasha must not hear of his losses.

IRINA. I don't suppose she cares.

(TCHEBUTYKIN, *who has only just got off his bed—he has been resting after dinner—comes into the dining-room combing his beard, then sits down to the table and takes a newspaper out of his pocket.*)

MASHA. Here he is . . . has he paid his rent?

IRINA (*laughs*). No. Not a kopek for eight months. Evidently he has forgotten.

MASHA (*laughs*). How gravely he sits. (*They all laugh; a pause.*)

IRINA. Why are you so quiet, Alexandr Ignatyevitch?

VERSHININ. I don't know. I am longing for tea. I'd give half my life for a glass of tea. I have had nothing to eat since the morning.

TCHEBUTYKIN. Irina Sergeyevna!

IRINA. What is it?

TCHEBUTYKIN. Come here. *Venez ici.* (IRINA *goes and sits down at the table.*) I can't do without you. (IRINA *lays out the cards for patience.*)

VERSHININ. Well, if they won't bring tea, let us discuss something.

TUSENBACH. By all means. What?

VERSHININ. What? Let us dream . . . for instance of the life that will come after us, in two or three hundred years.

TUSENBACH. Well? When we are dead, men will fly in balloons, change the fashion of their coats, will discover a sixth sense, perhaps, and develop it, but life will remain just the same, difficult, full of mysteries and happiness. In a thousand years man will sigh just the same, "Ah, how hard life is," and yet just as now he will be afraid of death and not want it.

VERSHININ (*after a moment's thought*). Well, I don't know. . . . It seems to me that everything on earth is bound to change by degrees and is already changing before our eyes. In two or three hundred, perhaps in a thousand years —the time does not matter—a new, happy life will come. We shall have no share in that life, of course, but we are living for it, we are working, well, yes, and suffering for it, we are creating it—and that alone is the purpose of our existence, and is our happiness, if you like.

(MASHA *laughs softly*.)

TUSENBACH. What is it?

MASHA. I don't know. I've been laughing all day.

VERSHININ. I was at the same school as you were, I did not go to the Military Academy; I read a great deal, but I do not know how to choose my books, and very likely I read quite the wrong things, and yet the longer I live the more I want to know. My hair is turning grey, I am almost an old man, but I know so little, oh so little! But all the same I fancy that I do know and thoroughly grasp what is essential and matters most. And how I should like to make you see that there is no happiness for us, that there ought not to be and will not be. . . . We must work and work, and happiness is the portion of our remote descendants (*a pause*). If it is not for me, at least it is for the descendants of my descendants. . . .

(FEDOTIK and RODDEY *appear in the dining-room; they sit down and sing softly, playing the guitar*.)

TUSENBACH. You think it's no use even dreaming of happiness! But what if I am happy?

VERSHININ. No.

TUSENBACH (*flinging up his hands and laughing*). It is clear we don't understand each other. Well, how am I to convince you?

(MASHA *laughs softly*.)

TUSENBACH (*holds up a finger to her*). Laugh! (*To* VERSHININ) Not only in two or three hundred years but in a million years life will be just the same; it does not change, it remains stationary, following its own laws which we have nothing to do with or which, anyway, we shall never find out. Migratory birds, cranes for instance, fly backwards and forwards, and whatever ideas, great or small, stray through their minds, they will still go on flying just the same without knowing where or why. They fly and will continue to fly, however philosophic they may become; and it doesn't matter how philosophical they are so long as they go on flying. . . .

MASHA. But still there is a meaning?

TUSENBACH. Meaning. . . . Here it is snowing. What meaning is there in that? (*A pause.*)

MASHA. I think man ought to have faith or ought to seek a faith, or else his life is empty, empty. . . . To live and not to understand why cranes fly; why children are born; why there are stars in the sky. . . . One must know what one is living for or else it is all nonsense and waste (*a pause*).

VERSHININ. And yet one is sorry that youth is over. . . .

MASHA. Gogol says: it's dull living in this world, friends!

TUSENBACH. And I say: it is difficult to argue with you, my friends, God bless you. . . .

TCHEBUTYKIN (*reading the newspaper*). Balzac was married at Berditchev.
(IRINA *hums softly.*)

TCHEBUTYKIN. I really must put that down in my book (*writes*) Balzac was married at Berditchev (*reads the paper*).

IRINA (*lays out the cards for patience, dreamily*). Balzac was married at Berditchev.

TUSENBACH. The die is cast. You know, Marya Sergeyevna, I've resigned my commission.

MASHA. So I hear. And I see nothing good in that. I don't like civilians.

TUSENBACH. Never mind . . . (*gets up*). I am not good-looking enough for a soldier. But that does not matter, though . . . I am going to work. If only for one day in my life, to work so that I come home at night tired out and fall asleep as soon as I get into bed . . . (*going into the dining-room*). Workmen must sleep soundly!

FEDOTIK (*to* IRINA). I bought these chalks for you just now as I passed the shop. . . . And this penknife. . . .

IRINA. You've got into the way of treating me as though I were little, but I am grown up, you know . . . (*takes the chalks and the penknife, joyfully*). How lovely!

FEDOTIK. And I bought a knife for myself . . . look . . . one blade, and another blade, a third, and this is for the ears, and here are scissors, and that's for cleaning the nails. . . .

RODDEY (*loudly*). Doctor, how old are you?

TCHEBUTYKIN. I? Thirty-two (*laughter*).

FEDOTIK. I'll show you another patience . . . (*lays out the cards*).
(*The samovar is brought in;* ANFISA *is at the samovar; a little later* NATASHA *comes in and is also busy at the table;* SOLYONY *comes in, and after greeting the others sits down at the table.*)

VERSHININ. What a wind there is!

MASHA. Yes. I am sick of the winter. I've forgotten what summer is like.

IRINA. It's coming out right, I see. We shall go to Moscow.

FEDOTIK. No, it's not coming out. You see, the eight is over the two of spades (*laughs*). So that means you won't go to Moscow.

TCHEBUTYKIN (*reads from the newspaper*). Tsi-tsi-kar. Smallpox is raging here.

ANFISA (*going up to* MASHA). Masha, come to tea, my dear. (*To* VERSHININ) Come, your honour . . . excuse me, sir, I have forgotten your name. . . .

MASHA. Bring it here, nurse, I am not going there.

IRINA. Nurse!

ANFISA. I am coming!

NATASHA (*to* SOLYONY). Little babies understand very well. "Good morning Bobik, good morning, darling," I said. He looked at me in quite a special way. You think I say that because I am a mother, but no, I assure you! He is an extraordinary child.

SOLYONY. If that child were mine, I'd fry him in a frying-pan and eat him. (*Takes his glass, comes into the drawing-room and sits down in a corner.*)

NATASHA (*covers her face with her hands*). Rude, ill-bred man!

MASHA. Happy people don't notice whether it is winter or summer. I fancy if I lived in Moscow I should not mind what the weather was like. . . .

VERSHININ. The other day I was reading the diary of a French minister written in prison. The minister was condemned for the Panama affair. With what enthusiasm and delight he describes the birds he sees from the prison window, which he never noticed before when he was a minister. Now that he is released, of course he notices birds no more than he did before. In the same way, you won't notice Moscow when you live in it. We have no happiness and never do have, we only long for it.

TUSENBACH (*takes a box from the table*). What has become of the sweets?

IRINA. Solyony has eaten them.

TUSENBACH. All?

ANFISA (*handing tea*). There's a letter for you, sir.

VERSHININ. For me? (*Takes the letter.*) From my daughter (*reads*). Yes, of course. . . . Excuse me, Marya Sergeyevna, I'll slip away. I won't have tea (*gets up in agitation*). Always these upsets. . . .

MASHA. What is it? Not a secret?

VERSHININ (*in a low voice*). My wife has taken poison again. I must go. I'll slip off unnoticed. Horribly unpleasant it all is. (*Kisses* MASHA'S *hand*) My fine, dear, splendid woman. . . . I'll go this way without being seen . . . (*goes out*).

ANFISA. Where is he off to? I've just given him his tea. . . . What a man.

MASHA (*getting angry*). Leave off! Don't pester, you give one no peace . . . (*goes with her cup to the table*). You bother me, old lady.

ANFISA. Why are you so huffy? Darling!

(*Andrey's voice:* "ANFISA!")

ANFISA (*mimicking*). Anfisa! he sits there. . . . (*goes out*).

MASHA (*by the table in the dining-room, angrily*). Let me sit down! (*Mixes the cards on the table.*) You take up all the table with your cards. Drink your tea!

IRINA. How cross you are, Masha!

MASHA. If I'm cross, don't talk to me. Don't interfere with me.

TCHEBUTYKIN (*laughing*). Don't touch her, don't touch her!

MASHA. You are sixty, but you talk rot like a schoolboy.

NATASHA (*sighs*). Dear Masha, why make use of such expressions in conversation? With your attractive appearance I tell you straight out, you would be simply fascinating in a well-bred social circle if it were not for the things you say. *Je vous prie, pardonnez-moi, Marie, mais vous avez des manières un peu grossières.*

TUSENBACH (*suppressing a laugh*). Give me . . . give me . . . I think there is some brandy there.

NATASHA. *Il paraît que mon Bobik déjà ne dort pas,* he is awake. He is not well to-day. I must go to him, excuse me. . . . (*goes out*).

IRINA. Where has Alexandr Ignatyevitch gone?

MASHA. Home. Something queer with his wife again.

TUSENBACH (*goes up to* SOLYONY *with a decanter of brandy in his hand*). You always sit alone, thinking, and there's no making out what you think about. Come, let us make it up. Let us have a drink of brandy. (*They drink.*) I shall have to play the piano all night, I suppose, play all sorts of trash. . . . Here goes!

SOLYONY. Why make it up? I haven't quarrelled with you.

TUSENBACH. You always make me feel as though something had gone wrong between us. You are a queer character, there's no denying that.

SOLYONY (*declaims*). I am strange, who is not strange! Be not wrath, Aleko!

TUSENBACH. I don't see what Aleko has got to do with it. . . .

SOLYONY. When I am *tête-à-tête* with somebody, I am all right, just like anyone else, but in company I am depressed, ill at ease and . . . say all sorts of idiotic things, but at the same time I am more conscientious and straight-forward than many. And I can prove it. . . .

TUSENBACH. I often feel angry with you, you are always attacking me when we are in company, and yet I somehow like you. Here goes, I am going to drink a lot to-day. Let's drink!

SOLYONY. Let us (*drinks*). I have never had anything against you, Baron. But I have the temperament of Lermontov. (*In a low voice*) In fact I am rather like Lermontov to look at . . . so I am told (*takes out scent-bottle and sprinkles scent on his hands*).

TUSENBACH. I have sent in my papers. I've had enough of it! I have been thinking of it for five years and at last I have come up to the scratch. I am going to work.

SOLYONY (*declaims*). Be not wrath, Aleko. . . . Forget, forget thy dreams. . . .

(*While they are talking* ANDREY *comes in quietly with a book and sits down by a candle.*)

TUSENBACH I am going to work.

TCHEBUTYKIN (*coming into the drawing-room with* IRINA). And the food too was real Caucasian stuff: onion soup and for the meat course *tchehartma.* . . .

SOLYONY. *Tcheremsha* is not meat at all, it's a plant rather like our onion.

TCHEBUTYKIN. No, my dear soul, it's not onion, but mutton roasted in a special way.

SOLYONY. But I tell you that *tcheremsha* is an onion.

TCHEBUTYKIN. And I tell you that *tchehartma* is mutton.

SOLYONY. And I tell you that *tcheremsha* is an onion.

TCHEBUTYKIN. What's the use of my arguing with you? You have never been to the Caucasus or eaten *tchehartma.*

SOLYONY. I haven't eaten it because I can't bear it. *Tcheremsha* smells like garlic.

ANDREY (*imploringly*). That's enough! Please!

TUSENBACH. When are the Carnival party coming?

IRINA. They promised to come at nine, so they will be here directly.

TUSENBACH (*embraces* ANDREY *and sings*). "Oh my porch, oh my new porch . . ."

ANDREY (*dances and sings*). "With posts of maple wood. . . ."

TCHEBUTYKIN (*dances*). "And lattice work complete . . ." (*laughter*).

TUSENBACH (*kisses* ANDREY). Hang it all, let us have a drink. Andryusha, let us drink to our everlasting friendship. I'll go to the University when you do, Andryusha.

SOLYONY. Which? There are two universities in Moscow.

ANDREY. There is only one university in Moscow.

SOLYONY. I tell you there are two.

ANDREY. There may be three for aught I care. So much the better.

SOLYONY. There are two universities in Moscow! (*A murmur and hisses.*) There are two universities in Moscow: the old one and the new one. And if you don't care to hear, if what I say irritates you, I can keep quiet. I can even go into another room (*goes out at one of the doors*).

TUSENBACH. Bravo, bravo! (*laughs*) Friends, begin, I'll sit down and play! Funny fellow that Solyony. . . . (*Sits down to the piano and plays a waltz.*)

MASHA (*dances a waltz alone*). The baron is drunk, the baron is drunk, the baron is drunk.

(*Enter* NATASHA.)

NATASHA (*to* TCHEBUTYKIN). Ivan Romanitch! (*Says something to* TCHEBUTYKIN, *then goes out softly.* TCHEBUTYKIN *touches* TUSENBACH *on the shoulder and whispers something to him.*)

IRINA. What is it?

TCHEBUTYKIN. It's time we were going. Good night.

TUSENBACH. Good night. It's time to be going.

IRINA. But I say . . . what about the Carnival party?

ANDREY (*with embarrassment*). They won't be coming. You see, dear,

Natasha says Bobik is not well, and so . . . In fact I know nothing about it, and don't care either.

IRINA (*shrugs her shoulders*). Bobik is not well!

MASHA. Well, it's not the first time we've had to lump it! If we are turned out, we must go. (*To* IRINA) It's not Bobik that is ill, but she is a bit . . . (*taps her forehead with her finger*). Petty, vulgar creature!

(ANDREY *goes by door on right to his own room,* TCHEBUTYKIN *following him; they are saying good-bye in the dining-room.*)

FEDOTIK. What a pity! I was meaning to spend the evening, but of course if the child is ill . . . I'll bring him a toy to-morrow.

RODDEY (*loudly*). I had a nap to-day after dinner on purpose, I thought I would be dancing all night. . . . Why, it's only nine o'clock.

MASHA. Let us go into the street; there we can talk. We'll decide what to do.

(*Sounds of* "Good-bye! Good night!" *The good-humoured laugh of* TUSENBACH *is heard. All go out.* ANFISA *and the maidservant clear the table and put out the light. There is the sound of the nurse singing.* ANDREY *in his hat and coat, and* TCHEBUTYKIN *come in quietly.*)

TCHEBUTYKIN. I never had time to get married, because life has flashed by like lightning and because I was passionately in love with your mother, who was married.

ANDREY. One shouldn't get married. One shouldn't, because it's boring.

TCHEBUTYKIN. That's all very well, but what about loneliness? Say what you like, it's a dreadful thing to be lonely, my dear boy. . . . But no matter, though!

ANDREY. Let's make haste and go.

TCHEBUTYKIN. What's the hurry? We have plenty of time.

ANDREY. I am afraid my wife may stop me.

TCHEBUTYKIN. Oh!

ANDREY. I am not going to play to-day, I shall just sit and look on. I don't feel well. . . . What am I to do, Ivan Romanitch, I am so short of breath?

TCHEBUTYKIN. It's no use asking me! I don't remember, dear boy. . . . I don't know. . . .

ANDREY. Let us go through the kitchen. (*They go out.*)

(*A ring, then another ring; there is a sound of voices and laughter.*)

IRINA (*enters*). What is it?

ANFISA (*in a whisper*). The mummers, all dressed up (*a ring*).

IRINA. Nurse, dear, say there is no one at home. They must excuse us.

(ANFISA *goes out.* IRINA *walks about the room in hesitation; she is excited. Enter* SOLYONY.)

SOLYONY (*in perplexity*). No one here. . . . Where are they all?

IRINA. They have gone home.

SOLYONY. How queer. Are you alone here?

IRINA. Yes (*a pause*). Good night.

SOLYONY. I behaved tactlessly, without sufficient restraint just now. But you are not like other people, you are pure and lofty, you see the truth. You alone can understand me. I love you, I love you deeply, infinitely.

IRINA. Good night! You must go.

SOLYONY. I can't live without you (*following her*). Oh, my bliss! (*Through his tears*) Oh, happiness! Those glorious, exquisite, marvellous eyes such as I have never seen in any other woman.

IRINA (*coldly*). Don't, Vassily Vassilyitch!

SOLYONY. For the first time I am speaking of love to you, and I feel as though I were not on earth but on another planet (*rubs his forehead*). But there, it does not matter. There is no forcing kindness, of course. . . . But there must be no happy rivals. . . . There must not. . . . I swear by all that is sacred I will kill any rival. . . . O exquisite being!

(NATASHA *passes with a candle*.)

NATASHA (*peeps in at one door, then at another and passes by the door that leads to her husband's room*). Andrey is there. Let him read. Excuse me, Vassily Vassilyitch, I did not know you were here, and I am in my dressing-gown. . . .

SOLYONY. I don't care. Good-bye! (*Goes out.*)

NATASHA. You are tired, my poor, dear little girl! (*kisses* IRINA). You ought to go to bed earlier. . . .

IRINA. Is Bobik asleep?

NATASHA. He is asleep, but not sleeping quietly. By the way, dear, I keep meaning to speak to you, but either you are out or else I haven't the time. . . . I think Bobik's nursery is cold and damp. And your room is so nice for a baby. My sweet, my dear, you might move for a time into Olya's room!

IRINA (*not understanding*). Where?

(*The sound of a three-horse sledge with bells driving up to the door.*)

NATASHA. You would be in the same room with Olya, and Bobik in your room. He is such a poppet. I said to him to-day, "Bobik, you are mine, you are mine!" and he looked at me with his funny little eyes. (*A ring.*) That must be Olya. How late she is!

(*The maid comes up to* NATASHA *and whispers in her ear.*)

NATASHA. Protopopov? What a queer fellow he is! Protopopov has come, and asks me to go out with him in his sledge (*laughs*). How strange men are! . . . (*A ring*) Somebody has come. I might go for a quarter of an hour. . . . (*To the maid*) Tell him I'll come directly. (*A ring*) You hear . . . it must be Olya (*goes out*).

(*The maid runs out;* IRINA *sits lost in thought;* KULIGIN, OLGA *and* VERSHININ *come in.*)

KULIGIN. Well, this is a surprise! They said they were going to have an evening party.

VERSHININ. Strange! And when I went away half an hour ago they were expecting the Carnival people. . . .

IRINA. They have all gone.

KULIGIN. Has Masha gone too? Where has she gone? And why is Protc.. popov waiting below with his sledge? Whom is he waiting for?

IRINA. Don't ask questions. . . . I am tired.

KULIGIN. Oh, you little cross-patch. . . .

OLGA. The meeting is only just over. I am tired out. Our headmistress is ill and I have to take her place. Oh, my head, my head does ache; oh, my head! (*Sits down.*) Andrey lost two hundred roubles yesterday at cards. . . . The whole town is talking about it. . . .

KULIGIN. Yes, I am tired out by the meeting too (*sits down*).

VERSHININ. My wife took it into her head to give me a fright, she nearly poisoned herself. It's all right now, and I'm glad, it's a relief. . . . So we are to go away? Very well, then, I will say good night. Fyodor Ilyitch, let us go somewhere together! I can't stay at home, I absolutely can't. . . . Come along!

KULIGIN. I am tired. I am not coming (*gets up*). I am tired. Has my wife gone home?

IRINA. I expect so.

KULIGIN (*kisses* IRINA's *hand*). Good-bye! I have all day to-morrow and next day to rest. Good night! (*Going*) I do want some tea. I was reckoning on spending the evening in pleasant company. . . . *O fallacem hominum spem!* . . . Accusative of exclamation.

VERSHININ. Well, then, I must go alone (*goes out with* KULIGIN, *whistling*).

OLGA. My head aches, oh, how my head aches. . . . Andrey has lost at cards. . . . The whole town is talking about it. . . . I'll go and lie down (*is going*). To-morrow I shall be free. . . . Oh, goodness, how nice that is! To-morrow I am free, and the day after I am free. . . . My head does ache, oh, my head . . . (*goes out*).

IRINA (*alone*). They have all gone away. There is no one left.

(*A concertina plays in the street, the nurse sings.*)

NATASHA (*in a fur cap and coat crosses the dining-room, followed by the maid*). I shall be back in half an hour. I shall only go a little way (*goes out*).

IRINA (*left alone, in dejection*). Oh, to go to Moscow, to Moscow!

CURTAIN.

ACT III

The Bedroom of OLGA *and* IRINA. *On left and right beds with screens round them. Past two o'clock in the night. Behind the scenes a bell is ringing on account of a fire in the town, which has been going on for some time. It can be seen that no one in the house has gone to bed yet. On the sofa* MASHA *is lying, dressed as usual in black. Enter* OLGA *and* ANFISA.

ANFISA. They are sitting below, under the stairs. . . . I said to them, "Come upstairs; why, you mustn't stay there"—they only cried. "We don't know where father is," they said. "What if he is burnt!" What an idea! And the poor souls in the yard . . . they are all undressed too.

OLGA (taking clothes out of the cupboard). Take this grey dress . . . and this one . . . and the blouse too . . . and that skirt, nurse. . . . Oh, dear, what a dreadful thing! Kirsanov Street is burnt to the ground, it seems. . . . Take this . . . take this . . . (throws clothes into her arms). The Vershinins have had a fright, poor things. . . . Their house was very nearly burnt. Let them stay the night here . . . we can't let them go home. . . . Poor Fedotik has had everything burnt, he has not a thing left. . . .

ANFISA. You'had better call Ferapont, Olya darling, I can't carry it all.

OLGA (rings). No one will answer the bell (at the door). Come here, whoever is there! (Through the open door can be seen a window red with fire; the fire brigade is heard passing the house). How awful it is! And how sickening!

(Enter FERAPONT.)

OLGA. Here take these, carry them downstairs. . . . The Kolotilin young ladies are downstairs . . . give it to them . . . and give this too.

FERAPONT. Yes, miss. In 1812 Moscow was burnt too. . . . Mercy on us! The French marvelled.

OLGA. You can go now.

FERAPONT. Yes, miss (goes out).

OLGA. Nurse darling, give them everything. We don't want anything, give it all to them. . . . I am tired, I can hardly stand on my feet. . . . We mustn't let the Vershinins go home. . . . The little girls can sleep in the drawing-room, and Alexandr Ignatyevitch down below at the baron's. . . . Fedotik can go to the baron's, too, or sleep in our dining-room. . . . As illluck will have it, the doctor is drunk, frightfully drunk, and no one can be put in his room. And Vershinin's wife can be in the drawing-room too.

ANFISA (wearily). Olya darling, don't send me away; don't send me away!

OLGA. That's nonsense, nurse. No one is sending you away.

ANFISA (lays her head on OLGA's shoulder). My own, my treasure, I work, I do my best. . . . I'm getting weak, everyone will say "Be off!" And where am I to go? Where? I am eighty. Eighty-one.

OLGA. Sit down, nurse darling. . . . You are tired, poor thing . . . (makes her sit down). Rest, dear good nurse. . . . How pale you are!

(Enter NATASHA)

NATASHA. They are saying we must form a committee at once for the assistance of those whose houses have been burnt. Well, that's a good idea. Indeed, one ought always to be ready to help the poor, it's the duty of the rich. Bobik and baby Sophie are both asleep, sleeping as though nothing were happening. There are such a lot of people everywhere, wherever one goes, the house is full. There is influenza in the town now; I am so afraid the children may get it.

OLGA (*not listening*). In this room one does not see the fire, it's quiet here.

NATASHA. Yes . . . my hair must be untidy (*in front of the looking-glass*). They say I have grown fatter . . . but it's not true! Not a bit! Masha is asleep. she is tired out, poor dear. . . . (*To* ANFISA *coldly*) Don't dare to sit down in my presence! Get up! Go out of the room! (ANFISA *goes out; a pause*). Why you keep that old woman, I can't understand!

OLGA (*taken aback*). Excuse me, I don't understand either. . . .

NATASHA. She is no use here. She is a peasant; she ought to be in the country. . . . You spoil people! I like order in the house! There ought to be no useless servants in the house. (*Strokes her cheek.*) You are tired, poor darling. Our headmistress is tired! When baby Sophie is a big girl and goes to the high-school, I shall be afraid of you.

OLGA. I shan't be headmistress.

NATASHA. You will be elected, Olya. That's a settled thing.

OLGA. I shall refuse. I can't. . . . It's too much for me . . . (*drinks water*). You were so rude to nurse just now. . . . Excuse me, I can't endure it. . . . It makes me feel faint.

NATASHA (*perturbed*). Forgive me, Olya; forgive me. . . . I did not mean to hurt your feelings.

(MASHA *gets up, takes her pillow, and goes out in a rage.*)

OLGA. You must understand, my dear, it may be that we have been strangely brought up, but I can't endure it. . . . Such an attitude oppresses me, it makes me ill. . . . I feel simply unnerved by it. . . .

NATASHA. Forgive me; forgive me . . . (*kisses her*).

OLGA. The very slightest rudeness, a tactless word, upsets me. . . .

NATASHA. I often say too much, that's true, but you must admit, dear, that she might just as well be in the country.

OLGA. She has been thirty years with us.

NATASHA. But now she can't work! Either I don't understand, or you won't understand me. She is not fit for work. She does nothing but sleep or sit still.

OLGA. Well, let her sit still.

NATASHA (*surprised*). How, sit still? Why, she is a servant. (*Through tears*) I don't understand you, Olya. I have a nurse to look after the children as well as a wet nurse for baby, and we have a housemaid and a cook, what do we want that old woman for? What's the use of her?

(*The alarm bell rings behind the scenes.*)

OLGA. This night has made me ten years older.

NATASHA. We must come to an understanding, Olya. You are at the high-school, I am at home; you are teaching while I look after the house, and if I say anything about the servants, I know what I'm talking about; I do know what I am talking about. . . . And that old thief, that old hag . . . (*stamps*), that old witch shall clear out of the house to-morrow! . . . I won't have people annoy me! I won't have it! (*Feeling that she has gone too far*) Really, if you don't move downstairs, we shall always be quarrelling. It's awful.

(*Enter* KULIGIN.)

KULIGIN. Where is Masha? It's time to be going home. The fire is dying down, so they say (*stretches*). Only one part of the town has been burnt, and yet there was a wind; it seemed at first as though the whole town would be destroyed (*sits down*). I am exhausted. Olya, my dear . . . I often think if it had not been for Masha I should have married you. You are so good. . . . I am tired out (*listens*).

OLGA. What is it?

KULIGIN. It is unfortunate the doctor should have a drinking bout just now; he is helplessly drunk. Most unfortunate (*gets up*). Here he comes, I do believe. . . . Do you hear? Yes, he is coming this way . . . (*laughs*). What a man he is, really. . . . I shall hide (*goes to the cupboard and stands in the corner*). Isn't he a ruffian!

OLGA. He has not drunk for two years and now he has gone and done it . . . (*walks away with* NATASHA *to the back of the room*).

(TCHEBUTYKIN *comes in; walking as though sober without staggering, he walks across the room, stops, looks round; then goes up to the washing-stand and begins to wash his hands.*)

TCHEBUTYKIN (*morosely*). The devil take them all . . . damn them all. They think I am a doctor, that I can treat all sorts of complaints, and I really know nothing about it, I have forgotten all I did know, I remember nothing, absolutely nothing. (OLGA *and* NATASHA *go out unnoticed by him.*) The devil take them. Last Wednesday I treated a woman at Zasyp—she died, and it's my fault that she died. Yes . . . I did know something twenty-five years ago, but now I remember nothing, nothing. Perhaps I am not a man at all but only pretend to have arms and legs and head; perhaps I don't exist at all and only fancy that I walk about, eat and sleep (*weeps*). Oh, if only I did not exist! (*Leaves off weeping, morosely*) I don't care! I don't care a scrap! (*a pause*) Goodness knows. . . . The day before yesterday there was a conversation at the club: they talked about Shakespeare, Voltaire. . . . I have read nothing, nothing at all, but I looked as though I had read them. And the others did the same as I did. The vulgarity! The meanness! And that woman I killed on Wednesday came back to my mind . . . and it all came back to my mind and everything seemed nasty, disgusting and all awry in my soul. . . . I went and got drunk. . . .

(*Enter* IRINA, VERSHININ *and* TUSENBACH; TUSENBACH *is wearing a fashionable new civilian suit.*)

IRINA. Let us sit here. No one will come here.

VERSHININ. If it had not been for the soldiers, the whole town would have been burnt down. Splendid fellows! (*Rubs his hands with pleasure.*) They are first-rate men! Splendid fellows!

KULIGIN (*going up to them*). What time is it?

TUSENBACH. It's past three. It's getting light already.

IRINA. They are all sitting in the dining-room. No one seems to think of

going. And that Solyony of yours is sitting there too. . . . (*To* TCHEBUTYKIN)
You had better go to bed, doctor.

TCHEBUTYKIN. It's all right. . . . Thank you! (*Combs his beard.*)

KULIGIN (*laughs*). You are a bit fuddled, Ivan Romanitch! (*Slaps him on the shoulder.*) Bravo! *In vino veritas*, the ancients used to say.

TUSENBACH. Everyone is asking me to get up a concert for the benefit of the families whose houses have been burnt down.

IRINA. Why, who is there? . . .

TUSENBACH. We could get it up, if we wanted to. Marya Sergeyevna plays the piano splendidly, to my thinking.

KULIGIN. Yes, she plays splendidly.

IRINA. She has forgotten. She has not played for three . . . or four years.

TUSENBACH. There is absolutely no one who understands music in this town, not one soul, but I do understand and on my honour I assure you that Marya Sergeyevna plays magnificently, almost with genius.

KULIGIN. You are right, Baron. I am very fond of her; Masha, I mean. She is a good sort.

TUSENBACH. To be able to play so gloriously and to know that no one understands you!

KULIGIN (*sighs*). Yes. . . . But would it be suitable for her to take part in a concert? (*a pause*) I know nothing about it, my friends. Perhaps it would be all right. There is no denying that our director is a fine man, indeed a very fine man, very intelligent, but he has such views. . . . Of course it is not his business, still if you like I'll speak to him about it.

(TCHEBUTYKIN *takes up a china clock and examines it.*)

VERSHININ. I got dirty all over at the fire. I am a sight (*a pause*). I heard a word dropped yesterday about our brigade being transferred ever so far away. Some say to Poland, and others to Tchita.

TUSENBACH. I've heard something about it too. Well! The town will be a wilderness then.

IRINA. We shall go away too.

TCHEBUTYKIN (*drops the clock, which smashes*). To smithereens!

KULIGIN (*picking up the pieces*). To smash such a valuable thing—oh, Ivan Romanitch, Ivan Romanitch! I should give you minus zero for conduct!

IRINA. That was mother's clock.

TCHEBUTYKIN. Perhaps. . . . Well, if it was hers, it was. Perhaps I did not smash it, but it only seems as though I had. Perhaps it only seems to us that we exist, but really we are not here at all. I don't know anything—nobody knows anything. (*By the door*) What are you staring at? Natasha has got a little affair on with Protopopov, and you don't see it. . . . You sit here and see nothing, while Natasha has a little affair on with Protopopov . . . (*sings*). May I offer you this date? . . . (*Goes out.*)

VERSHININ. Yes . . . (*laughs*). How very queer it all is, really! (*a pause*) When the fire began I ran home as fast as I could. I went up and saw our house was safe and sound and out of danger, but my little girls were standing in the doorway in their nightgowns; their mother was nowhere to be seen, people were bustling about, horses and dogs were running about, and my children's faces were full of alarm, horror, entreaty, and I don't know what; it wrung my heart to see their faces. My God, I thought, what more have these children to go through in the long years to come! I took their hands and ran along with them, and could think of nothing else but what more they would have to go through in this world! (*a pause*) When I came to your house I found their mother here, screaming, angry.

(MASHA *comes in with the pillow and sits down on the sofa.*)

VERSHININ. And while my little girls were standing in the doorway in their nightgowns and the street was red with the fire, and there was a fearful noise, I thought that something like it used to happen years ago when the enemy would suddenly make a raid and begin plundering and burning. . . . And yet, in reality, what a difference there is between what is now and has been in the past! And when a little more time has passed—another two or three hundred years—people will look at our present manner of life with horror and derision, and everything of to-day will seem awkward and heavy, and very strange and uncomfortable. Oh, what a wonderful life that will be—what a wonderful life! (*Laughs*) Forgive me, here I am airing my theories again! Allow me to go on. I have such a desire to talk about the future. I am in the mood (*a pause*). It's as though everyone were asleep. And so, I say, what a wonderful life it will be! Can you only imagine? . . . There are only three of your sort in the town now, but in generations to come there will be more and more and more; and the time will come when everything will be changed and be as you would have it; they will live in your way, and later on you too will be out of date—people will be born who will be better than you. . . . (*laughs*). I am in such a strange state of mind to-day. I have a fiendish longing for life . . . (*sings*). Young and old are bound by love, and precious are its pangs . . . (*laughs*).

MASHA. Tram-tam-tam!

VERSHININ. Tam-tam!

MASHA. Tra-ra-ra?

VERSHININ. Tra-ta-ta! (*Laughs*)

(*Enter* FEDOTIK.)

FEDOTIK (*dances*). Burnt to ashes! Burnt to ashes! Everything I had in the world (*laughter*).

IRINA. A queer thing to joke about. Is everything burnt?

FEDOTIK (*laughs*). Everything I had in the world. Nothing is left. My guitar is burnt, and the camera and all my letters. . . . And the note-book I meant to give you—that's burnt too.

(*Enter* SOLYONY.)

IRINA. No; please go, Vassily Vassilyitch. You can't stay here.

SOLYONY. How is it the baron can be here and I can't?

VERSHININ. We must be going, really. How is the fire?

SOLYONY. They say it is dying down. No, I really can't understand why the baron may be here and not I (*takes out a bottle of scent and sprinkles himself*).

VERSHININ. Tram-tam-tam!

MASHA. Tram-tam!

VERSHININ (*laughs, to* SOLYONY). Let us go into the dining-room.

SOLYONY. Very well; we'll make a note of it. I might explain my meaning further, but fear I may provoke the geese . . . (*looking at* TUSENBACH). Chook, chook, chook! . . . (*Goes out with* VERSHININ *and* FEDOTIK.)

IRINA. How that horrid Solyony has made the room smell of tobacco! . . . (*In surprise*) The baron is asleep! Baron, baron!

TUSENBACH (*waking up*). I am tired, though. . . . The brickyard. I am not talking in my sleep. I really am going to the brickyard directly, to begin work. . . . It's nearly settled. (*To* IRINA, *tenderly*) You are so pale and lovely and fascinating. . . . It seems to me as though your paleness sheds a light through the dark air. . . . You are melancholy; you are dissatisfied with life. . . . Ah, come with me; let us go and work together!

MASHA. Nikolay Lvovitch, do go!

TUSENBACH (*laughing*). Are you here? I didn't see you . . . (*kisses* IRINA's *hand*). Good-bye, I am going. . . . I look at you now, and I remember as though it were long ago how on your name-day you talked of the joy of work, and were so gay and confident. . . . And what a happy life I was dreaming of then! What has become of it? (*Kisses her hand.*) There are tears in your eyes. Go to bed, it's getting light . . . it is nearly morning. . . . If it were granted to me to give my life for you!

MASHA. Nikolay Lvovitch, do go! Come, really. . . .

TUSENBACH. I am going (*goes out*).

MASHA (*lying down*). Are you asleep, Fyodor?

KULIGIN. Eh?

MASHA. You had better go home.

KULIGIN. My darling Masha, my precious girl! . . .

IRINA. She is tired out. Let her rest, Fedya.

KULIGIN. I'll go at once. . . . My dear, charming wife! . . . I love you, my only one! . . .

MASHA (*angrily*). Amo, amas, amat; amamus, amatis, amant.

KULIGIN (*laughs*). Yes, really she is wonderful. You have been my wife for seven years, and it seems to me as though we were only married yesterday. Honour bright! Yes, really you are a wonderful woman! I am content, I am content, I am content!

MASHA. I am bored, I am bored, I am bored! . . . (*Gets up and speaks, sitting down*) And there's something I can't get out of my head. . . . It's simply revolting. It sticks in my head like a nail; I must speak of it. I mean about Andrey. . . . He has mortgaged this house in the bank and his wife has grabbed all the money, and you know the house does not belong to him alone, but to us four! He ought to know that, if he is a decent man.

KULIGIN. Why do you want to bother about it, Masha? What is it to you? Andryusha is in debt all round, so there it is.

MASHA. It's revolting, anyway (*lies down*).

KULIGIN. We are not poor. I work—I go to the high-school, and then I give private lessons. . . . I do my duty. . . . There's no nonsense about me. *Omnia mea mecum porto*, as the saying is.

MASHA. I want nothing, but it's the injustice that revolts me (*a pause*). Go, Fyodor.

KULIGIN (*kisses her*). You are tired, rest for half an hour, and I'll sit and wait for you. . . . Sleep . . . (*goes*). I am content. I am content, I am content (*goes out*).

IRINA. Yes, how petty our Andrey has grown, how dull and old he has become beside that woman! At one time he was working to get a professorship and yesterday he was boasting of having succeeded at last in becoming a member of the Rural Board. He is a member, and Protopopov is chairman. . . . The whole town is laughing and talking of it and he is the only one who sees and knows nothing. . . . And here everyone has been running to the fire while he sits still in his room and takes no notice. He does nothing but play his violin . . . (*nervously*). Oh, it's awful, awful, awful! (*Weeps*) I can't bear it any more, I can't! I can't, I can't!

(OLGA *comes in and begins tidying up her table.*)

IRINA (*sobs loudly*). Turn me out, turn me out, I can't bear it any more!

OLGA (*alarmed*). What is it? What is it, darling?

IRINA (*sobbing*). Where? Where has it all gone? Where is it? Oh, my God, my God! I have forgotten everything, everything . . . everything is in a tangle in my mind. . . . I don't remember the Italian for window or ceiling . . . I am forgetting everything; every day I forget something more and life is slipping away and will never come back, we shall never, never go to Moscow. . . . I see that we shan't go. . . .

OLGA. Darling, darling. . . .

IRINA (*restraining herself*). Oh, I am wretched. . . . I can't work, I am not going to work. I have had enough of it, enough of it! I have been a telegraph clerk and now I have a job in the town council and I hate and despise every bit of the work they give me. . . . I am nearly twenty-four, I have been working for years, my brains are drying up, I am getting thin and old and ugly and there is nothing, nothing, not the slightest satisfaction, and time is passing and one feels that one is moving away from a real, fine life, moving farther and farther away and being drawn into the depths. I am in despair and I don't know how it is I am alive and have not killed myself yet.

OLGA. Don't cry, my child, don't cry. It makes me miserable.

IRINA. I am not crying, I am not crying. . . . It's over. . . . There, I am not crying now. I won't . . . I won't.

OLGA. Darling, I am speaking to you as a sister, as a friend, if you care for my advice, marry the baron!

(IRINA *weeps*.)

OLGA (*softly*). You know you respect him, you think highly of him. . . . It's true he is ugly, but he is such a thoroughly nice man, so good. . . . One doesn't marry for love, but to do one's duty. . . . That's what I think, anyway, and I would marry without love. Whoever proposed to me I would marry him, if only he were a good man. . . I would even marry an old man. . . .

IRINA. I kept expecting we should move to Moscow and there I should meet my real one. I've been dreaming of him, loving him. . . . But it seems that was all nonsense, nonsense. . . .

OLGA (*puts her arms round her sister*). My darling, lovely sister, I understand it all; when the baron left the army and came to us in a plain coat, I thought he looked so ugly that it positively made me cry. . . . He asked me, "Why are you crying?" How could I tell him! But if God brought you together I should be happy. That's a different thing, you know, quite different.

(NATASHA *with a candle in her hand walks across the stage from door on right to door on left without speaking*.)

MASHA (*sits up*). She walks about as though it were she had set fire to the town.

OLGA. Masha, you are silly. The very silliest of the family, that's you. Please forgive me (*a pause*).

MASHA. I want to confess my sins, dear sisters. My soul is yearning. I am going to confess to you and never again to anyone. . . . I'll tell you this minute (*softly*). It's my secret, but you must know everything. . . . I can't be silent . . . (*a pause*). I am in love, I am in love. . . . I love that man. . . . You have just seen him. . . . Well, I may as well say it straight out. I love Vershinin.

OLGA (*going behind her screen*). Leave off. I don't hear anyway.

MASHA. But what am I to do? (*Clutches her head*.) At first I thought him queer . . . then I was sorry for him . . . then I came to love him . . . to love him with his voice, his words, his misfortunes, his two little girls. . . .

OLGA (*behind the screen*). I don't hear you anyway. Whatever silly things you say I shan't hear them.

MASHA. Oh, Olya, you are silly. I love him—so that's my fate. It means that that's my lot. . . . And he loves me. . . . It's all dreadful. Yes? Is it wrong? (*Takes* IRINA *by the hand and draws her to herself*.) Oh, my darling. . . . How are we going to live our lives, what will become of us? . . . When one reads a novel it all seems stale and easy to understand, but when you are in love yourself you see that no one knows anything and we all have to settle things for ourselves. . . . My darling, my sister. . . . I have confessed it to you, now I'll hold my tongue. . . . I'll be like Gogol's madman . . . silence . . . silence. . . .

(*Enter* ANDREY *and after him* FERAPONT.)

ANDREY (*angrily*). What do you want? I can't make it out.

FERAPONT (*in the doorway, impatiently*). I've told you ten times already, Andrey Sergeyevitch.

ANDREY. In the first place I am not Andrey Sergeyevitch, but your honour, to you!

FERAPONT. The firemen ask leave, your honour, to go through the garden on their way to the river. Or else they have to go round and round, an awful nuisance for them.

ANDREY. Very good. Tell them, very good. (FERAPONT *goes out*). I am sick of them. Where is Olga? (OLGA *comes from behind the screen*.) I've come to ask you for the key of the cupboard, I have lost mine. You've got one, it's a little key.

(OLGA *gives him the key in silence;* IRINA *goes behind her screen; a pause.*)

ANDREY. What a tremendous fire! Now it's begun to die down. Hang it all, that Ferapont made me so cross I said something silly to him. Your honour . . . (*a pause*). Why don't you speak, Olya? (*a pause*) It's time to drop this foolishness and sulking all about nothing. . . . You are here, Masha, and you too, Irina—very well, then, let us have things out thoroughly, once for all. What have you against me? What is it?

OLGA. Leave off, Andryusha. Let us talk to-morrow (*nervously*). What an agonizing night!·

ANDREY (*greatly confused*). Don't excite yourself. I ask you quite coolly, what have you against me? Tell me straight out.

(VERSHININ'S *voice:* "Tram-tam-tam!")

MASHA (*standing up, loudly*). Tra-ta-ta! (*To* OLGA) Good night, Olya, God bless you . . . (*Goes behind the screen and kisses* IRINA.) Sleep well. . . . Good night, Andrey. You'd better leave them now, they are tired out . . . you can go into things to-morrow (*goes out*).

OLGA. Yes, really, Andryusha, let us put it off till to-morrow . . . (*goes behind her screen*). It's time we were in bed.

ANDREY. I'll say what I have to say and then go. Directly. . . . First, you have something against Natasha, my wife, and I've noticed that from the very day of my marriage. Natasha is a splendid woman, conscientious, straightforward and honourable—that's my opinion! I love and respect my wife, do you understand? I respect her, and I insist on other people respecting her too. I repeat, she is a conscientious, honourable woman, and all your disagreements are simply caprice, or rather the whims of old maids. Old maids never like and never have liked their sisters-in-law—that's the rule (*a pause*). Secondly, you seem to be cross with me for not being a professor, not working at something learned. But I am in the service of the Zemstvo, I am a member of the Rural Board, and I consider this service just as sacred and elevated as the service of learning. I am a member of the Rural Board and I am proud of it, if you care to know . . . (*a pause*). Thirdly . . . there's something else I have to say. . . . I have mortgaged the house without asking your permission. . . . For that I am to blame, yes, and I ask your pardon for it. I was driven to it by my debts . . . thirty-five thousand. . . . I am not gambling now—I gave up cards long ago; but the chief thing I can say in self-defence is that you are, so to say, of the privileged sex—you get a pension . . . while I had not . . . my wages, so to speak . . . (a pause).

KULIGIN (at the door). Isn't Masha here? (Perturbed) Where is she? It's strange . . . (goes out).

ANDREY. They won't listen. Natasha is an excellent, conscientious woman (paces up and down the stage in silence, then stops). When I married her, I thought we should be happy . . . happy, all of us. . . . But, my God! (Weeps) Dear sisters, darling sisters, you must not believe what I say, you mustn't believe it . . . (goes out).

KULIGIN (at the door, uneasily). Where is Masha? Isn't Masha here? How strange! (Goes out.)

(The firebell rings in the street. The stage is empty.)

IRINA (behind the screen). Olya! Who is that knocking on the floor?

OLGA. It's the doctor, Ivan Romanitch. He is drunk.

IRINA. What a troubled night! (a pause) Olya! (Peeps out from behind the screen.) Have you heard? The brigade is going to be taken away; they are being transferred to some place very far off.

OLGA. That's only a rumour.

IRINA. Then we shall be alone. . . . Olya!

OLGA. Well?

IRINA. My dear, my darling, I respect the baron, I think highly of him, he is a fine man—I will marry him, I consent, only let us go to Moscow! I entreat you, do let us go! There's nothing in the world better than Moscow! Let us go, Olya! Let us go!

CURTAIN.

ACT IV

Old garden of the PROZOROVS' *house. A long avenue of fir trees, at the end of which is a view of the river. On the farther side of the river there is a wood. On the right the verandah of the house; on the table in it are bottles and glasses; evidently they have just been drinking champagne. It is twelve o'clock in the day. People pass occasionally from the street across the garden to the river; five soldiers pass rapidly.*

TCHEBUTYKIN, *in an affable mood, which persists throughout the act, is sitting in an easy chair in the garden, waiting to be summoned; he is wearing a military cap and has a stick.* IRINA, KULIGIN *with a decoration on his breast and with no moustache, and* TUSENBACH, *standing on the ve-randah, are saying good-bye to* FEDOTIK *and* RODDEY, *who are going down the steps; both officers are in marching uniform.*

TUSENBACH (*kissing* FEDOTIK). You are a good fellow; we've got on so happily together. (*Kisses* RODDEY.) Once more. . . . Good-bye, my dear boy. . .

IRINA. Till we meet again!

FEDOTIK. No, it's good-bye for good; we shall never meet again.

KULIGIN. Who knows! (*Wipes his eyes, smiles.*) Here I am crying too.

IRINA. We shall meet some day.

FEDOTIK. In ten years, or fifteen perhaps? But then we shall scarcely recognise each other—we shall greet each other coldly . . . (*Takes a snapshot*) Stand still. . . . Once more, for the last time.

RODDEY (*embraces* TUSENBACH). We shall not see each other again. . . . (*Kisses* IRINA's *hand.*) Thank you for everything, everything. . . .

FEDOTIK (*with vexation*). Oh, do wait!

TUSENBACH. Please God we shall meet again. Write to us. Be sure to write to us.

RODDEY (*taking a long look at the garden*). Good-bye, trees! (*Shouts*) Halloo! (*a pause*) Good-bye, echo!

KULIGIN. I shouldn't wonder if you get married in Poland. . . . Your Polish wife will clasp you in her arms and call you *kochany!* (*Laughs*)

FEDOTIK (*looking at his watch*). We have less than an hour. Of our battery only Solyony is going on the barge; we are going with the rank and file. Three divisions of the battery are going to-day and three more to-morrow—and peace and quiet will descend upon the town.

TUSENBACH. And dreadful boredom too.

RODDEY. And where is Marya Sergeyevna?

KULIGIN. Masha is in the garden.

FEDOTIK. We must say good-bye to her.

RODDEY. Good-bye. We must go, or I shall begin to cry . . . (*Hurriedly embraces* TUSENBACH *and* KULIGIN *and kisses* [RINA's *hand.*) We've had a splendid time here.

FEDOTIK (*to* KULIGIN). This is a little souvenir for you . . . a note-book with a pencil. . . . We'll go down here to the river . . . (*As they go away both look back.*)

RODDEY (*shouts*). Halloo-oo!

KULIGIN (*shouts*). Good-bye!

(RODDEY *and* FEDOTIK *meet* MASHA *in the background and say good-bye to her; she walks away with them.*)

IRINA. They've gone . . . (*Sits down on the bottom step of the verandah.*)

TCHEBUTYKIN. They have forgotten to say good-bye to me.

IRINA. And what were you thinking about?

TCHEBUTYKIN. Why, I somehow forget, too. But I shall see them again soon, I am setting off to-morrow. Yes . . . I have one day more. In a year I shall be on the retired list. Then I shall come here again and shall spend the rest of my life near you. . . . There is only one year now before I get my pension. (*Puts a newspaper into his pocket and takes out another.*) I shall come here to you and arrange my life quite differently. . . . I shall become such a quiet . . . God-fearing . . well-behaved person.

IRINA. Well, you do need to arrange your life differently, dear Ivan Romanitch. You certainly ought to somehow.

TCHEBUTYKIN. Yes, I feel it. (*Softly hums.*) "Tarara-boom-dee-ay—Tarara-boom-dee-ay."

KULIGIN. Ivan Romanitch is incorrigible! Incorrigible!

TCHEBUTYKIN. You ought to take me in hand. Then I should reform.

IRINA. Fyodor has shaved off his moustache. I can't bear to look at him!

KULIGIN. Why, what's wrong?

TCHEBUTYKIN. I might tell you what your countenance looks like now, but I really can't.

KULIGIN. Well! It's the thing now, *modus vivendi*. Our headmaster is clean-shaven and now I am second to him I have taken to shaving too. Nobody likes it, but I don't care. I am content. With moustache or without moustache I am equally content (*sits down*).

(*In the background* ANDREY *is wheeling a baby asleep in a perambulator.*)

IRINA. Ivan Romanitch, darling, I am dreadfully uneasy. You were on the boulevard yesterday, tell me what was it that happened?

TCHEBUTYKIN. What happened? Nothing. Nothing much (*reads the newspaper*). It doesn't matter!

KULIGIN. The story is that Solyony and the baron met yesterday on the boulevard near the theatre. . . .

TUSENBACH. Oh, stop it! Really . . . (*with a wave of his hand walks away into the house*).

KULIGIN. Near the theatre. . . . Solyony began pestering the baron and he couldn't keep his temper and said something offensive. . . .

TCHEBUTYKIN. I don't know. It's all nonsense.

KULIGIN. A teacher at a divinity school wrote "nonsense" at the bottom of an essay and the pupil puzzled over it thinking it was a Latin word . . . (*laughs*). It was fearfully funny. . . . They say Solyony is in love with Irina and hates the baron. . . . That's natural. Irina is a very nice girl.

(*From the background behind the scenes,* "Aa-oo! Halloo!")

IRINA (*starts*). Everything frightens me somehow to-day (*a pause*). All my things are ready, after dinner I shall send off my luggage. The baron and I are to be married to-morrow, to-morrow we go to the brickyard and the day after that I shall be in the school. A new life is beginning. God will help me! How will it fare with me? When I passed my exam. as a teacher I felt so appy, so blissful, that I cried . . . (*a pause*). The cart will soon be coming or my things. . . .

KULIGIN. That's all very well, but it does not seem serious. It's all nothing but ideas and very little that is serious. However, I wish you success with all my heart.

TCHEBUTYKIN (*moved to tenderness*). My good, delightful darling. . . . My heart of gold. . . .

KULIGIN. Well, to-day the officers will be gone and everything will go on in the old way. Whatever people may say, Masha is a true, good woman. I love her dearly and am thankful for my lot! . . . People have different lots in life. . . . There is a man called Kozyrev serving in the Excise here. He was at school with me, but he was expelled from the fifth form because he could never understand *ut consecutivum*. Now he is frightfully poor and ill, and when I meet him I say, "How are you, *ut consecutivum?*" "Yes," he says, "just so—*consecutivum*" . . . and then he coughs. . . . Now I have always been successful, I am fortunate, I have even got the order of the Stanislav of the second degree and I am teaching others that *ut consecutivum*. Of course I am clever, cleverer than very many people, but happiness does not lie in that . . . (*a pause*).

(*In the house the "Maiden's Prayer" is played on the piano.*)

IRINA. To-morrow evening I shall not be hearing that "Maiden's Prayer," shan't be meeting Protopopov . . . (*a pause*). Protopopov is sitting there in the drawing-room; he has come again to-day. . . .

KULIGIN. The headmistress has not come yet?

IRINA. No. They have sent for her. If only you knew how hard it is for me to live here alone, without Olya. . . . Now that she is headmistress and lives at the high-school and is busy all day long, I am alone, I am bored, I have nothing to do, and I hate the room I live in. . . . I have made up my mind, since I am not fated to be in Moscow, that so it must be. It must be destiny. There is no help for it. . . . It's all in God's hands, that's the truth. When Nikolay Lvovitch made me an offer again . . . I thought it over and made up my mind. . . . He is a good man, it's wonderful really how good he is. . . . And I suddenly felt as though my soul had grown wings, my heart felt so light and again I longed for work, work. . . . Only something happened yesterday, there is some mystery hanging over me.

TCHEBUTYKIN. Nonsense.

NATASHA (*at the window*). Our headmistress!

KULIGIN. The headmistress has come. Let us go in (*goes into the house with* IRINA).

TCHEBUTYKIN (*reads the newspaper, humming softly*). "Tarara-boom-dee-ay."

(MASHA *approaches; in the background* ANDREY *is pushing the perambulator.*)

MASHA. Here he sits, snug and settled.

TCHEBUTYKIN. Well, what then?

MASHA (*sits down*). Nothing . . . (*a pause*). Did you love my mother?

TCHEBUTYKIN. Very much.

MASHA. And did she love you?

TCHEBUTYKIN (*after a pause*). That I don't remember.

MASHA. Is my man here? It's just like our cook Marfa used to say about he policeman: is my man here?

TCHEBUTYKIN. Not yet.

MASHA. When you get happiness by snatches, by little bits, and then lose i as I am losing it, by degrees one grows coarse and spiteful . . . (*Points to he bosom*) I'm boiling here inside . . . (*Looking at* ANDREY, *who is pushing th perambulator*) Here is our Andrey. . . . All our hopes are shattered. Thou sands of people raised the bell, a lot of money and of labour was spent on i and it suddenly fell and smashed. All at once, for no reason whatever. That just how it is with Andrey. . . .

ANDREY. When will they be quiet in the house? There is such a noise.

TCHEBUTYKIN. Soon (*looks at his watch*). My watch is an old-fashione one with a repeater . . . (*winds his watch, it strikes*). The first, the secon and the fifth batteries are going at one o'clock (*a pause*). And I am going to morrow.

ANDREY. For good?

TCHEBUTYKIN. I don't know. Perhaps I shall come back in a year. Thoug goodness knows. . . . It doesn't matter one way or another.

(*There is the sound of a harp and violin being played far away in th street.*)

ANDREY. The town will be empty. It's as though one put an extinguishe over it (*a pause*). Something happened yesterday near the theatre; everyon is talking of it, and I know nothing about it.

TCHEBUTYKIN. It was nothing. Foolishness. Solyony began annoying th baron and he lost his temper and insulted him, and it came in the end t Solyony's having to challenge him (*looks at his watch*). It's time, I fancy . . . It was to be at half-past twelve in the Crown forest that we can from here beyond the river . . . Piff-paff! (*Laughs*) Solyony imagines he is Lermontov and even writes verses. Joking apart, this is his third duel.

MASHA. Whose?

TCHEBUTYKIN. Solyony's.

MASHA. And the baron's?

TCHEBUTYKIN. What about the baron? (*a pause*)

MASHA. My thoughts are in a muddle. . . . Anyway, I tell you, you ough not to let them do it. He may wound the baron or even kill him.

TCHEBUTYKIN. The baron is a very good fellow, but one baron more or les in the world, what does it matter? Let them! It doesn't matter. (*Beyond th garden a shout of* "Aa-oo! Halloo!") You can wait. That is Skvortsov, th second, shouting. He is in a boat (*a pause*).

ANDREY. In my opinion to take part in a duel, or to be present at it even
in the capacity of a doctor, is simply immoral.

TCHEBUTYKIN. That only seems so. . . . We are not real, nothing in the
world is real, we don't exist, but only seem to exist. . . . Nothing matters!

MASHA. How they keep on talking, talking all day long (*goes*). To live in
such a climate, it may snow any minute, and then all this talk on the top of
it (*stops*). I am not going indoors, I can't go in there. . . . When Vershinin
comes, tell me . . . (*goes down the avenue*). And the birds are already flying
south . . . (*looks up*). Swans or geese. . . . Darlings, happy things. . . .
(*goes out*).

ANDREY. Our house will be empty. The officers are going, you are going,
Irina is getting married, and I shall be left in the house alone.

TCHEBUTYKIN. What about your wife?

(*Enter* FERAPONT *with papers.*)

ANDREY. A wife is a wife. She is a straightforward, upright woman, good-
natured, perhaps, but for all that there is something in her which makes her
no better than some petty, blind, hairy animal. Anyway she is not a human
being. I speak to you as to a friend, the one man to whom I can open my soul.
I love Natasha, that is so, but sometimes she seems to me wonderfully vulgar,
and then I don't know what to think, I can't account for my loving her or,
anyway, having loved her.

TCHEBUTYKIN (*gets up*). I am going away to-morrow, my boy, perhaps
we shall never meet again, so this is my advice to you. Put on your cap, you
know, take your stick and walk off . . . walk off and just go, go without
looking back. And the farther you go, the better (*a pause*). But do as you like!
It doesn't matter. . . .

(SOLYONY *crosses the stage in the background with two officers; seeing*
TCHEBUTYKIN *he turns towards him; the officers walk on.*)

SOLYONY. Doctor, it's time! It's half-past twelve (*greets* ANDREY).

TCHEBUTYKIN. Directly. I am sick of you all. (*To* ANDREY) If anyone asks
for me, Andryusha, say I'll be back directly . . . (*sighs*). Oho-ho-ho!

SOLYONY. He had not time to say alack before the bear was on his back
(*walks away with the doctor*). Why are you croaking, old chap?

TCHEBUTYKIN. Come!

SOLYONY. How do you feel?

TCHEBUTYKIN (*angrily*). Like a pig in clover.

SOLYONY. The old chap need not excite himself. I won't do anything much,
I'll only shoot him like a snipe (*takes out scent and sprinkles his hands*). I've
used a whole bottle to-day, and still they smell. My hands smell like a corpse
(*a pause*). Yes. . . . Do you remember the poem? "And, restless, seeks the
stormy ocean, as though in tempest there were peace." . . .

TCHEBUTYKIN. Yes. He had not time to say alack before the bear was on
his back (*goes out with* SOLYONY. *Shouts are heard:* "Halloo! Oo-oo!" ANDREY
and FERAPONT *come in*).

FERAPONT. Papers for you to sign. . . .

ANDREY (*nervously*). Let me alone! Let me alone! I entreat you! (*Walk away with the perambulator.*)

FERAPONT. That's what the papers are for—to be signed (*retires into th background*).

(*Enter* IRINA *and* TUSENBACH *wearing a straw hat;* KULIGIN *crosses th stage shouting* "Aa-oo, Masha, aa-oo!")

TUSENBACH. I believe that's the only man in the town who is glad that th officers are going away.

IRINA. That's very natural (*a pause*). Our town will be empty now.

TUSENBACH. Dear, I'll be back directly.

IRINA. Where are you going?

TUSENBACH. I must go into the town, and then . . to see my comrade off.

IRINA. That's not true. . . . Nikolay, why are you so absent-minded to-day? (*a pause*) What happened yesterday near the theatre?

TUSENBACH (*with a gesture of impatience*). I'll be here in an hour and with you again (*kisses her hands*). My beautiful one . . . (*looks into her face*). For five years now I have loved you and still I can't get used to it, and you seem to me more and more lovely. What wonderful, exquisite hair! What eyes! I shall carry you off to-morrow, we will work, we will be rich, my dreams will come true. You shall be happy. There is only one thing, one thing: you don't love me!

IRINA. That's not in my power! I'll be your wife and be faithful and obedient, but there is no love, I can't help it (*weeps*). I've never been in love in my life! Oh, I have so dreamed of love, I've been dreaming of it for years day and night, but my soul is like a wonderful piano of which the key has been lost (*a pause*). You look uneasy.

TUSENBACH. I have not slept all night. There has never been anything in my life so dreadful that it could frighten me, and only that lost key frets at my heart and won't let me sleep. . . . Say something to me . . . (*a pause*). Say something to me. . . .

IRINA. What? What am I to say to you? What?

TUSENBACH. Anything.

IRINA. There, there! (*a pause*)

TUSENBACH. What trifles, what little things suddenly *à propos* of nothing acquire importance in life! One laughs at them as before, thinks them non-sense, but still one goes on and feels that one has not the power to stop. Don't let us talk about it! I am happy. I feel as though I were seeing these pines, these maples, these birch trees for the first time in my life, and they all seem to be looking at me with curiosity and waiting. What beautiful trees, and, really, how beautiful life ought to be under them! (*A shout of* "Halloo! Aa-oo!") I must be off; it's time. . . . See, that tree is dead, but it waves in the wind with the others. And so it seems to me that if I die I shall still have part in life, one way or another. Good-bye, my darling . . . (*kisses her hands*). Those papers of yours you gave me are lying under the calendar on my table.

IRINA. I am coming with you.

TUSENBACH (*in alarm*). No, no! (*Goes off quickly, stops in the avenue.*) Irina!

IRINA. What is it?

TUSENBACH (*not knowing what to say*). I didn't have any coffee this morning. Ask them to make me some (*goes out quickly*).

(IRINA *stands lost in thought, then walks away into the background of the scene and sits down on the swing. Enter* ANDREY *with the perambulator, and* FERAPONT *comes into sight.*)

FERAPONT. Andrey Sergeyevitch, the papers aren't mine; they are Government papers. I didn't invent them.

ANDREY. Oh, where is it all gone? What has become of my past, when I was young, gay, and clever, when my dreams and thoughts were exquisite, when my present and my past were lighted up by hope? Why on the very threshold of life do we become dull, grey, uninteresting, lazy, indifferent, useless, unhappy? . . . Our town has been going on for two hundred years—there are a hundred thousand people living in it; and there is not one who is not like the rest, not one saint in the past, or the present, not one man of learning, not one artist, not one man in the least remarkable who could inspire envy or a passionate desire to imitate him. . . . They only eat, drink, sleep, and then die . . . others are born, and they also eat and drink and sleep, and not to be bored to stupefaction they vary their lives by nasty gossip, vodka, cards, litigation; and the wives deceive their husbands, and the husbands tell lies and pretend that they see and hear nothing, and an overwhelmingly vulgar influence weighs upon the children, and the divine spark is quenched in them and they become the same sort of pitiful, dead creatures, all exactly alike, as their fathers and mothers. . . . (*To* FERAPONT, *angrily*) What do you want?

FERAPONT. Eh? There are papers to sign.

ANDREY. You bother me!

FERAPONT (*handing him the papers*). The porter from the local treasury was saying just now that there was as much as two hundred degrees of frost in Petersburg this winter.

ANDREY. The present is hateful, but when I think of the future, it is so nice! I feel so light-hearted, so free. A light dawns in the distance, I see freedom. I see how I and my children will become free from sloth, from kvass, from goose and cabbage, from sleeping after dinner, from mean, parasitic living. . . .

FERAPONT. He says that two thousand people were frozen to death. The people were terrified. It was either in Petersburg or Moscow, I don't remember.

ANDREY (*in a rush of tender feeling*). My dear sisters, my wonderful sisters! (*Through tears*) Masha, my sister!

NATASHA (*in the window*). Who is talking so loud out there? Is that you Andryusha? You will wake baby Sophie. *Il ne faut pas faire de bruit, l Sophie est dormée déjà. Vous êtes un ours.* (*Getting angry*) If you want t talk, give the perambulator with the baby to somebody else. Ferapont, tak the perambulator from the master!

FERAPONT. Yes, ma'am (*takes the pram*).

ANDREY (*in confusion*). I am talking quietly.

NATASHA (*petting her child, inside the room*). Bobik! Naughty Bobik! Littl rascal!

ANDREY (*looking through the papers*). Very well, I'll look through then and sign what wants signing, and then you can take them back to the Boarc . . . (*Goes into the house reading the papers;* FERAPONT *pushes the prar farther into the garden.*)

NATASHA (*speaking indoors*). Bobik, what is mamma's name? Darling darling! And who is this? This is auntie Olya. Say to auntie, "Good morning Olya!"

> (*Two wandering musicians, a man and a girl, enter and play a violi and a harp; from the house enter* VERSHININ *with* OLGA *and* ANFIS♦ *and stand for a minute listening in silence;* IRINA *comes up.*)

OLGA. Our garden is like a public passage; they walk and ride through Nurse, give those people something.

ANFISA (*gives money to the musicians*). Go away, and God bless you, m dear souls! (*The musicians bow and go away.*) Poor things. People don't pla᾽ if they have plenty to eat. (*To* IRINA) Good morning, Irisha! (*Kisses her.* Aye, aye, my little girl, I am having a time of it! Living in the high-school in a government flat, with dear Olya—that's what the Lord has vouchsafe᷄ me in my old age! I have never lived so well in my life, sinful woman tha᷄ I am. . . . It's a big flat, and I have a room to myself and a bedstead. All a᷄ the government expense. I wake up in the night and, O Lord, Mother of Go᷄ there is no one in the world happier than I!

VERSHININ (*looks at his watch*). We are just going, Olga Sergeyevna. It᾽ time to be off (*a pause*). I wish you everything, everything. . . . Where i Marya Sergeyevna?

IRINA. She is somewhere in the garden. . . . I'll go and look for her.

VERSHININ. Please be so good. I am in a hurry.

ANFISA. I'll go and look for her too. (*Shouts*) Mashenka, aa-oo! (*Goes wit♦ IRINA into the farther part of the garden.*) Aa-oo! Aa-oo!

VERSHININ. Everything comes to an end. Here we are parting (*looks at hi᾽ watch*). The town has given us something like a lunch; we have been drinkin᷄ champagne, the mayor made a speech. I ate and listened, but my heart wa᷄ here, with you all . . . (*looks round the garden*). I've grown used to you. . .

OLGA. Shall we ever see each other again?

VERSHININ. Most likely not (*a pause*). My wife and two little girls will sta᾽

re for another two months; please, if anything happens, if they need any-
ing . . .

OLGA. Yes, yes, of course. Set your mind at rest (*a pause*). By to-morrow
ere won't be a soldier in the town—it will all turn into a memory, and of
urse for us it will be like beginning a new life . . . (*a pause*). Nothing
rns out as we would have it. I did not want to be a headmistress, and yet
am. It seems we are not to live in Moscow. . . .

VERSHININ. Well. . . . Thank you for everything. . . . Forgive me if any-
ing was amiss. . . . I have talked a great deal: forgive me for that too—
n't remember evil against me.

OLGA (*wipes her eyes*). Why doesn't Masha come?

VERSHININ. What else am I to say to you at parting? What am I to theorise
out? . . . (*Laughs*) Life is hard. It seems to many of us blank and hopeless;
t yet we must admit that it goes on getting clearer and easier, and it looks as
ough the time were not far off when it will be full of happiness (*looks at his
atch*). It's time for me to go! In old days men were absorbed in wars, filling
their existence with marches, raids, victories, but now all that is a thing of
e past. leaving behind it a great void which there is so far nothing to fill:
manity is searching for it passionately, and of course will find it. Ah, if
ly it could be quickly! (*a pause*) If, don't you know, industry were united
th culture and culture with industry . . . (*Looks at his watch*) But, I say,
's time for me to go. . . .

OLGA. Here she comes.

(MASHA *comes in.*)

VERSHININ. I have come to say good-bye. . . .

(OLGA *moves a little away to leave them free to say good-bye.*)

MASHA (*looking into his face*). Good-bye . . . (*a prolonged kiss*).

OLGA. Come, come. . . .

(MASHA *sobs violently.*)

VERSHININ. Write to me. . . . Don't forget me! Let me go! . . . Time is
! . . Olga Sergeyevna, take her, I must . . . go . . . I am late . . .
Much moved, kisses OLGA's *hands; then again embraces* MASHA *and quickly
es off.*)

OLGA. Come, Masha! Leave off, darling.

(*Enter* KULIGIN.)

KULIGIN (*embarrassed*). Never mind, let her cry—let her. . . . My good
asha, my dear Masha! . . . You are my wife, and I am happy, anyway.
. . I don't complain; I don't say a word of blame. . . . Here Olya is my
itness. . . . We'll begin the old life again, and I won't say one word, not
hint. . . .

MASHA (*restraining her sobs*). By the sea-strand an oak-tree green. . . .
pon that oak a chain of gold. . . . Upon that oak a chain of gold. . . . I
n going mad. . . . By the sea-strand . . . an oak-tree green. . . .

OLGA. Calm yourself, Masha. . . Calm yourself. . . . Give her som
water.

MASHA. I am not crying now. . . .

KULIGIN. She is not crying now . . . she is good. . . .

(*The dim sound of a far-away shot.*)

MASHA. By the sea-strand an oak-tree green, upon that oak a chain of golc
. . . The cat is green . . . the oak is green. . . . I am mixing it up . .
(*drinks water*). My life is a failure. . . . I want nothing now. . . . I sha
be calm directly. . . . It doesn't matter. . . . What does "strand" mean
Why do these words haunt me? My thoughts are in a tangle.

(*Enter* IRINA.)

OLGA. Calm yourself, Masha. Come, that's a good girl. Let us go indoor

MASHA (*angrily*). I am not going in. Let me alone! (*Sobs, but at onc
checks herself.*) I don't go into that house now and I won't.

IRINA. Let us sit together, even if we don't say anything. I am going awa
to-morrow, you know . . . (*a pause*).

KULIGIN. I took a false beard and moustache from a boy in the third forr
yesterday, just look . . . (*puts on the beard and moustache*). I look like th
German teacher . . . (*laughs*). Don't I? Funny creatures, those boys.

MASHA. You really do look like the German teacher.

OLGA (*laughs*). Yes.

(MASHA *weeps.*)

IRINA. There, Masha!

KULIGIN. Awfully like. . . .

(*Enter* NATASHA.)

NATASHA (*to the maid*). What? Mr. Protopopov will sit with Sophie, an
let Andrey Sergeyitch wheel Bobik up and down. What a lot there is to d
with children . . . (*To* IRINA) Irina, you are going away to-morrow, wha
a pity. Do stay just another week. (*Seeing* KULIGIN *utters a shriek; the latte
laughs and takes off the beard and moustache.*) Well, what next, you gave m
such a fright! (*To* IRINA) I am used to you and do you suppose that I don'
feel parting with you? I shall put Andrey with his violin into your room—le
him saw away there!—and we will put baby Sophie in his room. Adorable, de
lightful baby! Isn't she a child! To-day she looked at me with such eyes an
said "Mamma"!

KULIGIN. A fine child, that's true.

NATASHA. So to-morrow I shall be all alone here (*sighs*). First of all I shal
have this avenue of fir trees cut down, and then that maple. . . . It looks s
ugly in the evening. . . . (*To* IRINA.) My dear, that sash does not suit you a
all. . . . It's in bad taste. You want something light. And then I shall hav
flowers, flowers planted everywhere, and there will be such a scent. . .
(*Severely*) Why is there a fork lying about on that seat? (*Going into th
house, to the maid*) Why is there a fork lying about on this seat. I ask you
(*Shouts*) Hold your tongue!

KULIGIN. She is at it!

(*Behind the scenes the band plays a march; they all listen.*)

OLGA. They are going.

(*Enter* TCHEBUTYKIN.)

MASHA. Our people are going. Well . . . a happy journey to them! (*To her husband*) We must go home. . . . Where are my hat and cape?

KULIGIN. I took them into the house . . . I'll get them directly. . . .

OLGA. Yes, now we can go home, it's time.

TCHEBUTYKIN. Olga Sergeyevna!

OLGA. What is it? (*a pause*) What?

TCHEBUTYKIN. Nothing. . . . I don't know how to tell you. (*Whispers in her ear.*)

OLGA (*in alarm*). It can't be!

TCHEBUTYKIN. Yes . . . such a business. . . . I am so worried and worn out, I don't want to say another word. . . . (*With vexation*). But there, it doesn't matter!

MASHA. What has happened?

OLGA (*puts her arms round* IRINA). This is a terrible day. . . . I don't know how to tell you, my precious. . . .

IRINA. What is it? Tell me quickly, what is it? For God's sake! (*Cries*)

TCHEBUTYKIN. The baron has just been killed in a duel.

IRINA (*weeping quietly*). I knew, I knew. . . .

TCHEBUTYKIN (*in the background of the scene sits down on a garden seat*). I am worn out . . . (*takes a newspaper out of his pocket*). Let them cry. . . . (*Sings softly.*) "Tarara-boom-dee-ay" . . . It doesn't matter.

(*The three sisters stand with their arms round one another.*)

MASHA. Oh, listen to that band! They are going away from us; one has gone altogether, gone forever. We are left alone to begin our life over again. . . . We've got to live . . . we've got to live. . . .

IRINA (*lays her head on* OLGA's *bosom*). A time will come when everyone will know what all this is for, why there is this misery; there will be no mysteries and, meanwhile, we have got to live . . . we have got to work, only to work! To-morrow I shall go alone; I shall teach in the school, and I will give all my life to those to whom it may be of use. Now it's autumn; soon winter will come and cover us with snow, and I will work, I will work.

OLGA (*embraces both her sisters*). The music is so gay, so confident, and one longs for life! O my God! Time will pass, and we shall go away for ever, and we shall be forgotten, our faces will be forgotten, our voices, and how many there were of us; but our sufferings will pass into joy for those who will live after us, happiness and peace will be established upon earth, and they will remember kindly and bless those who have lived before. Oh, dear sisters, our life is not ended yet. We shall live! The music is so gay, so joyful, and it seems as though a little more and we shall know what we are living for, why we are suffering. . . . If we only knew—if we only knew!

(*The music grows more and more subdued;* KULIGIN, *cheerful and smiling, brings the hat and cape;* ANDREY *pushes the perambulator in
which* BOBIK *is sitting.*)

TCHEBUTYKIN (*humming softly*). "Tarara-boom-dee-ay!" (*Reads his
paper.*) It doesn't matter, it doesn't matter.

OLGA. If we only knew, if we only knew!

CURTAIN.

UNCLE VANYA

SCENES FROM COUNTRY LIFE, IN FOUR ACTS

First performed in 1899

CHARACTERS IN THE PLAY

ALEXANDR VLADIMIROVITCH SEREBRYAKOV (*a retired Professor*).

YELENA ANDREYEVNA (*his wife, aged 27*).

SOFYA ALEXANDROVNA (SONYA) (*his daughter by his first wife*).

MARYA VASSILYEVNA VOYNITSKY (*widow of a Privy Councillor and mother of Professor's first wife*).

IVAN PETROVITCH VOYNITSKY (*her son*).

MIHAIL LVOVITCH ASTROV (*a Doctor*).

ILYA ILYITCH TELYEGIN (*a Landowner reduced to poverty*).

MARINA (*an old Nurse*).

A LABOURER.

The action takes place on SEREBRYAKOV'S *estate.*

ACT I

Garden. Part of the house can be seen with the verandah. In the avenue under an old poplar there is a table set for tea. Garden seats and chairs; on one of the seats lies a guitar. Not far from the table there is a swing. Between two and three o'clock on a cloudy afternoon.
MARINA, *a heavy old woman, slow to move, is sitting by the samovar, knitting a stocking, and* ASTROV *is walking up and down near her.*

MARINA (*pours out a glass of tea*). Here, drink it, my dear.
ASTROV (*reluctantly takes the glass*). I don't feel much like it.
MARINA. Perhaps you would have a drop of vodka?
ASTROV. No. I don't drink vodka every day. Besides, it's so sultry (*a pause*). Nurse, how many years have we known each other?
MARINA (*pondering*). How many? The Lord help my memory. . . . You came into these parts . . . when? Vera Petrovna, Sonitchka's mother, was living then. You came to see us two winters before she died. . . . Well, that must be eleven years ago. (*After a moment's thought*) Maybe even more. . . .
ASTROV. Have I changed much since then?
MARINA. Very much. You were young and handsome in those days, and now you have grown older. And you are not as good-looking. There's another thing too—you take a drop of vodka now.
ASTROV. Yes. . . . In ten years I have become a different man. And what's the reason of it? I am overworked, nurse. From morning till night I am always on my legs, not a moment of rest, and at night one lies under the bedclothes in continual terror of being dragged out to a patient. All these years that you have known me I have not had one free day. I may well look old! And the life in itself is tedious, stupid, dirty. . . . This life swallows one up completely. There are none but queer people about one—they are a queer lot, all of them —and when one has lived two or three years among them, by degrees one turns queer too, without noticing it. It's inevitable (*twisting his long moustache*). Ough, what a huge moustache I've grown . . . a stupid moustache. . . . I've turned into a queer fish, nurse. I haven't grown stupid yet, thank God! My brains are in their place, but my feelings are somehow blunter. There is nothing I want, nothing I care about, no one I am fond of . . . except you, perhaps—I am fond of you (*kisses her on the head*). I had a nurse like you when I was a child.

149

MARINA. Perhaps you would like something to eat?

ASTROV. No. In the third week of Lent I went to Malitskoe, where there was an epidemic . . . spotted typhus . . . in the huts the people were lying about in heaps. There was filth, stench, smoke . . . calves on the ground with the sick . . . little pigs about too. I was hard at work all day, did not sit down for a minute, and hadn't a morsel of food, and when I got home they wouldn't let me rest. They brought me a signalman from the line. I laid him on the table to operate upon him, and he went and died under the chloroform. And just when they weren't wanted, my feelings seemed to wake up again, and I was as conscience-stricken as though I had killed him on purpose. I sat down shut my eyes like this, and thought: those who will live a hundred or two hundred years after us, for whom we are struggling now to beat out a road, will they remember and say a good word for us? Nurse, they won't, you know!

MARINA. Men will not remember, but God will remember.

ASTROV. Thank you for that. That's a good saying.

(*Enter* VOYNITSKY.)

VOYNITSKY (*comes out of the house; he has had a nap after lunch and looks rumpled; he sits down on the garden-seat and straightens his fashionable tie*). Yes . . . (*a pause*). Yes. . . .

ASTROV. Had a good sleep?

VOYNITSKY. Yes . . . very (*yawns*). Ever since the Professor and his wife have been here our life has been turned topsy-turvy. I sleep at the wrong time, at lunch and dinner I eat all sorts of messes, I drink wine—it's not good for one! In old days I never had a free moment. Sonya and I used to work in grand style, but now Sonya works alone, while I sleep and eat and drink. It's bad!

MARINA (*shaking her head*). Such goings-on! The Professor gets up at twelve o'clock, and the samovar is boiling all the morning waiting for him. Before they came we always had dinner about one o'clock, like other people, and now they are here we have it between six and seven. The Professor spends the night reading and writing, and all at once, at two o'clock in the morning, he'll ring his bell. Goodness me! What is it? Tea! People have to be waked out of their sleep to get him the samovar. What goings-on!

ASTROV. And will they be here much longer?

VOYNITSKY (*whistles*). A hundred years. The Professor has made up his mind to settle here.

MARINA. Look now! The samovar has been on the table for the last two hours, and they've gone for a walk.

VOYNITSKY. They are coming. They are coming! Don't worry.

(*There is a sound of voices; from the farther part of the garden enter* SEREBRYAKOV, YELENA ANDREYEVNA, SONYA *and* TELYEGIN *returning from a walk.*)

SEREBRYAKOV. Lovely, lovely! . . . Exquisite views!

TELYEGIN. Remarkable, your Excellency.

SONYA. We'll go to the plantation to-morrow, father. Shall we?

VOYNITSKY. Tea is ready!

SEREBRYAKOV. My friends, be so kind as to send my tea into the study for me. I have something more I must do to-day.

SONYA. You will be sure to like the plantation.

(YELENA ANDREYEVNA, SEREBRYAKOV, *and* SONYA *go into the house.* TELYEGIN *goes to the table and sits down beside* MARINA.)

VOYNITSKY. It's hot, stifling; but our great man of learning is in his great-coat and goloshes, with an umbrella and gloves too.

ASTROV. That shows that he takes care of himself.

VOYNITSKY. And how lovely she is! How lovely! I've never seen a more beautiful woman.

TELYEGIN. Whether I drive through the fields, Marina Timofeyevna, or walk in the shady garden, or look at this table, I feel unutterably joyful. The weather is enchanting, the birds are singing, we are all living in peace and concord—what more could one wish for? (*Taking his glass*) I am truly grateful to you!

VOYNITSKY (*dreamily*). Her eyes . . . an exquisite woman!

ASTROV. Tell us something, Ivan Petrovitch.

VOYNITSKY (*listlessly*). What am I to tell you?

ASTROV. Is there nothing new?

VOYNITSKY. Nothing. Everything is old. I am just as I always was, perhaps worse, for I have grown lazy. I do nothing but just grumble like some old crow. My old magpie *maman* is still babbling about the rights of women. With one foot in the grave, she is still rummaging in her learned books for the dawn of a new life.

ASTROV. And the Professor?

VOYNITSKY. The Professor, as before, sits in his study writing from morning till dead of night. "With furrowed brow and racking brains, We write and write and write, And ne'er a word of praise we hear, Our labours to requite." Poor paper! He had much better be writing his autobiography. What a superb subject! A retired professor, you know—an old dry-as-dust, a learned fish. Gout, rheumatism, migraine, envy and jealousy have affected his liver. The old fish is living on his first wife's estate, living there against his will because he can't afford to live in the town. He is forever complaining of his misfortunes, though, as a matter of fact, he is exceptionally fortunate. (*Nervously*) Just think how fortunate! The son of a humble sacristan, he has risen to university distinctions and the chair of a professor; he has become "your Excellency," the son-in-law of a senator, and so on, and so on. All that is no great matter, though. But just take this. The man has been lecturing and writing about art for twenty-five years, though he knows absolutely nothing about art. For twenty-five years he has been chewing over other men's ideas about realism, naturalism, and all sorts of nonsense; for twenty-five years he has been lecturing and writing on things all intelligent people know about already and stupid ones aren't interested in—so for twenty-five years he has been simply wasting his time. And with all that, what conceit! What pretensions! He has retired, and not a living soul knows anything about him; he is absolutely unknown. So that for twenty-five years all he has done is to keep a better man out of a job! But just look at him: he struts about like a demi-god!

ASTROV. Come, I believe you are envious.

VOYNITSKY. Yes, I am. And the success he has with women! Don Juan is not in it. His first wife, my sister, a lovely, gentle creature, pure as this blue sky, noble, generous, who had more suitors than he has had pupils, loved him as only pure angels can love beings as pure and beautiful as themselves. My mother adores him to this day, and he still inspires in her a feeling of devout awe. His second wife, beautiful, intelligent—you have just seen her—has married him in his old age, sacrificed her youth, her beauty, her freedom, her brilliance, to him. What for? Why?

ASTROV. Is she faithful to the Professor?

VOYNITSKY. Unhappily, she is.

ASTROV. Why unhappily?

VOYNITSKY. Because that fidelity is false from beginning to end. There is plenty of fine sentiment in it, but no logic. To deceive an old husband whom one can't endure is immoral; but to try and stifle her piteous youth and living feeling—that's not immoral.

TELYEGIN (*in a tearful voice*). Vanya, I can't bear to hear you talk like that. Come, really! Anyone who can betray wife or husband is a person who can't be trusted and who might betray his country.

VOYNITSKY (*with vexation*). Dry up, Waffles!

TELYEGIN. Excuse me, Vanya. My wife ran away from me with the man she loved the day after our wedding, on the ground of my unprepossessing appearance. But I have never been false to my vows. I love her to this day and am faithful to her. I help her as far as I can, and I gave all I had for the education of her children by the man she loved. I have lost my happiness, but my pride has been left to me. And she? Her youth is over, her beauty, in accordance with the laws of nature, has faded, the man she loved is dead. . . What has she left?

(*Enter* SONYA *and* YELENA ANDREYEVNA *and a little later,* MARYA VASSILYEVNA *with a book; she sits down and reads. They hand her tea, and she drinks it without looking at it.*)

SONYA (*hurriedly to the nurse.*) Nurse, darling, some peasants have come. Go and speak to them. I'll look after the tea.

(*Exit Nurse.* YELENA ANDREYEVNA *takes her cup and drinks it sitting in the swing.*)

ASTROV (*to* YELENA ANDREYEVNA). I've come to see your husband. You wrote to me that he was very ill—rheumatism and something else—but it appears he is perfectly well.

YELENA. Last night he was poorly, complaining of pains in his legs, but to-day he is all right. . . .

ASTROV. And I have galloped twenty miles at break-neck speed! But there, it doesn't matter! it's not the first time. I shall stay with you till to-morrow to make up for it, and anyway I shall sleep *quantum satis*.

SONYA. That's splendid! It's not often you stay the night with us. I expect you've not had dinner?

ASTROV. No, I haven't.

SONYA. Oh, well, you will have some dinner, then! We have dinner now between six and seven (*drinks tea*). The tea is cold!

TELYEGIN. The temperature in the samovar has perceptibly dropped.

YELENA. Never mind, Ivan Ivanitch; we will drink it cold.

TELYEGIN. I beg your pardon, I am not Ivan Ivanitch, but Ilya Ilyitch—Ilya Ilyitch Telyegin, or, as some people call me on account of my pock-marked face, Waffles. I stood godfather to Sonetchka; and his Excellency, your husband, knows me very well. I live here now on your estate. If you've been so kind as to observe it, I have dinner with you every day.

SONYA. Ilya Ilyitch is our helper, our right hand. (*Tenderly*) Let me give you another cup, godfather.

MARYA. Ach!

SONYA. What is it, grandmamma?

MARYA. I forgot to tell Alexandr—I am losing my memory—I got a letter to-day from Harkov, from Pavel Alexeyevitch . . . he has sent his new pamphlet.

ASTROV. Is it interesting?

MARYA. It's interesting, but it's rather queer. He is attacking what he himself maintained seven years ago. It's awful.

VOYNITSKY. There's nothing awful in it. Drink your tea, *maman*.

MARYA. But I want to talk.

VOYNITSKY. But we have been talking and talking for fifty years and reading pamphlets. It's about time to leave off.

MARYA. You don't like listening when I speak; I don't know why. Forgive my saying so, Jean, but you have so changed in the course of the last year that I hardly know you. You used to be a man of definite principles, of elevating ideas.

VOYNITSKY. Oh, yes! I was a man of elevating ideas which elevated nobody (*a pause*). . . . A man of elevating ideas . . . you could not have made a more malignant joke! Now I am forty-seven. Till last year I tried, like you, to blind myself with all your pedantic rubbish on purpose to avoid seeing life as it is—and thought I was doing the right thing. And now, if only you knew! I can't sleep at night for vexation, for rage that I so stupidly wasted the time when I might have had everything from which my age now shuts me out.

SONYA Uncle Vanya, it's so dreary!

MARYA (*to her son*). You seem to be blaming your former principles. It is not they that are to blame, but yourself. You forget that principles alone are no use—a dead letter. You ought to have been working.

VOYNITSKY. Working? It is not everyone who can be a writing machine like your Herr Professor.

MARYA. What do you mean by that?

SONYA (*in an imploring voice*). Grandmamma! Uncle Vanya! I entreat you!

VOYNITSKY. I'll hold my tongue—hold my tongue and apologise.

(*A pause.*)

YELENA. What a fine day! It's not too hot.

(*A pause.*)

VOYNITSKY. A fine day to hang oneself!

(TELYEGIN *tunes the guitar.* MARINA *walks to and fro near the house, calling a hen.*)

MARINA. Chook, chook, chook!

SONYA. Nurse, darling, what did the peasants come about?

MARINA. It's the same thing—about the waste land again. Chook, chook, chook!

SONYA. Which is it you are calling?

MARINA. Speckly has gone off somewhere with her chickens. . . . The crows might get them (*walks away*).

(TELYEGIN *plays a polka; they all listen to him in silence. Enter a labourer.*)

LABOURER. Is the doctor here? (*To* ASTROV) If you please, Mihail Lvovitch, they have sent for you.

ASTROV. Where from?

LABOURER. From the factory.

ASTROV (*with vexation*). Much obliged to you. Well, I suppose I must go (*looks round him for his cap*). What a nuisance, hang it!

SONYA. How annoying it is, really! Come back from the factory to dinner.

ASTROV. No. It will be too late. "How should I? . . . How could I? . . ." (*To the labourer*) Here, my good man, you might get me a glass of vodka, anyway. (*Labourer goes off.*) "How should I? . . . How could I? . . ." (*Finds his cap.*) In one of Ostrovsky's plays there is a man with a big moustache and little wit—that's like me. Well, I have the honour to wish you all good-bye. (*To* YELENA ANDREYEVNA) If you ever care to look in upon me, with Sofya Alexandrovna, I shall be truly delighted. I have a little estate, only ninety acres, but there is a model garden and nursery such as you wouldn't find for hundreds of miles round—if that interests you. Next to me is the government plantation. The forester there is old and always ill, so that I really look after all the work.

YELENA. I have been told already that you are very fond of forestry. Of course, it may be of the greatest use, but doesn't it interfere with your real work? You are a doctor.

ASTROV. Only God knows what is one's real work.

YELENA. And is it interesting?

ASTROV. Yes, it is interesting work.

VOYNITSKY (*ironically*). Very much so!

YELENA (*to* ASTROV). You are still young—you don't look more than thirty-six or thirty-seven . . . and it cannot be so interesting as you say. Nothing but trees and trees. I should think it must be monotonous.

SONYA. No, it's extremely interesting. Mihail Lvovitch plants fresh trees every year, and already they have sent him a bronze medal and a diploma. He tries to prevent the old forests being destroyed. If you listen to him you will agree with him entirely. He says that forests beautify the country, that they teach man to understand what is beautiful and develop a lofty attitude of mind. Forests temper the severity of the climate. In countries where the climate is mild, less energy is wasted on the struggle with nature, and so man is softer and milder. In such countries people are beautiful, supple and sensitive; their language is elegant and their movements are graceful. Art and learning flourish among them, their philosophy is not gloomy, and their attitude to women is full of refined courtesy.

VOYNITSKY (*laughing*). Bravo, bravo! That's all charming but not convincing; so (*to* ASTROV) allow me, my friend, to go on heating my stoves with logs and building my barns of wood.

ASTROV. You can heat your stoves with peat and build your barns of brick. Well, I am ready to let you cut down wood as you need it, but why destroy the forests? The Russian forests are going down under the axe. Millions of trees are perishing, the homes of wild animals and birds are being laid waste, the rivers are dwindling and drying up, wonderful scenery is disappearing never to return; and all because lazy man has not the sense to stoop down and pick up the fuel from the ground. (*To* YELENA ANDREYEVNA) Am I not right, madam? One must be an unreflecting savage to burn this beauty in one's stove, to destroy what we cannot create. Man is endowed with reason and creative force to increase what has been given him; but hitherto he has not created but destroyed. There are fewer and fewer forests, the rivers are drying up, the wild creatures are becoming extinct, the climate is ruined, and every day the earth is growing poorer and more hideous. (*To* VOYNITSKY) Here you are looking at me with irony, and all I say seems to you not serious and—perhaps I really am a crank. But when I walk by the peasants' woods which I have saved from cutting down, or when I hear the rustling of the young copse planted by my own hands, I realise that the climate is to some extent in my power, and that if in a thousand years man is to be happy I too shall have had some small hand in it. When I plant a birch tree and see it growing green and swaying in the wind my soul is filled with pride, and I . . . (*seeing the labourer, who has brought a glass of vodka on a tray*). However (*drinks*), it's time for me to go. Probably the truth of the matter is that I am a crank. I have the honour to take my leave! (*Goes towards the house.*)

SONYA (*takes his arm and goes with him*). When are you coming to us?

ASTROV. I don't know.

SONYA. Not for a month again?

(ASTROV *and* SONYA *go into the house;* MARYA VASSILYEVNA *and* TELYE-
GIN *remain at the table;* YELENA ANDREYEVNA *walks towards the
verandah.*)

YELENA. You have been behaving impossibly again, Ivan Petrovitch. Why
need you have irritated Marya Vassilyevna and talked about a writing machine! And at lunch to-day you quarrelled with Alexandr again. How petty it
is!

VOYNITSKY. But if I hate him?

YELENA. There is no reason to hate Alexandr; he is like everyone else. He
is no worse than you are.

VOYNITSKY. If you could see your face, your movements! You are too
indolent to live! Ah, how indolent!

YELENA. Ach! indolent and bored! Everyone abuses my husband; everyone
looks at me with compassion, thinking, "Poor thing! she has got an old husband." This sympathy for me, oh, how well I understand it! As Astrov said
just now, you all recklessly destroy the forests, and soon there will be nothing
left on the earth. In just the same way you recklessly destroy human beings,
and soon, thanks to you, there will be no fidelity, no purity, no capacity for
sacrifice left on earth! Why is it you can never look with indifference at a
woman unless she is yours? Because—that doctor is right—there is a devil of
destruction in all of you. You have no feeling for the woods, nor the birds,
nor for women, nor for one another!

VOYNITSKY. I don't like this moralising.

(*A pause.*)

YELENA. That doctor has a weary, sensitive face. An interesting face. Sonya
is evidently attracted by him; she is in love with him, and I understand her
feeling. He has come three times since I have been here, but I am shy and
have not once had a proper talk with him, or been nice to him. He thinks I am
disagreeable. Most likely that's why we are such friends, Ivan Petrovitch, that
we are both such tiresome, tedious people. Tiresome! Don't look at me like
that, I don't like it.

VOYNITSKY. How else can I look at you, since I love you? You are my happiness, my life, my youth! I know the chances of your returning my feeling are
nil, non-existent, but I want nothing, only let me look at you, listen to your
voice. . . .

YELENA. Hush, they may hear you! (*They go into the house.*)

VOYNITSKY (*following her*). Let me speak of my love, don't drive me away
—that alone will be the greatest happiness for me. . . .

YELENA. This is agonising.

(*Both go into the house.* TELYEGIN *strikes the strings and plays a polka.*
MARYA VASSILYEVNA *makes a note on the margin of a pamphlet.*)

CURTAIN.

ACT II

Dining-room in Serebryakov's *house. Night. A watchman can be heard tapping in the garden.*
  Serebryakov, *sitting in an arm-chair before an open window, dozing, and* Yelena Andreyevna *sitting beside him, dozing too.*

Serebryakov (*waking*). Who is it? Sonya, is it you?
Yelena. It's me.
Serebryakov. You, Lenotchka! . . . I am in unbearable pain.
Yelena. Your rug has fallen on the floor (*wrapping it round his legs*). I'll shut the window, Alexandr.
Serebryakov. No, I feel suffocated. . . . I just dropped asleep and I dreamed that my left leg did not belong to me. I was awakened by the agonising pain. No, it's not gout; it's more like rheumatism. What time is it now?
Yelena. Twenty minutes past twelve (*a pause*).
Serebryakov. Look for Batyushkov in the library in the morning. I believe we have his works.
Yelena. What?
Serebryakov. Look for Batyushkov in the morning. I remember we did have him. But why is it so difficult for me to breathe?
Yelena. You are tired. This is the second night you have not slept.
Serebryakov. I have been told that Turgenev got *angina pectoris* from gout. I am afraid I may have it. Hateful, detestable old age. Damnation take it! Since I have grown old I have grown hateful to myself. And you must all hate the sight of me.
Yelena. You talk of your age as though we were all responsible for it.
Serebryakov. I am most of all hateful to you.
  (Yelena Andreyevna *gets up and sits down farther away.*)
Serebryakov. Of course, you are right. I am not a fool, and I understand. You are young and strong and good-looking. You want life and I am an old man, almost a corpse. Do you suppose I don't understand? And, of course, it is stupid of me to go on living. But wait a little, I shall soon set you all free. I shan't have to linger on much longer.
Yelena. I am worn out . . . for God's sake be quiet!
Serebryakov. It seems that, thanks to me, everyone is worn out, depressed, wasting their youth, and I am the only one enjoying life and satisfied. Oh, yes, of course!
Yelena. Be quiet! You make me miserable!
Serebryakov. I make everyone miserable. Of course.

YELENA (*through tears*). It's insufferable! Say, what is it you want of me?

SEREBRYAKOV. Nothing.

YELENA. Well, be quiet then. I implore you!

SEREBRYAKOV. It's a strange thing, Ivan Petrovitch may speak and that old idiot, Marya Vassilyevna, and there is nothing against it, everyone listens—but if I say a word everyone begins to feel miserable. They dislike the very sound of my voice. Well, suppose I am disagreeable, egoistic and tyrannical—haven't I a right, even in my old age, to think of myself? Haven't I earned it? Haven't I the right, I ask you, to be quiet in my old age, to be cared for by other people?

YELENA. No one is disputing your rights. (*The window bangs in the wind.*) The wind has got up; I'll shut the window (*shuts the window*). There will be rain directly. No one disputes your rights.

(*A pause; the watchman in the garden taps and sings.*)

SEREBRYAKOV. After devoting all one's life to learning, after growing used to one's study, to one's lecture-room, to the society of honourable colleagues—all of a sudden to find oneself here in this vault, every day to see stupid people, to hear foolish conversation. I want life, I like success, I like fame, I like distinction, renown, and here—it's like being an exile. Every moment to be grieving for the past, watching the successes of others, dreading death. I can't bear it! It's too much for me! And then they won't forgive me my age!

YELENA. Wait a little, have patience: in five or six years I shall be old too.

(*Enter* SONYA.)

SONYA. Father, you told us to send for Doctor Astrov yourself, and now that he has come you won't see him. It isn't nice. You've troubled him for nothing.

SEREBRYAKOV. What good is your Astrov to me? He knows as much about medicine as I do about astronomy.

SONYA. We can't send for all the great medical authorities here for your gout.

SEREBRYAKOV. I am not going to talk to that crazy crank.

SONYA. That's as you please (*sits down*). It doesn't matter to me.

SEREBRYAKOV. What's the time?

YELENA. Nearly one o'clock.

SEREBRYAKOV. I feel stifled. . . . Sonya, fetch me my drops from the table.

SONYA. In a minute (*gives him the drops*).

SEREBRYAKOV (*irritably*). Oh, not those! It's no use asking for anything!

SONYA. Please don't be peevish. Some people may like it, but please spare me! I don't like it. And I haven't the time. I have to get up early in the morning, we are hay-making to-morrow.

(*Enter* VOYNITSKY *in a dressing-gown with a candle in his hand.*)

VOYNITSKY. There's a storm coming on. (*A flash of lightning.*) There, look! Hélène and Sonya, go to bed. I have come to take your place.

SEREBRYAKOV (*frightened*). No, no! Don't leave me with him. No! He will be the death of me with his talking!

VOYNITSKY. But you must let them have some rest! This is the second night they have had no sleep.

SEREBRYAKOV. Let them go to bed, but you go too. Thank you. I entreat you to go. For the sake of our past friendship, don't make any objections! We'll talk some other time.

VOYNITSKY (*mockingly*). Our past friendship. . . . Past . . .

SONYA. Be quiet, Uncle Vanya.

SEREBRYAKOV (*to his wife*). My love, don't leave me alone with him! He will be the death of me with his talking!

VOYNITSKY. This is really getting laughable.

(*Enter* MARINA *with a candle.*)

SONYA. You ought to be in bed, nurse darling! It's late.

MARINA. The samovar has not been cleared. One can't very well go to bed.

SEREBRYAKOV. Everyone is kept up, everyone is worn out. I am the only one enjoying myself.

MARINA (*going up to* SEREBRYAKOV *tenderly*). Well, master dear, is the pain so bad? I have a grumbling pain in my legs too, such a pain (*tucks the rug in*). You've had this trouble for years. Vera Petrovna, Sonetchka's mother, used to be up night after night with you, wearing herself out. How fond she was of you! (*a pause*) The old are like little children, they like someone to be sorry for them; but no one feels for the old (*kisses* SEREBRYAKOV *on the shoulder*). Come to bed, dear . . . come, my honey. . . . I'll give you some lime-flower tea and warm your legs . . . and say a prayer for you. . . .

SEREBRYAKOV (*moved*). Let us go, Marina.

MARINA. I have such a grumbling pain in my legs myself, such a pain (*together with* SONYA *leads him off*). Vera Petrovna used to be crying, and breaking her heart over you. . . . You were only a mite then, Sonetchka, and had no sense. . . . Come along, come along, sir . . .

(SEREBRYAKOV, SONYA *and* MARINA *go out.*)

YELENA. I am quite worn out with him. I can hardly stand on my feet.

VOYNITSKY. You with him, and I with myself. This is the third night I have had no sleep.

YELENA. It's dreadful in this house. Your mother hates everything except her pamphlets and the Professor; the Professor is irritated, he does not trust me, and is afraid of you; Sonya is angry with her father, angry with me and has not spoken to me for a fortnight; you hate my husband and show open contempt for your mother; I am overwrought and have been nearly crying twenty times to-day. . . . It's dreadful in this house.

VOYNITSKY. Let us drop this moralising.

YELENA. You are a well-educated and intelligent man, Ivan Petrovitch, and I should have thought you ought to understand that the world is not being destroyed through fire or robbery, but through hatred, enmity and all this petty wrangling. . . . It ought to be your work to reconcile everyone, and not to grumble.

VOYNITSKY. Reconcile me to myself first! My precious . . . (*bends down and kisses her hand*).

YELENA. Don't! (*Draws away her hand.*) Go away!

VOYNITSKY. The rain will be over directly and everything in nature will be refreshed and sigh with relief. But the storm has brought no relief to me. Day and night the thought that my life has been hopelessly wasted weighs on me like a nightmare. I have no past, it has been stupidly wasted on trifles, and the present is awful in its senselessness. Here you have my life and my love! What use to make of them? What am I to do with them? My passion is wasted in vain like a ray of sunshine that has fallen into a pit, and I am utterly lost, too.

YELENA. When you talk to me about your love, I feel stupid and don't know what to say. Forgive me, there is nothing I can say to you (*is about to go out*). Good night.

VOYNITSKY (*barring her way*). And if you knew how wretched I am at the thought that by my side, in this same house, another life is being wasted, too —yours! What are you waiting for? What cursed theory holds you back? Understand, do understand . . .

YELENA (*looks at him intently*). Ivan Petrovitch, you are drunk!

VOYNITSKY. I may be, I may be . . .

YELENA. Where is the doctor?

VOYNITSKY. He is in there . . . he is staying the night with me. It may be, it may be . . . anything may be!

YELENA. You have been drinking again to-day. What's that for?

VOYNITSKY. There's a semblance of life in it, anyway. . . . Don't prevent me, Hélène!

YELENA. You never used to drink, and you did not talk so much. . . . Go to bed! You bore me.

VOYNITSKY (*kisses her hand*). My precious . . . marvellous one!

YELENA (*with vexation*). Don't. This is really hateful (*goes out*).

VOYNITSKY (*alone*). She is gone . . . (*a pause*). Ten years ago I used to meet her at my sister's. Then she was seventeen and I was thirty-seven. Why didn't I fall in love with her then and make her an offer? It might easily have happened then! And now she would have been my wife. . . . Yes. . . . Now we should both have been awakened by the storm; she would have been frightened by the thunder, I should have held her in my arms and whispered, "Don't be frightened, I am here." Oh, wonderful thoughts, what happiness; it makes me laugh with delight—but, my God, my thoughts are in a tangle. Why am I old? Why doesn't she understand me? Her fine phrases, her lazy morality, her nonsensical lazy theories about the ruin of the world—all that is absolutely hateful to me (*a pause*). Oh, how I have been cheated! I adored that Professor, that pitiful gouty invalid, and worked for him like an ox. Sonya and I squeezed every farthing out of the estate; we haggled over linseed oil, peas, curds, like greedy peasants; we grudged ourselves every morsel to save up halfpence and farthings and send him thousands of roubles. I was proud of him and his learning; he was my life, the breath of my being. All his writings and utterances seemed to me inspired by genius. . . . My God, and now! Here he is retired, and now one can see the sum total of his life. He leaves not one page of work behind him, he is utterly unknown, he is nothing—a soap bubble! And I have been cheated. . .   I see it—stupidly cheated. . . .

(*Enter* Astrov *in his coat, but without waistcoat or tie; he is a little drunk; he is followed by* Telyegin *with the guitar.*)

Astrov. Play something!

Telyegin. Everyone is asleep!

Astrov. Play!

(Telyegin *begins playing softly.*)

Astrov (*to* Voynitsky). Are you alone? No ladies here? (*Putting his arms akimbo sings*) "Dance my hut and dance my stove, the master has no bed to lie on." The storm woke me. Jolly good rain. What time is it?

Voynitsky. Goodness knows.

Astrov. I thought I heard Yelena Andreyevna's voice.

Voynitsky. She was here a minute ago.

Astrov. A fine woman. (*Examines the medicine bottles on the table.*) Medicines! What a lot of prescriptions! From Harkov, from Moscow, from Tula. He has bored every town with his gout. Is he really ill or shamming?

Voynitsky. He is ill (*a pause*).

Astrov. Why are you so melancholy to-day? Are you sorry for the Professor, or what?

Voynitsky. Let me alone.

Astrov. Or perhaps you are in love with the Professor's lady?

Voynitsky. She is my friend.

Astrov. Already?

Voynitsky. What do you mean by "already"?

Astrov. A woman can become a man's friend only in the following sequence: first agreeable acquaintance, then mistress, then friend.

Voynitsky. A vulgar theory.

Astrov. What? Yes . . . I must own I am growing vulgar. You see, I am drunk too. As a rule I get drunk like this once a month. When I am in this condition I become coarse and insolent in the extreme. I don't stick at anything then. I undertake the most difficult operations and do them capitally. I make the most extensive plans for the future; I don't think of myself as a crank at such times, but believe that I am being of immense service to humanity—immense! And I have my own philosophy of life at such times, and all you, my good friends, seem to me such insects . . . microbes! (*To* Telyegin.) Waffles, play!

Telyegin. My dear soul, I'd be delighted to do anything for you, but do realise—everyone is asleep!

Astrov. Play!

(TELYEGIN *begins playing softly.*)

ASTROV. We must have a drink. Come along, I fancy we have still some brandy left. And as soon as it is daylight, we will go to my place. Right? I have an assistant who never says "right," but "roight." He is an awful scoundrel. So we will go, shall we? (*Sees* SONYA *entering*) Excuse me, I have no tie on. (*Goes out hurriedly,* TELYEGIN *following him.*)

SONYA. Uncle Vanya, you have been drinking with the doctor again. You are a nice pair! He has always been like that, but why do you do it? It's so unsuitable at your age.

VOYNITSKY. Age makes no difference. When one has no real life, one has to live on illusions. It's better than nothing, anyway.

SONYA. The hay is all cut, it rains every day, it's all rotting, and you are living in illusions. You have quite given up looking after things. . . . I have to work alone, and am quite done up. . . . (*Alarmed*) Uncle, you have tears in your eyes!

VOYNITSKY. Tears? Not a bit of it . . . nonsense. . . . You looked at me just now so like your dear mother. My darling . . . (*eagerly kisses her hands and face*). My sister . . . my dear sister . . . where is she now? If she knew! Ah, if she knew!

SONYA. What, uncle? Knew what?

VOYNITSKY. It's painful, useless. . . . Never mind. . . . Afterwards . . . it's nothing . . . I am going (*goes out*).

SONYA (*knocks at the door*). Mihail Lvovitch, you are not asleep, are you? One minute!

ASTROV (*through the door*). I am coming! (*A minute later he comes out with his waistcoat and tie on.*) What can I do for you?

SONYA. Drink yourself, if it does not disgust you, but I implore you, don't let my uncle drink! It's bad for him.

ASTROV. Very good. We won't drink any more (*a pause*). I am just going home. That's settled and signed. It will be daylight by the time they have put the horses in.

SONYA. It is raining. Wait till morning.

ASTROV. The storm is passing over, we shall only come in for the end of it. I'm going. And please don't send for me again to see your father. I tell him it's gout and he tells me it's rheumatism; I ask him to stay in bed and he sits in a chair. And to-day he wouldn't speak to me at all.

SONYA. He is spoiled. (*Looks into the sideboard*) Won't you have something to eat?

ASTROV. Well, perhaps.

SONYA. I like eating at night. I believe there is something in the sideboard. They say he's been a great favourite with the ladies, and women have spoiled him. Here, have some cheese. (*Both stand at the sideboard and eat.*)

ASTROV. I have had nothing to eat all day, only drink. Your father has a difficult temper. (*Takes a bottle from the sideboard.*) May I? (*Drinks a glass.*)

There is no one here and one may speak frankly. Do you know, it seems to me that I could not exist in your house for a month, I should be choked by the atmosphere. . . . Your father, who is entirely absorbed in his gout and his books, Uncle Vanya with his melancholy, your grandmother, and your stepmother too. . . .

SONYA. What about my stepmother?

ASTROV. Everything ought to be beautiful in a human being: face, and dress, and soul, and ideas. She is beautiful, there is no denying that, but . . . You know she does nothing but eat, sleep, walk about, fascinate us all by her beauty—nothing more. She has no duties, other people work for her. . . . That's true, isn't it? And an idle life cannot be pure (*a pause*). But perhaps I am too severe. I am dissatisfied with life like your Uncle Vanya, and we are both growing peevish.

SONYA. Are you dissatisfied with life, then?

ASTROV. I love life as such, but our life, our everyday provincial life in Russia, I can't endure. I despise it with every fibre of my being. And as for my own personal life, there is absolutely nothing nice in it, I can assure you. You know when you walk through a forest on a dark night, and a light gleams in the distance, you do not notice your weariness, nor the darkness, nor the sharp twigs that lash you in the face. . . . I work—as you know—harder than anyone in the district, fate is for ever lashing at me; at times I am unbearably miserable, but I have no light in the distance. I expect nothing for myself; I am not fond of my fellow creatures. . . . It's years since I cared for anyone.

SONYA. You care for no one at all?

ASTROV. No one. I feel a certain affection for your nurse—for the sake of old times. The peasants are too much alike, undeveloped, living in dirt, and it is difficult to get on with the educated people. They are all wearisome. Our good friends are small in their ideas, small in their feelings, and don't see beyond their noses—or, to put it plainly, they are stupid. And those who are bigger and more intelligent are hysterical, morbidly absorbed in introspection and analysis. . . . They are for ever whining; they are insanely given to hatred and slander; they steal up to a man sideways, and look at him askance and decide "Oh, he is a neurotic!" or "he is posing." And when they don't know what label to stick on my forehead, they say "he is a queer fellow, very queer!" I am fond of forestry—that's queer; I don't eat meat—that's queer too. There is no direct, genuine, free attitude to people and to nature left among them. . . . None, none! (*Is about to drink.*)

SONYA (*prevents him*). No, please, I beg you, don't drink any more!

ASTROV. Why not?

SONYA. It's so out of keeping with you! You are so refined, you have such a soft voice. . . . More than that even, you are unlike everyone else I know— you are beautiful. Why, then, do you want to be like ordinary people who drink and play cards? Oh, don't do it, I entreat you! You always say that people don't create but only destroy what heaven gives them. Then why do you destroy yourself, why? You mustn't, you mustn't, I beseech you, I implore you!

ASTROV (*holds out his hand to her*). I won't drink any more!

SONYA. Give me your word.

ASTROV. My word of honour.

SONYA (*presses his hand warmly*). Thank you!

ASTROV. Enough! I have come to my senses. You see, I am quite sober now and I will be so to the end of my days (*looks at his watch*). And so, as I was saying, my time is over, it's too late for me. . . . I have grown old, I have worked too hard, I have grown vulgar, all my feelings are blunted, and I believe I am not capable of being fond of anyone. I don't love anyone . . . and I don't believe I ever shall. What still affects me is beauty. That does stir me. I fancy if Yelena Andreyevna, for example, wanted to, she could turn my head in one day. . . . But that's not love, that's not affection . . . (*covers his face with his hands and shudders*).

SONYA. What is it?

ASTROV. Nothing. . . . In Lent one of my patients died under chloroform.

SONYA. You ought to forget that by now (*a pause*). Tell me, Mihail Lvovitch . . . if I had a friend or a younger sister, and if you found out that she . . . well, suppose that she loved you, how would you take that?

ASTROV (*shrugging his shoulders*). I don't know. Nohow, I expect. I should give her to understand that I could not care for her . . . and my mind is taken up with other things. Anyway, if I am going, it is time to start. Goodbye, my dear girl, or we shall not finish till morning (*presses her hand*). I'll go through the drawing-room if I may, or I am afraid your uncle may detain me (*goes out*).

SONYA (*alone*). He has said nothing to me. . . . His soul and his heart are still shut away from me, but why do I feel so happy? (*Laughs with happiness.*) I said to him, you are refined, noble, you have such a soft voice. . . . Was it inappropriate? His voice trembles and caresses one . . . I still feel it vibrating in the air. And when I spoke to him of a younger sister, he did not understand. . . . (*Wringing her hands*) Oh, how awful it is that I am not beautiful! How awful it is! And I know I am not, I know it, I know it! . . . Last Sunday, as people were coming out of church, I heard them talking about me, and one woman said: "She is a sweet generous nature, but what a pity she is so plain. . . ." Plain. . . .

(*Enter* YELENA ANDREYEVNA.)

YELENA (*opens the window*). The storm is over. What delicious air! (*a pause*) Where is the doctor?

SONYA. He is gone (*a pause*).

YELENA. Sophie!

SONYA. What is it?

YELENA. How long are you going to be sulky with me? We have done each other no harm. Why should we be enemies? Let us make it up. . . .

SONYA. I wanted to myself . . . (*embraces her*). Don't let us be cross any more.

YELENA. That's right. (*Both are agitated.*)

SONYA. Has father gone to bed?

YELENA. No, he is sitting in the drawing-room. . . . We don't speak to each other for weeks, and goodness knows why. . . . (*Seeing that the sideboard is open*) How is this?

SONYA. Mihail Lvovitch has been having some supper.

YELENA. And there is wine too. . . . Let us drink to our friendship.

SONYA. Yes, let us.

YELENA. Out of the same glass . . . (*fills it*). It's better so. So now we are friends?

SONYA. Friends. (*They drink and kiss each other.*) I have been wanting to make it up for ever so long, but somehow I felt ashamed . . . (*cries*).

YELENA. Why are you crying?

SONYA. It's nothing.

YELENA. Come, there, there . . . (*weeps*). I am a queer creature, I am crying too . . . (*a pause*). You are angry with me because you think I married your father from interested motives. . . . If that will make you believe me, I will swear it—I married him for love. I was attracted by him as a learned, celebrated man. It was not real love, it was all made up; but I fancied at the time that it was real. It's not my fault. And ever since our marriage you have been punishing me with your clever, suspicious eyes.

SONYA. Come, peace! peace! Let us forget.

YELENA. You mustn't look like that—it doesn't suit you. You must believe in everyone—there is no living if you don't (*a pause*).

SONYA. Tell me honestly, as a friend . . . are you happy?

YELENA. No.

SONYA. I knew that. One more question. Tell me frankly, wouldn't you have liked your husband to be young?

YELENA. What a child you are still! Of course I should! (*Laughs*) Well, ask something else, ask away. . . .

SONYA. Do you like the doctor?

YELENA. Yes, very much.

SONYA (*laughs*). Do I look silly . . . yes? He has gone away, but I still hear his voice and his footsteps, and when I look at the dark window I can see his face. Do let me tell you. . . . But I can't speak so loud; I feel ashamed. Come into my room, we can talk there. You must think me silly? Own up. . . . Tell me something about him.

YELENA. What am I to tell you?

SONYA. He is clever. . . . He understands everything, he can do anything. . . . He doctors people, and plants forests too. . . .

YELENA. It is not a question of forests and medicine. . . . My dear, you must understand he has a spark of genius! And you know what that means?

Boldness, freedom of mind, width of outlook. . . . He plants a tree and is already seeing what will follow from it in a thousand years, already he has visions of the, happiness of humanity. Such people are rare, one must love them. . . . He drinks, he is sometimes a little coarse—but what does that matter? A talented man cannot keep spotless in Russia. Only think what sort of life that doctor has! Impassable mud on the roads, frosts, snowstorms, the immense distances, the coarse savage peasants, poverty and disease all around him—it is hard for one who is working and struggling day after day in such surroundings to keep spotless and sober till he is forty (*kisses her*). I wish you happiness with all my heart; you deserve it . . . (*gets up*). But I am a tiresome, secondary character. . . . In music and in my husband's house, and in all the love affairs, everywhere in fact, I have always played a secondary part. As a matter of fact, if you come to think of it, Sonya, I am very, very unhappy! (*Walks up and down the stage in agitation.*) There is no happiness in this world for me, none! Why do you laugh?

SONYA (*laughs, hiding her face*). I am so happy . . . so happy!

YELENA. I have a longing for music. I should like to play something.

SONYA. Do play something! (*Embraces her.*) I can't sleep. . . . Play something!

YELENA. In a minute. Your father is not asleep. Music irritates him when he is ill. Go and ask his leave. If he doesn't object, I'll play. Go!

SONYA. Very well (*goes out*).

(*Watchman taps in the garden.*)

YELENA. It's a long time since I have played the piano. I shall play and cry, cry like an idiot. (*In the window*) Is that you tapping, Yefim?

WATCHMAN'S VOICE. Yes.

YELENA. Don't tap, the master is unwell.

WATCHMAN'S VOICE. I am just going (*whistles*). Hey there, good dog! Come, lad! Good dog! (*A pause.*)

SONYA (*returning*). We mustn't!

CURTAIN.

ACT III

The drawing-room in SEREBRYAKOV'S *house. Three doors: on the right, on the left and in the middle. Daytime.*

VOYNITSKY *and* SONYA *seated, and* YELENA ANDREYEVNA *walking about the stage, thinking.*

VOYNITSKY. The Herr Professor has graciously expressed a desire that we should all gather together in this room at one o'clock to-day (*looks at his watch*). It is a quarter to. He wishes to make some communication to the world.

YELENA. Probably some business matter.

VOYNITSKY. He has no business. He spends his time writing twaddle, grumbling and being jealous.

SONYA (*in a reproachful tone*). Uncle!

VOYNITSKY. Well, well, I am sorry (*Motioning towards* YELENA ANDREY-EVNA) Just look at her! she is so lazy that she almost staggers as she walks. Very charming! Very!

YELENA. You keep buzzing and buzzing away all day—aren't you tired of it? (*Miserably*) I am bored to death. I don't know what I'm to do.

SONYA (*shrugging her shoulders*). Isn't there plenty to do? If only you cared to do it.

YELENA. For instance?

SONYA. You could help us with the estate, teach the children or look after the sick. There's plenty to do. When father and you were not here, Uncle Vanya and I used to go to the market ourselves and sell the flour.

YELENA. I don't know how to do such things. And they are not interesting. It's only in novels with a purpose that people teach and doctor the peasants. How am I, all of a sudden, *à propos* of nothing, to go and teach them or doctor them?

SONYA. Well, I don't see how one can help doing it. Wait a little, and you too will get into the way of it (*puts her arm round her*). Don't be depressed, dear (*laughs*). You are bored and don't know what to do with yourself, and boredom and idleness are catching. Look at Uncle Vanya—he does nothing but follow you about like a shadow. I have left my work and run away to talk to you. I have grown lazy—I can't help it! The doctor, Mihail Lvovitch, used to come and see us very rarely, once a month; it was difficult to persuade him to come, and now he drives over every day. He neglects his forestry and his patients. You must be a witch.

VOYNITSKY. Why be miserable? (*Eagerly*) Come, my precious, my splendid one, be sensible! You have mermaid blood in your veins—be a mermaid! Let yourself go for once in your life! Make haste and fall head over ears in love with some water-sprite—and plunge headlong into the abyss so that the Herr Professor and all of us may throw up our hands in amazement!

YELENA (*angrily*). Leave me in peace! How cruel it is! (*Is about to go out.*)

VOYNITSKY (*prevents her*). Come, come, my dearest, forgive me. . . . I apologise (*kisses her hand*). Peace!

YELENA. You would drive an angel out of patience, you know.

VOYNITSKY. As a sign of peace and harmony I'll fetch you a bunch of roses; I gathered them for you this morning. Autumn roses—exquisite, mournful roses . . . (*goes out*).

SONYA. Autumn roses—exquisite, mournful roses. . . . (*Both look out of window.*)

YELENA. It's September already. However are we to get through the winter here? (*a pause*) Where is the doctor?

SONYA. In Uncle Vanya's room. He is writing something. I am glad Uncle Vanya is gone. I want to talk to you.

YELENA. What about?

SONYA. What about! (*Lays her head on* YELENA'S *bosom.*)

YELENA. Come, there, there . . . (*strokes her head*).

SONYA. I am not good-looking.

YELENA. You have beautiful hair.

SONYA. No! (*Looks round so as to see herself in the looking-glass.*) No! When a woman is plain, she is always told "You have beautiful eyes, you have beautiful hair." . . . I have loved him for six years. I love him more than my own mother. Every moment I am conscious of him. I feel the touch of his hand and I watch the door. I wait, expecting him every moment to come in. And here you see I keep coming to you simply to talk of him. Now' he is here every day, but he doesn't look at me—doesn't see me. . . That's such agony! I have no hope at all—none, none! (*In despair*) Oh, my God, give me strength . . . I have been praying all night. . . . I often go up to him, begin talking to him, look into his eyes. I have no pride left, no strength to control myself. I couldn't keep it in and told Uncle Vanya yesterday that I love him. . . . And all the servants know I love him. Everybody knows it.

YELENA. And he?

SONYA. No. He doesn't notice me.

YELENA (*musing*). He is a strange man. . . Do you know what? Let me speak to him. . . . I'll do it carefully—hint at it . . . (*a pause*). Yes, really —how much longer are you to remain in uncertainty? Let me!

(SONYA *nods her head in consent.*)

YELENA. That's right. It won't be difficult to find out whether he loves you or not. Don't you be troubled, darling; don't be uneasy. I'll question him so tactfully that he won't notice it. All we want to find out is yes or no (*a pause*). If it's no, he had better not come here, had he?

(SONYA *nods in agreement.*)

YELENA. It's easier to bear when one doesn't see the man. We won't put things off; we will question him straight away. He was meaning to show me some charts. Go and tell him that I want to see him.

SONYA (*in violent agitation*). You will tell me the whole truth?

YELENA. Yes, of course. It seems to me that the truth, however dreadful it is, is not so dreadful as uncertainty. Rely on me, dear.

SONYA. Yes, yes . . . I shall tell him you want to see his charts (*is going, and stops in the doorway*) . . . No, uncertainty is better. . . One has hope, at least. . . .

YELENA. What do you say?

SONYA. Nothing (*goes out*).

YELENA (*alone*). Nothing is worse than knowing somebody else's secret and not being able to help. (*Musing*) He is not in love with her—that's evident; but why should he not marry her? She is not good-looking, but she would be a capital wife for a country doctor at his age. She is so sensible, so kind and pure-hearted. . . . No, that's not it . . . (*a pause*). I understand the poor child. In the midst of desperate boredom, with nothing but grey shadows wandering about instead of human beings, with only dull commonplaces to listen to, among people who can do nothing but eat, drink and sleep—he sometimes appears on the scene unlike the rest, handsome, interesting, fascinating, like a bright moon rising in the darkness. . . . To yield to the charm of such a man . . forget oneself . . . I believe I am a little fascinated myself. Yes, I feel bored when he does not come, and even now I am smiling when I think of him. . . . That Uncle Vanya says I have mermaid's blood in my veins. "Let yourself go for once in your life." Well, perhaps that's what I ought to do. . . . If I could fly, free as a bird, away from all of you—from your sleepy faces, from your talk, forget your existence. . . . But I am cowardly and diffident. . . . My conscience troubles me. . . . He comes here every day. I guess why he comes, and already I have a guilty feeling. I am ready to throw myself on my knees before Sonya, to beg her pardon, to cry. . . .

ASTROV (*comes in with a chart*). Good day! (*Shakes hands.*) You wanted to see my handiwork.

YELENA. You promised yesterday to show me. . . . Can you spare the time?

ASTROV. Oh, of course! (*Spreads the map on a card table and fixes it with drawing pins.*) Where were you born?

YELENA (*helping him*). In Petersburg.

ASTROV. And where did you study?

YELENA. At the School of Music.

ASTROV. I expect this won't be interesting to you.

YELENA. Why not? It's true that I don't know the country, but I have read a great deal.

ASTROV. I have my own table here, in this house . . . in Ivan Petrovitch's room. When I am so exhausted that I feel completely stupefied, I throw everything up and fly here and amuse myself with this for an hour or two. . . . Ivan Petrovitch and Sofya Alexandrovna click their counting beads, and I sit beside them at my table and daub away—and I feel snug and comfortable, and the cricket churrs. But I don't allow myself that indulgence too often—only once a month. . . . (*Pointing to the map*) Now, look here! It's a picture of our district as it was fifty years ago. The dark and light green stands for forest; half of the whole area was covered with forest. Where there is a network of red over the green, elks and wild goats were common. . . . I show both the flora and the fauna here. On this lake there were swans, geese and ducks, and the old people tell us there were "a power" of birds of all sorts, no end of them; they flew in clouds. Besides the villages and hamlets, you see scattered here and there all sorts of settlements—little farms, monasteries of

Old Believers, water-mills. . . . Horned cattle and horses were numerous. That is shown by the blue colour. For instance, the blue colour lies thick on this neighbourhood. Here there were regular droves of horses, and every homestead had three on an average (*a pause*). Now look lower down. That's how it was twenty-five years ago. Already, you see, only a third of the area is under forest. There are no goats left, but there are elks. Both the green and the blue are paler. And so it goes on and on. Let us pass to the third part— a map of the district as it is at present. There is green here and there, but only in patches; all the elks have vanished, and the swans and the caper-cailzies too. . . . Of the old settlements and farms and monasteries and mills there is not a trace. In fact, it's a picture of gradual and unmistakable de-generation which will, apparently, in another ten or fifteen years be complete. You will say that it is the influence of civilisation—that the old life must naturally give way to the new. Yes, I understand that. If there were highroads and railways on the site of these ruined forests, if there were works and fac-tories and schools, the peasants would be healthier, better off, more intelligent; but, you see, there is nothing of the sort! There are still the same swamps and mosquitoes, the same lack of roads, and poverty, and typhus and diphtheria and fires in the district. . . . We have here a degeneration that is the result of too severe a struggle for existence. This degeneration is due to inertia, ignorance, to the complete lack of understanding, when a man, cold, hungry and sick, simply to save what is left of life, to keep his children alive, in-stinctively, unconsciously clutches at anything to satisfy his hunger and warm himself and destroys everything heedless of the morrow. . . . Almost every-thing has been destroyed already, but nothing as yet has been created to take its place. (*Coldly*) I see from your face that it doesn't interest you. '

YELENA. But I understand so little about all that. . . .

ASTROV. There's nothing to understand in it; it simply doesn't interest you.

YELENA. To speak frankly, I am thinking of something else. Forgive me. I want to put you through a little examination, and I am troubled and don't know how to begin.

ASTROV. An examination?

YELENA. Yes, an examination . . . but not a very formidable one. Let us sit down. (*They sit down.*) It concerns a certain young lady. We will talk like honest people, like friends, without beating about the bush. Let us talk and forget all about it afterwards. Yes?

ASTROV. Yes.

YELENA. It concerns my step-daughter Sonya. You like her, don't you?

ASTROV. Yes, I have a respect for her.

YELENA. Does she attract you as a woman?

ASTROV (*after a pause*). No.

YELENA. A few words more, and I have done. Have you noticed nothing?

ASTROV. Nothing.

YELENA (*taking him by the hand*). You do not love her . . . I see it from

our eyes. . . . She is unhappy. . . . Understand that and . . . give up com-
ng here.

ASTROV (*gets up*). My day is over. Besides, I have too much to do (*shrug-
ing his shoulders*). What time have I for such things? (*He is confused.*)

YELENA. Ough! What an unpleasant conversation! I am trembling as though
'd been carrying a ton weight. Well, thank God, that's over! Let us forget it.
.et it be as though we had not spoken at all, and . . . and go away. You are
in intelligent man . . . you'll understand (*a pause*). I feel hot all over.

ASTROV. If you had spoken a month or two ago I might, perhaps, have con-
idered it; but now . . . (*he shrugs his shoulders*). And if she is unhappy,
hen of course . . . There's only one thing I can't understand: what induced
ou to go into it? (*Looks into her eyes and shakes his finger at her*) You are
. sly one!

YELENA. What does that mean?

ASTROV (*laughs*). Sly! Suppose Sonya is unhappy—I am quite ready to
dmit it—but why need you go into it? (*Preventing her from speaking,
agerly*) Please don't try to look astonished. You know perfectly well what
rings me here every day. . . . Why, and on whose account, I am here, you
now perfectly well. You charming bird of prey, don't look at me like that,
am an old sparrow. . . .

YELENA (*perplexed*). Bird of prey! I don't understand.

ASTROV. A beautiful, fluffy weasel. . . . You must have a victim! Here I
iave been doing nothing for a whole month. I have dropped everything. I
eek you greedily—and you are awfully pleased at it, awfully. . . . Well, I
m conquered; you knew that before your examination (*folding his arms and
owing his head*). I submit. Come and devour me!

YELENA. You are mad!

ASTROV (*laughs through his teeth*). You—diffident. . . .

YELENA. Oh, I am not so bad and so mean as you think! I swear I'm not
tries to go out).

ASTROV (*barring the way*). I am going away to-day. I won't come here
igain, but . . . (*takes her hand and looks round*) where shall we see each
ither? Tell me quickly, where? Someone may come in; tell me quickly. . . .
Passionately) How wonderful, how magnificent you are! One kiss. . . . If I
ould only kiss your fragrant hair. . . .

YELENA. I assure you . . .

ASTROV (*preventing her from speaking*). Why assure me? There's no need.
No need of unnecessary words. . . . Oh, how beautiful you are! What hands!
Kisses her hands.)

YELENA. That's enough . . . go away . . . (*withdraws her hands*). You
ire forgetting yourself.

ASTROV. Speak, speak! Where shall we meet to-morrow? (*Puts his arm
ound her waist.*) You see, it is inevitable; we must meet. (*Kisses her; at that

instant VOYNITSKY *comes in with a bunch of roses and stands still in the door way.)*

YELENA (*not seeing* VOYNITSKY). Spare me . . . let me go . . . (*lays he head on* ASTROV's *chest.)* No! (*Tries to go out.*)

ASTROV (*holding her by the waist*). Come to the plantation to-morrow . . . at two o'clock. . . . Yes? Yes? You'll come?

YELENA (*seeing* VOYNITSKY). Let me go! (*In extreme confusion goes to th window.*) This is awful!

VOYNITSKY (*lays the roses on a chair; in confusion wipes his face and hi neck with his handkerchief*). Never mind . . . no . . . never mind. . . .

ASTROV (*carrying it off with bravado*). The weather is not so bad to-day honoured Ivan Petrovitch. It was overcast in the morning, as though we were going to have rain, but now it is sunny. To tell the truth, the autumn ha turned out lovely . . . and the winter corn is quite promising (*rolls up the map*). The only thing is the days are getting shorter . . . (*goes out*).

YELENA (*goes quickly up to* VOYNITSKY). You will try—you will do you utmost that my husband and I should leave here to-day! Do you hear? Thi very day.

VOYNITSKY (*mopping his face*). What? Oh, yes . . . very well . . . I saw it all, Hélène—all. . . .

YELENA (*nervously*). Do you hear? I must get away from here to-day!

(*Enter* SEREBRYAKOV, TELYEGIN *and* MARINA.)

TELYEGIN. I don't feel quite the thing myself, your Excellency. I have been poorly for the last two days. My head is rather queer. . . .

SEREBRYAKOV. Where are the others? I don't like this house. It's a perfect labyrinth. Twenty-six huge rooms, people wander in different directions, and there is no finding anyone (*rings*). Ask Marya Vassilyevna and Yelena Andrey- evna to come here.

YELENA I am here.

SEREBRYAKOV. I beg you to sit down, friends.

SONYA (*going up to* YELENA ANDREYEVNA, *impatiently*). What did he say?

YELENA. Presently.

SONYA. You are trembling! You are agitated! (*Looking searchingly into her face*) I understand. . . . He said that he won't come here again . . . yes? (*a pause*) Tell me: yes?

(YELENA ANDREYEVNA *nods*.)

SEREBRYAKOV (*to* TELYEGIN). One can put up with illness, after all; but what I can't endure is the whole manner of life in the country. I feel as though I had been cast off the earth into some other planet. Sit down, friends, I beg! Sonya! (SONYA *does not hear him; she stands with her head drooping sorrowfully.*) Sonya! (*a pause*) She does not hear. (*To* MARINA) You sit down too, nurse. (*Nurse sits down, knitting a stocking.*) I beg you, my friends, hang your ears on the nail of attention, as the saying is (*laughs*).

VOYNITSKY (*agitated*). Perhaps I am not wanted? Can I go?

SEREBRYAKOV. No; it is you whom we need most.

VOYNITSKY. What do you require of me?

SEREBRYAKOV. Require of you. . . . Why are you cross? (*a pause*) If I have been to blame in any way, pray excuse me.

VOYNITSKY. Drop that tone. Let us come to business. What do you want?

(*Enter* MARYA VASSILYEVNA.)

SEREBRYAKOV. Here is mamán. I will begin, friends (*a pause*). I have invited you, gentlemen, to announce that the Inspector-General is coming. But let us lay aside jesting. It is a serious matter. I have called you together to ask for your advice and help, and, knowing your invariable kindness, I hope to receive it. I am a studious, bookish man, and have never had anything to do with practical life. I cannot dispense with the assistance of those who understand it, and I beg you, Ivan Petrovitch, and you, Ilya Ilyitch, and you, maman. . . . The point is that *manet omnes una nox*—that is, that we are all mortal. I am old and ill, and so I think it is high time to settle my worldly affairs so far as they concern my family. My life is over. I am not thinking of myself, but I have a young wife and an unmarried daughter (*a pause*). It is impossible for me to go on living in the country. We are not made for country life. But to live in town on the income we derive from this estate is impossible. If we sell the forest, for instance, that's an exceptional measure which we cannot repeat every year. We must take some steps which would guarantee us a permanent and more or less definite income. I have thought of such a measure, and have the honour of submitting it to your consideration. Omitting details I will put it before you in rough outline. Our estate yields on an average not more than two per cent. on its capital value. I propose to sell it. If we invest the money in suitable securities, we should get from four to five per cent., and I think we might even have a few thousand roubles to spare for buying a small villa in Finland.

VOYNITSKY. Excuse me . . . surely my ears are deceiving me! Repeat what you have said.

SEREBRYAKOV. To put the money in some suitable investment and with the remainder purchase a villa in Finland.

VOYNITSKY. Not Finland. . . . You said something else.

SEREBRYAKOV. I propose to sell the estate.

VOYNITSKY. That's it. You will sell the estate; superb, a grand idea. . . . And what do you propose to do with me, and your old mother and Sonya here?

SEREBRYAKOV. We will settle all that in due time. One can't go into everything at once.

VOYNITSKY. Wait a minute. It's evident that up to now I've never had a grain of common sense. Up to now I have always imagined that the estate belongs to Sonya. My father bought this estate as a dowry for my sister. Till now I have been simple; I did not interpret the law like a Turk, but thought that my sister's estate passed to Sonya.

SEREBRYAKOV. Yes, the estate belongs to Sonya. Who disputes it? Witho Sonya's consent I shall not venture to sell it. Besides, I am proposing to do for Sonya's benefit.

VOYNITSKY. It's inconceivable, inconceivable! Either I have gone out of r mind, or . . . or . . .

MARYA. Jean, don't contradict Alexandr. Believe me, he knows better th. we do what is for the best.

VOYNITSKY. No; give me some water (drinks water). Say what you like say what you like!

SEREBRYAKOV. I don't understand why you are so upset. I don't say that n plan is ideal. If everyone thinks it unsuitable, I will not insist on it.

(A pause.)

TELYEGIN (in confusion). I cherish for learning, your Excellency, not simp a feeling of reverence, but a sort of family feeling. My brother Grigo Ilyitch's wife's brother—perhaps you know him?—Konstantin Trofimit Lakedemonov, was an M.A. . . .

VOYNITSKY. Stop, Waffles; we are talking of business. . . . Wait a little later. . . . (To SEREBRYAKOV) Here, ask him. The estate was bought fro his uncle.

SEREBRYAKOV. Oh! why should I ask him? What for?

VOYNITSKY. The estate was bought at the time for ninety-five thousar roubles. My father paid only seventy thousand, and twenty-five thousar remained on mortgage. Now, listen. . . . The estate would never have bee bought if I had not renounced my share of the inheritance in favour of n sister, whom I loved dearly. What's more, I worked for ten years like a slaⁿ and paid off all the mortgage. . . .

SEREBRYAKOV. I regret that I broached the subject.

VOYNITSKY. The estate is free from debt and in a good condition on owing to my personal efforts. And now that I am old I am to be kicked o of it!

SEREBRYAKOV. I don't understand what you are aiming at.

VOYNITSKY. I have been managing this estate for twenty-five years. I haⁿ worked and sent you money like the most conscientious steward, and yc have never thanked me once in all these years. All that time—both when was young and now—you have given me five hundred roubles a year as salaⁿ —a beggarly wage!—and it never occurred to you to add a rouble to it.

SEREBRYAKOV. Ivan Petrovitch, how could I tell? I am not a practical maⁿ and don't understand these things. You could have added as much to it you chose.

VOYNITSKY. Why didn't I steal? How is it you don't all despise me becauⁿ I didn't steal? It would have been right and I shouldn't have been a paupⁿ now!

MARYA (sternly). Jean!

TELYEGIN (in agitation). Vanya, my dear soul, don't, don't . . . I am a f a tremble. . . . Why spoil our good relations? (*Kisses him*) You mustn't.

VOYNITSKY. For twenty-five years I have been here within these four walls
with mother, buried like a mole. . . . All our thoughts and feelings belonged
to you alone. By day we talked of you and your labours. We were proud of
you; with reverence we uttered your name. We wasted our nights reading
books and magazines for which now I have the deepest contempt!

TELYEGIN. Don't, Vanya, don't . . . I can't stand it. . . .

SEREBRYAKOV (*wrathfully*). I don't know what it is you want.

VOYNITSKY. To us you were a being of a higher order, and we knew your
articles by heart. . . . But now my eyes are opened! I see it all! You write of
art, but you know nothing about art! All those works of yours I used to love
are not worth a brass farthing! You have deceived us!

SEREBRYAKOV. Do stop him! I am going!

YELENA. Ivan Petrovitch, I insist on your being silent! Do you hear?

VOYNITSKY. I won't be silent. (*Preventing* SEREBRYAKOV *from passing*)
Stay! I have not finished. You have destroyed my life! I have not lived! I have
not lived! Thanks to you, I have ruined and wasted the best years of my life.
You are my bitterest enemy.

TELYEGIN. I can't bear it . . . I can't bear it . . . I must go (*goes out,
in violent agitation*).

SEREBRYAKOV. What do you want from me? And what right have you to
speak to me like this? You nonentity! If the estate is yours, take it. I don't
want it!

YELENA. I am going away from this hell this very minute (*screams*). I can't
put up with it any longer!

VOYNITSKY. My life is ruined! I had talent, I had courage, I had intelli-
gence! If I had had a normal life I might have been a Schopenhauer, a Dos-
toevsky. . . . Oh, I am talking like an idiot! I am going mad. . . . Mother,
I am in despair! Mother!

MARYA (*sternly*). Do as Alexandr tells you.

SONYA (*kneeling down before the nurse and huddling up to her*). Nurse,
darling! Nurse, darling!

VOYNITSKY. Mother! What am I to do? Don't speak; there's no need! I
know what I must do! (*To* SEREBRYAKOV) You shall remember me! (*Goes out
through middle door.*)

          (MARYA VASSILYEVNA *follows him.*)

SEREBRYAKOV. This is beyond everything! Take that madman away! I cannot live under the same roof with him. He is always there (*points to the middle door*)—almost beside me. . . . Let him move into the village, or into
the lodge, or I will move; but remain in the same house with him I cannot. . . .

YELENA (*to her husband*). We will leave this place to-day! We must pack
up this minute!

SEREBRYAKOV. An utterly insignificant creature!

SONYA (*on her knees, turns her head towards her father; hysterical through her tears*). You must be merciful, father! Uncle Vanya and I are so unhappy (*Mastering her despair*) You must be merciful! Remember how, when you were younger, Uncle Vanya and grandmamma sat up all night translating books for you, copying your manuscripts . . . all night . . . all night . . Uncle Vanya and I worked without resting—we were afraid to spend a farthing on ourselves and sent it all to you. . . . We did not eat the bread of idleness. I am saying it all wrong—all wrong; but you ought to understand us, father. You must be merciful!

YELENA (*in agitation, to her husband*). Alexandr, for God's sake make it up with him. . . . I beseech you!

SEREBRYAKOV. Very well, I will talk to him. . . . I am not accusing him of anything, I am not angry with him. But you must admit that his behaviour is strange, to say the least of it. Very well, I'll go to him (*goes out by middle door*).

YELENA. Be gentle with him, soothe him . . . (*follows him out*).

SONYA (*hugging Nurse*). Oh, nurse, darling! Nurse, darling!

MARINA. Never mind, child. The ganders will cackle a bit and leave off. . . . They will cackle and leave off. . . .

SONYA. Nurse, darling!

MARINA (*stroking her head*). You are shivering as though you were frozen! There, there. little orphan, God is merciful! A cup of lime-flower water, or raspberry tea, and it will pass. . . . Don't grieve, little orphan. (*Looking towards the middle door wrathfully*) What a to-do they make, the ganders! Plague take them!

(*A shot behind the scenes; a shriek from* YELENA ANDREYEVNA *is heard;* SONYA *shudders.*)

MARINA. Ough! Botheration take them!

SEREBRYAKOV (*runs in, staggering with terror*). Hold him! hold him! He is out of his mind!

(YELENA ANDREYEVNA *and* VOYNITSKY *struggle in the doorway.*)

YELENA (*trying to take the revolver from him*). Give it up! Give it up, I tell you!

VOYNITSKY. Let me go, Hélène! Let me go! (*Freeing himself from her, he runs in, looking for* SEREBRYAKOV) Where is he? Oh, here he is! (*Fires at him*) Bang! (*a pause*) Missed! Missed again! (*Furiously*) Damnation—damnation take it . . . (*Flings revolver on the floor and sinks on to a chair, exhausted.* SEREBRYAKOV *is overwhelmed;* YELENA *leans against the wall, almost fainting.*)

YELENA. Take me away! Take me away! Kill me . . . I can't stay here, I can't!

VOYNITSKY (*in despair*). Oh, what am I doing! What am I doing!

SONYA (*softly*). Nurse, darling! Nurse, darling!

CURTAIN.

ACT IV

VOYNITSKY's *room: it is his bedroom and also his office. In the window there is a big table covered with account books and papers of all sorts; a bureau, bookcases, scales. A smaller table, for* ASTROV; *on that table there are paints and drawing materials; beside it a big portfolio. A cage with a starling in it. On the wall a map of Africa, obviously of no use to anyone. A big sofa covered with American leather. To the left a door leading to other apartments. On the right a door into the hall; near door, on right, there is a doormat, that the peasants may not muddy the floor. An autumn evening. Stillness.*

TELYEGIN *and* MARINA *sitting opposite each other winding wool.*

TELYEGIN. You must make haste, Marina Timofeyevna, they will soon be calling us to say good-bye. They have already ordered the horses.

MARINA (*tries to wind more rapidly*). There is not much left.

TELYEGIN. They are going to Harkov. They'll live there.

MARINA. Much better so.

TELYEGIN. They've had a fright. . . . Yelena Andreyevna keeps saying, "I won't stay here another hour. Let us get away; let us get away." "We will stay at Harkov," she says; "we will have a look round and then send for our things. . . ." They are not taking much with them. It seems it is not ordained that they should live here, Marina Timofeyevna. It's not ordained. . . . It's the dispensation of Providence.

MARINA. It's better so. Look at the quarrelling and shooting this morning— a regular disgrace!

TELYEGIN. Yes, a subject worthy of the brush of Aïvazovsky.

MARINA. A shocking sight it was (*a pause*). We shall live again in the old way, as we used to. We shall have breakfast at eight, dinner at one, and sit down to supper in the evening; everything as it should be, like other people . . . like Christians (*with a sigh*). It's a long while since I have tasted noodles, sinner that I am!

TELYEGIN. Yes, it's a long time since they have given us noodles at dinner (*a pause*). A very long time. . . . As I was walking through the village this morning, Marina Timofeyevna, the man at the shop called after me, "You cadger, living upon other people." And it did hurt me so.

MARINA. You shouldn't take any notice of that, my dear. We all live upon God. Whether it's you or Sonya or Ivan Petrovitch, none of you sit idle, we all work hard! All of us. . . . Where is Sonya?

TELYEGIN. In the garden. She is still going round with the doctor looking for Ivan Petrovitch. They are afraid he may lay hands on himself.

MARINA. And where is his pistol?

TELYEGIN (*in a whisper*). I've hidden it in the cellar!

MARINA (*with a smile*). What goings-on!

(*Enter* VOYNITSKY *and* ASTROV *from outside.*)

VOYNITSKY. Let me alone. (*To* MARINA *and* TELYEGIN) Go away, leave me alone—if only for an hour! I won't endure being watched.

TELYEGIN. Certainly, Vanya (*goes out on tiptoe*).

MARINA. The gander says, ga-ga-ga! (*Gathers up her wool and goes out.*)

VOYNITSKY. Let me alone!

ASTROV. I should be delighted to. I ought to have gone away ages ago, but I repeat I won't go till you give back what you took from me.

VOYNITSKY. I did not take anything from you.

ASTROV. I am speaking in earnest, don't detain me. I ought to have gone long ago.

VOYNITSKY. I took nothing from you. (*Both sit down.*)

ASTROV. Oh! I'll wait a little longer and then, excuse me, I must resort to force. We shall have to tie your hands and search you. I am speaking quite seriously.

VOYNITSKY. As you please (*a pause*). To have made such a fool of myself: to have fired twice and missed him! I shall never forgive myself for that.

ASTROV. If you wanted to be playing with firearms, you would have done better to take a pop at yourself.

VOYNITSKY (*shrugging his shoulders*). It's queer. I made an attempt to commit murder and I have not been arrested; no one has sent for the police. So I am looked upon as a madman (*with a bitter laugh*). I am mad, but people are not mad who hide their crass stupidity, their flagrant heartlessness under the mask of a professor, a learned sage. People are not mad who marry old men and then deceive them before the eyes of everyone. I saw you kissing her! I saw!

ASTROV. Yes, I did kiss her, and that's more than you ever have!

VOYNITSKY (*looking towards the door*). No, the earth is mad to let you go on living on it!

ASTROV. Come, that's silly.

VOYNITSKY. Well, I am mad. I am not responsible. I have a right to say silly things.

ASTROV. That's a stale trick. You are not a madman: you are simply a crank. A silly fool. Once I used to look upon every crank as an invalid—as abnormal; but now I think it is the normal condition of man to be a crank. You are quite normal.

VOYNITSKY (*covers his face with his hands*). I am ashamed! If you only knew how ashamed I am! No pain can be compared with this acute shame (*miserably*). It's unbearable (*bends over the table*). What am I to do? What am I to do?

ASTROV. Nothing.

VOYNITSKY. Give me something! Oh, my God! I am forty-seven. If I live to be sixty, I have another thirteen years. It's a long time! How am I to get through those thirteen years? What shall I do? How am I to fill them up? Oh, you know . . . (*squeezing* ASTROV's *hand convulsively*); you know, if only one could live the remnant of one's life in some new way. Wake up on a still sunny morning and feel that one had begun a new life, that all the past was forgotten and had melted away like smoke (*weeps*). To begin a new life. . . . Tell me how to begin it . . . what to begin. . . .

ASTROV (*with vexation*). Oh, get away with you! New life, indeed! Our position—yours and mine—is hopeless.

VOYNITSKY. Yes?

ASTROV. I am convinced of it.

VOYNITSKY. Give me something. . . . (*Pointing to his heart*) I have a scalding pain here.

ASTROV (*shouts angrily*). Leave off! (*Softening*) Those who will live a hundred or two hundred years after us, and who will despise us for having lived our lives so stupidly and tastelessly—they will, perhaps, find a means of being happy; but we . . . There is only one hope for you and me. The hope that when we are asleep in our graves we may, perhaps, be visited by pleasant visions (*with a sigh*). Yes, old man, in the whole district there were only two decent, well-educated men: you and I. And in some ten years the common round of the trivial life here has swamped us, and has poisoned our life with its putrid vapours, and made us just as despicable as all the rest. (*Eagerly*) But don't try to put me off: give me what you took away from me.

VOYNITSKY. I took nothing from you.

ASTROV. You took a bottle of morphia out of my travelling medicine-chest (*a pause*). Look here, if you insist on making an end of yourself, go into the forest and shoot yourself. But give me back the morphia or else there will be talk and conjecture. People will think I have given it you. It will be quite enough for me to have to make your post-mortem. Do you think I shall find it interesting?

(*Enter* SONYA.)

VOYNITSKY. Leave me alone.

ASTROV (*to* SONYA). Sofya Alexandrovna, your uncle has taken a bottle of morphia out of my medicine-chest, and won't give it back. Tell him that it's . . . really stupid. And I haven't the time to waste. I ought to be going.

SONYA. Uncle Vanya, did you take the morphia? (*A pause*)

ASTROV. He did. I am certain of it.

SONYA. Give it back. Why do you frighten us? (*Tenderly*) Give it back, Uncle Vanya! I am just as unhappy, perhaps, as you are; but I am not going to give way to despair. I am bearing it, and will bear it, till my life ends of itself. . . . You must be patient too (*a pause*). Give it back! (*Kisses his hands.*) Dear, good uncle, darling! give it back! (*Weeps.*) You are kind, you will have pity on us and give it back. Be patient, uncle!—be patient!

VOYNITSKY (*takes the bottle out of the table-drawer and gives it to* ASTROV). There, take it! (*To* SONYA) But we must make haste and work, make haste and do something, or else I can't . . . I can't bear it.

SONYA. Yes, yes, work. As soon as we have seen our people off, we'll sit down to work. . . . (*Nervously turning over the papers on the table*) We have let everything go.

ASTROV (*puts the bottle into his case and tightens the straps*). Now I can set off.

(*Enter* YELENA.)

YELENA. Ivan Petrovitch, are you here? We are just starting. Go to Alexandr, he wants to say something to you.

SONYA. Go, Uncle Vanya. (*Takes* VOYNITSKY *by the arm*) Let us go. Father and you must be reconciled. That's essential.

(SONYA *and* VOYNITSKY *go out.*)

YELENA. I am going away. (*Gives* ASTROV *her hand*) Good-bye.

ASTROV. Already?

YELENA. The carriage is waiting.

ASTROV. Good-bye.

YELENA. You promised me to-day that you would go away.

ASTROV. I remember. I am just going (*a pause*). You have taken fright? (*Taking her hand*) Is it so terrible?

YELENA. Yes.

ASTROV. You had better stay, after all! What do you say? To-morrow in the plantation——

YELENA. No. It's settled. And I look at you so fearlessly just because it is settled. I have only one favour to ask of you: think better of me. I should like you to have a respect for me.

ASTROV. Ugh! (*Makes a gesture of impatience.*) Do stay, I ask you to. Do recognise, you have nothing to do in this world, you have no object in life, you have nothing to occupy your mind, and sooner or later you will give way to feeling—it's inevitable. And it had better not be at Harkov, or somewhere in Kursk, but here, in the lap of nature. . . . It's poetical, anyway, even the autumn is beautiful. . . . There is the forest plantation here, half-ruined homesteads in the Turgenev style. . . .

YELENA. How absurd you are. . . . I am angry with you, but yet . . . I shall think of you with pleasure. You are an interesting, original man. We shall never meet again, and so—why conceal it?—I was really a little bit in love with you. Come, let us shake hands and part friends. Don't remember evil against me.

ASTROV (*pressing her hand*). Yes, you had better go . . . (*musing*). You seem to be a good, warm-hearted creature, and yet there is something strange about your whole personality, as it were. You came here with your husband, and all of us who were at work, toiling and creating something, had to fling aside our work and attend to nothing all the summer but your husband's gout and you. The two of you have infected all of us with your idleness. I was attracted by you and have done nothing for a whole month, and, meanwhile, people have been ill, and the peasants have pastured their cattle in my woods, of young, half-grown trees. . . . And so, wherever you and your husband go, you bring destruction everywhere. . . . I am joking, of course, yet . . . it is strange. And I am convinced that if you had stayed here, the devastation would have been immense. I should have been done for . . . and you wouldn't have fared well either! Well, go away. *Finita la commedia!*

YELENA (*taking a pencil from his table and hurriedly putting it in her pocket*). I shall take this pencil as a keepsake.

ASTROV. It is strange. . . . We have been friends and all at once for some reason . . . we shall never meet again. So it is with everything in this world. . . . While there is no one here—before Uncle Vanya comes in with a nosegay —allow me to kiss you at parting. . . . Yes? (*Kisses her on the cheek*). That's right.

YELENA. I wish you all happiness. (*Looks round*) Well, so be it! For once in my life! (*Embraces him impulsively and both simultaneously draw rapidly apart from each other.*) I must go—I must go!

ASTROV. Make haste and go. Since the carriage is there, you had better set off.

YELENA. There's someone coming, I believe. (*Both listen.*)

ASTROV. *Finita!*

(*Enter* SEREBRYAKOV, VOYNITSKY, MARYA VASSILYEVNA, *with a book;* TELYEGIN *and* SONYA.)

SEREBRYAKOV (*to* VOYNITSKY). Let bygones be bygones. After what has happened, I have gone through and experienced so much in these few hours, that I believe I could write a whole treatise on the art of living for the benefit of posterity. I gladly accept your apologies and apologise myself. Good-bye! (*He and* VOYNITSKY *kiss each other three times.*)

VOYNITSKY. You shall receive regularly the same sum as hitherto. Everything shall be as before.

(YELENA ANDREYEVNA *embraces* SONYA.)

SEREBRYAKOV (*kisses* MARYA VASSILYEVNA's *hand*). Maman. . . .

MARYA (*kissing him*). Alexandr, have your photograph taken again and send it to me. You know how dear you are to me.

TELYEGIN. Good-bye, your Excellency! Don't forget us!

SEREBRYAKOV (*kissing his daughter*). Good-bye . . good-bye, everyone. (*Shaking hands with* ASTROV) Thanks for your pleasant company. I respect your way of thinking, your enthusiasms, your impulses, but permit an old man to add one observation to his farewell message: you must work, my friends! you must work! (*He bows to them all.*) I wish you all things good!

(*Goes out, followed by* MARYA VASSILYEVNA *and* SONYA.)

VOYNITSKY (*warmly kisses* YELENA ANDREYEVNA's *hand*). Good-bye. . . . Forgive me. . . . We shall never meet again.

YELENA (*moved*). Good-bye, dear Ivan Petrovitch (*kisses him on the head and goes out*).

ASTROV (*to* TELYEGIN). Waffles, tell them, by the way, to bring my carriage round too.

TELYEGIN. Certainly, my dear soul (*goes out*).

(*Only* ASTROV *and* VOYNITSKY *remain.*)

ASTROV (*clearing his paints from·the table and putting them away in his portmanteau*). Why don't you go and see them off?

VOYNITSKY. Let them go, I . . . I can't. My heart is too heavy. I must make haste and occupy myself with something. . . . Work! Work! (*Rummages among his papers on the table.*)

(*A pause; there is the sound of bells.*)

ASTROV. They've gone. The Professor is glad, I'll be bound. Nothing will tempt him back.

MARINA (*enters*). They've gone (*sits down in an easy chair and knits her stocking*).

SONYA (*enters*). They've gone (*wipes her eyes*). Good luck to them. (*To her uncle*) Well, Uncle Vanya, let us do something.

VOYNITSKY. Work, work. . . .

SONYA. It's ever so long since we sat at this table together (*lights the lamp on the table*). I believe there is no ink (*takes the inkstand, goes to the cupboard, and fills it with ink*). But I feel sad that they have gone.

(*MARYA VASSILYEVNA comes in slowly.*)

MARYA. They've gone (*sits down and becomes engrossed in reading*).

SONYA (*sits down to the table and turns over the pages of the account book*). First of all, Uncle Vanya, let us make out our accounts. We've neglected it all dreadfully. Someone sent for his account again to-day. Make it out. If you will do one account, I will do another.

VOYNITSKY (*writes*). "Delivered . . . to Mr. . . ." (*Both write in silence.*)

MARINA (*yawning*). I am ready for bye-bye.

ASTROV. How quiet it is! The pens scratch and the cricket churrs. It's warm and snug. I don't want to go. (*There is the sound of bells.*) There are my horses. . . . There is nothing left for me but to say good-bye to you, my friends—to say good-bye to my table—and be off! (*Packs up his maps in the portfolio.*)

MARINA. Why are you in such a hurry? You might as well stay.

ASTROV. I can't.

VOYNITSKY (*writes*). "Account delivered, two roubles and seventy-five kopeks."

(*Enter a* LABOURER.)

LABOURER. Mihail Lvovitch, the horses are ready.

ASTROV. I heard them. (*Hands him the medicine-chest, the portmanteau and the portfolio*) Here, take these. Mind you don't crush the portfolio.

LABOURER. Yes, sir.

ASTROV. Well? (*Goes to say good-bye.*)

SONYA. When shall we see you again?

ASTROV. Not before next summer, I expect. Hardly in the winter. . . . Of course, if anything happens, you'll let me know, and I'll come (*shakes hands*). Thank you for your hospitality, for your kindness—for everything, in fact. (*Goes up to nurse and kisses her on the head*) Good-bye, old woman.

MARINA. You are not going without tea?

ASTROV. I don't want any, nurse.

MARINA. Perhaps you'll have a drop of vodka?

ASTROV (*irresolutely*). Perhaps.

(MARINA *goes out.*)

ASTROV (*after a pause*). My trace-horse has gone a little lame. I noticed it yesterday when Petrushka was taking it to water.

VOYNITSKY. You must change his shoes.

ASTROV. I shall have to call in at the blacksmith's in Rozhdestvennoye. It can't be helped. (*Goes up to the map of Africa and looks at it*) I suppose in that Africa there the heat must be something terrific now!

VOYNITSKY. Yes, most likely.

MARINA (*comes back with a tray on which there is a glass of vodka and a piece of bread*). There you are.

(ASTROV *drinks the vodka.*)

MARINA. To your good health, my dear (*makes a low bow*). You should eat some bread with it.

ASTROV. No, I like it as it is. And now, good luck to you all. (*To* MARINA) Don't come out, nurse, there is no need.

(*He goes out;* SONYA *follows with a candle, to see him off;* MARINA *sits in her easy chair.*)

VOYNITSKY (*writes*). "February the second, Lenten oil, twenty pounds. February sixteenth, Lenten oil again, twenty pounds. Buckwheat . . ." (*a pause*).

(*The sound of bells.*)

MARINA. He has gone (*a pause*).

SONYA (*comes back and puts the candle on the table*). He has gone.

VOYNITSKY (*counts on the beads and writes down*). "Total . . . fifteen . . . twenty-five . . ."

(SONYA *sits down and writes.*)

MARINA (*yawns*). Lord have mercy on us!

(TELYEGIN *comes in on tiptoe, sits by the door and softly tunes the guitar.*)

VOYNITSKY (*to* SONYA, *passing his hand over her hair*). My child, how my heart aches! Oh, if only you knew how my heart aches!

SONYA. There is nothing for it. We must go on living! (*a pause*) We shall go on living, Uncle Vanya! We shall live through a long, long chain of days and weary evenings; we shall patiently bear the trials which fate sends us; we

shall work for others, both now and in our old age, and have no rest; and when our time comes we shall die without a murmur, and there beyond the grave we shall say that we have suffered, that we have wept, that life has been bitter to us, and God will have pity on us, and you and I, uncle, dear uncle, shall see a life that is bright, lovely, beautiful. We shall rejoice and look back at these troubles of ours with tenderness, with a smile—and we shall rest. I have faith, uncle; I have fervent, passionate faith. (*Slips on her knees before him and lays her head on his hands; in a weary voice:*) We shall rest!
(TELYEGIN *softly plays on the guitar.*)

SONYA. We shall rest! We shall hear the angels; we shall see all Heaven lit with radiance; we shall see all earthly evil, all our sufferings, drowned in mercy which will fill the whole world, and our life will be peaceful, gentle and sweet as a caress. I have faith, I have faith (*wipes away his tears with her handkerchief*). Poor Uncle Vanya, you are crying. (*Through her tears*) You have had no joy in your life, but wait, Uncle Vanya, wait. We shall rest (*puts her arms round him*). We shall rest! (*The Watchman taps.*)
(TELYEGIN *plays softly;* MARYA VASSILYEVNA *makes notes on the margin of her pamphlet;* MARINA *knits her stocking.*)

SONYA. We shall rest!

CURTAIN DROPS SLOWLY.

THE ANNIVERSARY

CHARACTERS IN THE PLAY

ANDREY ANDREYEVITCH SHIPUTCHIN (*Chairman of the Board of Management of the N—— Mutual Credit Bank, a youngish man with an eyeglass*).

TATYANA ALEXEYEVNA (*his wife, aged 25*).

KUZMA NIKOLAYEVITCH HIRIN (*the Bank Cashier, an old man*).

NASTASYA FYODOROVNA MERTCHUTKIN (*an old woman in a pelisse*).

MEMBERS OF THE BOARD OF MANAGEMENT.

BANK CLERKS.

The action takes place in the N—— Mutual Credit Bank.

THE ANNIVERSARY

The chairman's office. On the left a door leading to the counting-house. Two writing-tables. The office is furnished with pretensions to refined taste: velvet upholstery, flowers, statues, rugs. Telephone. Midday.
HIRIN *alone; he is wearing felt overboots.*

HIRIN (*shouts at the door*). Send someone to the chemist's for three penny-worth of valerian drops and tell them to bring some clean water to the chairman's office! Am I to tell you a hundred times? (*Goes to the table.*) I am utterly worn out. I have been writing for the last three days and nights without closing my eyes; from morning till night I am at work here, and from night till morning at home (*coughs*). And I feel ill all over! Shivering, feverish, coughing, my legs ache and there are all sorts of . . . stops and dashes before my eyes (*sits down*). That affected ass, our scamp of a chairman, will read a report to-day at the general meeting: "Our bank at present and in the future." A regular Gambetta . . . (*writes*). Two . . . one . . . one . . . six . . . nought . . . six. . . . He wants to cut a dash and so I have to sit here and work for him like a galley-slave! . . . He has put in nothing but the lyrical touches in the report and has left me to work for days together adding up figures, the devil flay his soul . . . (*counts on reckoning frame*). I can't endure the man (*writes*). One . . . three . . . seven . . . two . . . one . . . nought. . . . He promised to reward me for my work. If everything goes off well to-day and he succeeds in hoodwinking the public, he promised me a gold medal and a bonus of three hundred. . . . We shall see (*writes*). But if I get nothing for my trouble you must look out for yourself. . . . I am a hasty man. . . . I may do anything if I am worked up. . . . Yes!

(*Behind the scenes there is a noise of applause. Voice of* SHIPUTCHIN: "Thank you, thank you! I am touched!" *Enter* SHIPUTCHIN. *He is wearing a dress-coat and white tie; in his hands an album which has just been presented to him.*)

SHIPUTCHIN (*standing in the doorway and looking towards the counting-house*). I shall keep this present of yours, dear colleagues, to the day of my death in memory of the happiest days of my life! Yes, gentlemen! I thank you once more (*waves a kiss and walks up to* HIRIN). My dear, good Kuzma Nikolayevitch!

187

(*While he is on the stage* CLERKS *come in occasionally with papers for him to sign, and go out again.*)

HIRIN (*getting up*). I have the honour to congratulate you, Andrey Andreyevitch, on the fifteenth anniversary of our bank, and hope that . . .

SHIPUTCHIN (*presses his hand warmly*). Thank you, dear old man, thank you! In honour of this glorious occasion, in honour of the anniversary, I think we might even kiss each other. (*They kiss.*) I am very glad, very. Thanks for your good work, for everything! If I've done anything useful during my period of office as chairman of the Board of Management, I am indebted for it above all to my colleagues (*sighs*). Yes, old man, fifteen years, fifteen years as sure as my name's Shiputchin! (*Eagerly*) Well, what about my report? Is it getting on?

HIRIN. Yes. There are only five pages left.

SHIPUTCHIN. Good. Then by three o'clock it will be ready?

HIRIN. If nobody hinders me, I shall get it done. There's very little left to do.

SHIPUTCHIN. Splendid. Splendid, as sure as my name's Shiputchin! The general meeting will be at four o'clock. I say, my dear fellow, let me have the first half, I'll go over it. . . . Make haste, give it me (*takes the report*). . . . I expect great things from this report. . . . It's my *profession de foi,* or rather my fireworks . . . fireworks, as sure as my name's Shiputchin! (*sits down and reads the report*). I am devilish tired, though. . . . I had an attack of gout in the night, I spent all the morning racing about doing things, and then this excitement, this ovation . . . so upsetting! I am tired!

HIRIN (*writes*). Two . . . nought . . . nought . . . three . . . nine . . . two . . . nought. . . . The figures make my eyes dizzy. . . . Three . . . one . . . six . . . four . . . one . . . five . . . (*rattles the reckoning beads*).

SHIPUTCHIN. Another unpleasantness. . . . Your wife came to me this morning and complained of you again. She said that you ran after her and your sister-in-law with a knife yesterday. Kuzma Nikolayevitch, what next! Aie, aie!

HIRIN (*sourly*). I will venture, Andrey Andreyevitch, in honour of the anniversary, to ask a favour of you, and beg you, if only out of consideration for my working like a slave, not to meddle in my family affairs! I beg you!

SHIPUTCHIN (*sighs*). You have an impossibe temper, Kuzma Nikolayevitch! You are an excellent, estimable person, but with women you behave like some Jack the Ripper! You really do. I can't understand why you hate them so.

HIRIN. And I can't understand why you like them so! (*A pause.*)

SHIPUTCHIN. The clerks have just presented me with an album and the members of the Board, so I hear, are going to present me with an address and a silver tankard . . . (*playing with his eyeglass*). It's fine, as sure as my name's Shiputchin! . . . It's all to the good. . . . We must have a bit of splash for the sake of the bank, deuce take it! You are one of ourselves, you know all about it, of course. . . . I composed the address myself, I bought

the silver tankard myself too. . . . And there, the binding of the address cost
45 roubles. But we have to have that. They would never have thought of it
themselves (*looks round him*). Just look at the get-up of the place! Isn't it
fine? Here they tell me that it is petty of me to want the locks on the doors
to be polished and the clerks to wear fashionable ties, and to have a stout
porter at the entrance. Not a bit of it, my good sir! The locks on the doors
and the stout porter are not a petty matter. At home I may be a vulgarian,
I may eat and sleep like a pig and drink till I am crazy. . . .

HIRIN. No insinuations, please!

SHIPUTCHIN. Nobody is making insinuations! What an impossible temper
you have. . . . Well, as I was saying, at home I may be a vulgarian, a par-
venu, and give way to my habits, but here everything must be *en grand*. This
is the bank! Here every detail must be impressive, so to speak, and have an
imposing air! (*Picks up a scrap of paper from the floor and throws it into the
fire.*) What I do take credit for is having raised the reputation of the bank.
. . . Tone is a great thing! It's a great thing as sure as my name's Shiputchin.
(*Scrutinising* HIRIN) My dear fellow, the deputation from the shareholders
may be here any minute and you are in your felt overboots and that scarf
. . . and a reefer jacket of some nondescript colour. . . . You might have
put on a dress-coat or a black frock-coat, anyway. . . .

HIRIN. My health is more precious to me than your shareholders. I am
suffering from inflammation all over.

SHIPUTCHIN (*growing excited*). But you must own it's unsuitable? You
spoil the *ensemble!*

HIRIN. If the deputation comes in I can keep out of sight. It's no great
matter . . . (*writes*). Seven . . . one . . . seven . . . two . . . one . . .
five . . . nought. I don't like anything unsuitable myself. Seven . . . two
. . . nine . . . (*rattles the reckoning beads*). I can't stand anything unsuitable. For instance, you would have done better not to have invited ladies to
the anniversary dinner to-day!

SHIPUTCHIN. What nonsense!

HIRIN. I know you will let in a whole drawing-room full of them to make
a fine show, only mind they'll spoil it all for you. They are the source of every
trouble and mischief.

SHIPUTCHIN. Quite the opposite. Feminine society has an elevating influence!

HIRIN. Yes. . . . Your wife is highly cultured, I believe, but last Monday
she said something so appalling that I couldn't get over it for two days after.
All of a sudden, before outsiders, she blurted out: "Is it true that my husband
has bought the Dryazhko-Pryazhky shares which have fallen on the exchange?
Oh, my husband is so worried about them!" To say that before outsiders! And
what you want to be so open with them for, I can't understand! Do you want
them to get you into trouble?

SHIPUTCHIN. Come, that's enough, that's enough! This is all too gloomy for an anniversary. By the way, you remind me (*looks at his watch*). My better-half ought to be here directly. By rights I ought to have gone to the station to meet her, poor thing, but I haven't time and I'm . . . tired. To tell the truth I am not glad she is coming. That is, I am glad, but it would have been pleasanter for me if she had stayed another two days at her mother's. She will expect me to spend the whole evening with her, and meanwhile we have planned a little excursion when the dinner is over . . . (*shivers*). There, I am in a nervous shiver already. My nerves are so overstrained that I could burst into tears at the slightest provocation! No, I must be firm, as sure as my name's Shiputchin!

(*Enter* TATYANA ALEXEYEVNA *wearing a waterproof and with a travelling satchel slung across one shoulder.*)

SHIPUTCHIN. Bah! Talk about angels!

TATYANA ALEXEYEVNA. Darling! (*Runs to her husband; prolonged kiss.*)

SHIPUTCHIN. And we were just talking about you!

TATYANA ALEXEYEVNA (*breathlessly*). Have you missed me? Are you quite well? I haven't been home yet, I've come straight here from the station. I've got ever so much to tell you, ever so much. I can't wait . . . I won't take off my things, I've only looked in for a minute. (*To* HIRIN) How are you, Kuzma Nikolayevitch? (*To her husband*) Is everything all right at home?

SHIPUTCHIN. Quite. Why, you've grown plumper and prettier in the week. Well, what sort of journey did you have?

TATYANA ALEXEYEVNA. Splendid! Mamma and Katya send you their love. Vassily Andreyevitch asked me to give you a kiss from him (*kisses him*). Aunt sends you a jar of jam and they are all angry with you for not writing. Zina told me to give you a kiss from her (*kisses him*). Ah, if only you knew what happened! What happened! I am positively afraid to tell you! Oh, such a dreadful thing happened! But I see from your face you're not glad to see me.

SHIPUTCHIN. Quite the contrary . . . darling . . . (*kisses her*).

(HIRIN *coughs angrily.*)

TATYANA ALEXEYEVNA (*sighs*). Ah, poor Katya, poor Katya! I am so sorry for her, so frightfully sorry!

SHIPUTCHIN. It's our anniversary to-day, darling. The deputation from the shareholders may turn up here any minute and you are not dressed.

TATYANA ALEXEYEVNA. Really? The anniversary? I congratulate you, gentlemen. . . . I wish you . . . So there will be a party here to-day, a dinner? I like that. . . . And do you remember that splendid address you were so long making up for the shareholders? Will they read it to you to-day?

(HIRIN *coughs angrily.*)

SHIPUTCHIN (*in confusion*). We don't talk about that, darling. . . . Really, you had better go home.

TATYANA ALEXEYEVNA. In a minute, in a minute . . . I'll tell you all about it in one instant and then go. I'll tell you all about it from the very beginning.

Well . . . when you saw me off I sat down, do you remember, beside that stout lady and began reading? I don't like talking in the train. I went on reading for three stations and did not say a word to anyone. . . . Well, evening came on and I began to have such depressing thoughts, you know! There was a young man sitting opposite who was quite all right, not bad-looking, rather dark. . . . Well, we got into conversation. . . . A naval officer came up, then a student . . . (*laughs*). I told them I wasn't married. . . . How they flirted with me! We talked till midnight. The dark young man told some awfully funny stories and the naval officer kept singing. . . . My chest simply ached with laughing. And when the officer—ah, those naval men!—when the officer found out accidentally that my name was Tatyana, do you know what he sang? (*Sings in a bass voice*) "Onyegin, I will not disguise it, I love Tatyana madly!" . . . (*laughs*).

(HIRIN *coughs angrily.*)

SHIPUTCHIN. But, Tanyusha, we are hindering Kuzma Nikolayevitch. Go home, darling. Tell me later. . . .

TATYANA ALEXEYEVNA. Never mind, never mind, let him listen, it's interesting. I shall have finished directly. Seryozha came to the station to fetch me. A young man turned up too, a tax inspector I believe he was . . . quite all right, very nice, particularly his eyes. . . . Seryozha introduced him and he drove back with us. It was glorious weather. . . .

(*Voices behind the scenes:* "You can't, you can't! What do you want?"

Enter MADAME MERTCHUTKIN.)

MADAME MERTCHUTKIN (*in the doorway, waving the clerks off*). What are you holding me for? What next! I want to see the manager! . . . (*Comes in to* SHIPUTCHIN) . . . I have the honour, your Excellency . . . my name is Nastasya Fyodorovna Mertchutkin, wife of a provincial secretary.

SHIPUTCHIN. What can I do for you?

MADAME MERTCHUTKIN. You see, your Excellency, my husband, the provincial secretary Mertchutkin, has been ill for five months, and while he was laid up at home in the doctor's hands he was discharged from the service for no sort of reason, your Excellency. And when I went for his salary, they deducted, if you please, your Excellency, 24 roubles 36 kopeks from it. "What's that for?" I asked. "Well," they told me, "he borrowed that from the Mutual Benefit club and the other clerks stood security for him." How is that? How could he borrow it without my consent? That's not the way to do things, your Excellency! I am a poor woman, I earn my bread by taking in lodgers. . . . I am a weak, defenceless woman. . . . I have to put up with ill-usage from everyone and never hear a kind word.

SHIPUTCHIN. Excuse me (*takes her petition from her and reads it standing*).

TATYANA ALEXEYEVNA (*to* HIRIN). But I must tell you from the beginning. . . . Last week I suddenly got a letter from mamma. She wrote to me that a certain Mr. Grendilevsky had made my sister Katya an offer. An excellent, modest young man, but with no means and no definite position. And unluckily, only fancy, Katya was very much taken with him. What was to be done? Mamma wrote that I was to come at once and use my influence with Katya.

HIRIN (*surlily*). Excuse me, you put me out! You go on about mamma and Katya and I've lost count and don't know what I am doing.

TATYANA ALEXEYEVNA. As though that mattered! You ought to listen when a lady talks to you! Why are you so cross to-day? Are you in love? (*Laughs.*)

SHIPUTCHIN (*to* MADAME MERTCHUTKIN). Excuse me, what's this? I can make nothing of it.

TATYANA ALEXEYEVNA. You're in love! A-ha! he is blushing!

SHIPUTCHIN (*to his wife*). Tanyusha, go into the counting-house for a minute, darling. I shan't be long.

TATYANA ALEXEYEVNA. Very well (*goes out*).

SHIPUTCHIN. I can make nothing of it. Evidently you have come to the wrong place, madam. Your petition has nothing to do with us at all. You will have to apply to the department in which your husband was employed.

MADAME MERTCHUTKIN. Why, my dear sir, I have been to five places already and they would not even take the petition anywhere. I'd quite lost my head, but my son-in-law, Boris Matveyitch—God bless him for it—advised me to come to you. "You go to Mr. Shiputchin, mamma," he said, "he is an influential man, he can do anything for you." . . . Help me, your Excellency!

SHIPUTCHIN. We can do nothing for you, Madame Mertchutkin. You must understand: your husband, so far as I can see, served in the Army Medical Department, and our establishment is a purely private commercial undertaking, a bank. Surely you must understand that!

MADAME MERTCHUTKIN. Your Excellency, I have the doctor's certificate that my husband was ill! Here it is, if you will kindly look at it!

SHIPUTCHIN (*irritably*). Very good, I believe you, but I repeat it has nothing to do with us.

> (*Behind the scenes* TATYANA ALEXEYEVNA'S *laugh; then a masculine laugh.*)

SHIPUTCHIN (*glancing towards the door*). She is hindering the clerks there. (*To* MADAME MERTCHUTKIN) It's queer and absurd, indeed. Surely your husband must know where you ought to apply.

MADAME MERTCHUTKIN. He knows nothing, your Excellency. He keeps on "It's not your business, go away"—that's all I can get out of him.

SHIPUTCHIN. I repeat, madam: your husband was in the Army Medical Department, and this is a bank, a purely private commercial undertaking.

MADAME MERTCHUTKIN. Yes, yes, yes. . . . I understand, sir. In that case, your Excellency, tell them to pay me fifteen roubles at least! I agree to take part on account.

SHIPUTCHIN (*sighs*). Ough!

HIRIN. Andrey Andreyitch, at this rate I shall never have the report done!

SHIPUTCHIN. One minute. (*To* MADAME MERTCHUTKIN) There's no making you see reason. Do understand that to apply to us with such a petition is as strange as to send a petition for divorce to a chemist's, for instance, or to the Assaying Board.

(*A knock at the door*, TATYANA ALEXEYEVNA's *voice:* "Andrey, may I come in?")

SHIPUTCHIN (*shouts*). Wait a little, darling; in a minute! (*To* MADAME MERTCHUTKIN) You have not been paid your due, but what have we to do with it? Besides, madam, it's our anniversary to-day; we are busy . . . and someone may come in here at any minute. . . . Excuse me.

MADAME MERTCHUTKIN. Your Excellency, have pity on a lone lorn woman! I am a weak, defenceless woman. . . . I am worried to death. . . . I have a lawsuit with my lodgers, and I have to see to my husband's affairs and fly round looking after the house, and my son-in-law is out of a job.

SHIPUTCHIN. Madame Mertchutkin, I . . . No, excuse me, I cannot talk to you! My head is going round. . . . You are hindering us and wasting time . . . (*sighs, aside*). She's an idiot, as sure as my name is Shiputchin! (*To* HIRIN) Kuzma Nikolayevitch, please will you explain to Madame Mertchutkin . . . (*with a wave of his hand goes out of the office*).

HIRIN (*going up to* MADAME MERTCHUTKIN, *surlily*). What can I do for you?

MADAME MERTCHUTKIN. I am a weak, defenceless woman. . . . I look strong perhaps, but if you were to overhaul me there isn't one healthy fibre in me! I can scarcely keep on my feet, and my appetite is gone. I drank my cup of coffee this morning without the slightest relish.

HIRIN. I am asking you what I can do for you.

MADAME MERTCHUTKIN. Bid them pay me fifteen roubles, sir, and I'll take the rest in a month's time.

HIRIN. But you've been told already in plain words: this is a bank.

MADAME MERTCHUTKIN. Yes, yes. . . . And if necessary I can produce a medical certificate.

HIRIN. Have you got a head on your shoulders, or what?

MADAME MERTCHUTKIN. My dear man, I am asking for what is my due. I don't want other people's money.

HIRIN. I ask you, madam, have you got a head on your shoulders, or what? I'll be damned if I waste my time talking to you. I am busy. (*Points to the door*) Kindly walk out!

MADAME MERTCHUTKIN (*surprised*). And what about the money?

HIRIN. The fact is, what you've got on your shoulders is not a head, but this . . . (*taps with his finger on the table and then on his own forehead*).

MADAME MERTCHUTKIN (*offended*). What? Come, come! . . . Talk to your own wife like that. . . . My husband is a provincial secretary! You'd better look out!

HIRIN (*firing up, in a low voice*). Clear out!

MADAME MERTCHUTKIN. Come, come, come! . . . Look out!

HIRIN (*in a low voice*). If you don't leave the room this very minute, I'll send for the porter. Clear out! (*Stamps.*)

MADAME MERTCHUTKIN. Not a bit of it! I am not afraid of you. I've seen the likes of you. . . . You screw!

HIRIN. I don't believe I've ever in my life seen a nastier woman. . . . Ough! It makes me feel dizzy . . . (*breathing hard*). I tell you once more . . . do you hear? If you don't leave the room, you old scarecrow! I'll pound you to a jelly. I've such a temper, I might cripple you for life! I might commit a crime!

MADAME MERTCHUTKIN. More bark than bite. I'm not afraid of you. I've seen the likes of you.

HIRIN (*in despair*). I can't bear the sight of her! I feel ill! I can't stand it (*goes to the table and sits down*). They let loose a swarm of women on the bank: I can't write the report! I can't do it!

MADAME MERTCHUTKIN. I am not asking for other people's money: I am asking for my own—for what is my lawful due. Ah, the shameless fellow! He is sitting in a public office with his overboots on. . . . The lout!

(*Enter* SHIPUTCHIN *and* TATYANA ALEXEYEVNA.)

TATYANA ALEXEYEVNA (*following her husband in*). We went to an evening party at the Berezhnitskys'. Katya was wearing a pale blue foulard with light lace and a low neck. . . . It does suit her doing her hair up high, and I did it for her myself. . . . When she was dressed and had her hair done she looked simply fascinating!

SHIPUTCHIN (*by now suffering from migraine*). Yes, yes . . . fascinating! . . . They may come in here in a minute.

MADAME MERTCHUTKIN. Your Excellency!

SHIPUTCHIN (*despondently*). What now? What can I do for you?

MADAME MERTCHUTKIN. Your Excellency! (*Pointing to* HIRIN) Here, this man . . . he here, this man, tapped himself on the forehead and then tapped the table. . . . You told him to go into my case, and he is jeering at me and saying all sorts of things. I am a weak, defenceless woman.

SHIPUTCHIN. Very good, madam; I will go into it. . . . I will take steps. . . . Go away! Later. (*Aside*) My gout is coming on!

HIRIN (*goes quietly up to* SHIPUTCHIN). Andrey Andreyitch, send for the porter; let him kick her out! It's too much of a good thing!

SHIPUTCHIN (*in alarm*). No, no! She'll set up a squeal, and there are lots of flats in the building.

MADAME MERTCHUTKIN. Your Excellency!

HIRIN (*in a tearful voice*). But I've got to finish the report! I shan't finish it in time! . . . (*goes back to the table*). I can't do it!

MADAME MERTCHUTKIN. Your Excellency, when shall I receive the money? I need it to-day.

SHIPUTCHIN (*aside, with indignation*). A re-mar-kab-ly nasty woman. (*To her, softly*) Madam, I have told you already, this is a bank—a private commercial establishment.

MADAME MERTCHUTKIN. Do me a kindness, your Excellency! Be a father to me! . . . If the medical certificate is not enough, I can produce an affidavit from the police. Tell them to give me the money!

SHIPUTCHIN (*sighs heavily*). Ough!

TATYANA ALEXEYEVNA (*to* MADAME MERTCHUTKIN). Granny, you've been told that you are hindering them. It's too bad of you, really.

MADAME MERTCHUTKIN. My pretty lady, I've no one to take my part. I might just as well not eat or drink. I drank my cup of coffee this morning without the slightest relish.

SHIPUTCHIN (*exhausted, to* MADAME MERTCHUTKIN). How much do you want?

MADAME MERTCHUTKIN. Twenty-four roubles thirty-six kopeks.

SHIPUTCHIN. Very good (*takes a twenty-five rouble note out of his pocketbook and gives it to her*). Here is twenty-five roubles. Take it . . . and go!

(HIRIN *coughs angrily*.)

MADAME MERTCHUTKIN. Thank you kindly, your Excellency (*puts the money away*).

TATYANA ALEXEYEVNA (*sitting down by her husband*). It's time for me to go home (*looking at her watch*). . . . But I haven't finished my story. It won't take me a minute to tell you the rest, and then I am going. . . . Something so dreadful happened! And so we went to an evening party at the Berezhnitskys'. . . . It was all right—very jolly—but nothing special. . . . Of course, Katya's admirer Grendilevsky was there too. . . . Well, I had talked to Katya, I had cried; I'd used my influence; she had it out with Grendilevsky on that very evening and refused him. Well, I thought, everything is settled for the best: I had set mamma's mind at rest, I had saved Katya, and now I could be comfortable myself. . . . And what do you think? Just before supper Katya and I were walking along an avenue in the garden. . . . All of a sudden . . . (*excited*) all of a sudden we hear a shot. . . . No, I can't talk of it! (*Fans herself with her handkerchief.*) No, I can't!

SHIPUTCHIN (*sighs*). Ough!

TATYANA ALEXEYEVNA (*weeping*). We ran into the arbour, and there . . . there lay poor Grendilevsky . . . with a pistol in his hand. . . .

SHIPUTCHIN. No, I can't stand it! I can't stand it! (*To* MADAME MERTCHUTKIN) What more do you want?

MADAME MERTCHUTKIN. Your Excellency, couldn't you find another job for my husband?

TATYANA ALEXEYEVNA (*weeping*). He had aimed straight at his head . . . here. . . . Katya fell down fainting, poor darling! . . . And he lay there terribly frightened, and . . and asked us to send for a doctor. Soon a doctor arrived and . . . and saved the poor fellow. . . .

MADAME MERTCHUTKIN. Your Excellency, couldn't you find another job for my husband?

SHIPUTCHIN. No, I can't stand it! (*Weeps*) I can't stand it! (*Holds out both hands to* HIRIN *in despair.*) Turn her out! Turn her out, I implore you!

HIRIN (*going up to* TATYANA ALEXEYEVNA). Clear out!

SHIPUTCHIN. Not her, but this . . . this awful woman . . . (*points to* MADAME MERTCHUTKIN) this one!

HIRIN (*not understanding, to* TATYANA ALEXEYEVNA). Clear out! (*Stamps*) Clear out!

TATYANA ALEXEYEVNA. What? What are you about? Have you gone off your head?

SHIPUTCHIN. This is awful! I'm done for! Turn her out! Turn her out!

HIRIN (*to* TATYANA ALEXEYEVNA). Get out! I'll smash you! I'll make mincemeat of you! I'll do something criminal!

TATYANA ALEXEYEVNA (*runs away from him; he runs after her*). How dare you! You insolent creature! (*screams*). Andrey! Save me, Andrey! (*shrieks*).

SHIPUTCHIN (*runs after them*). Leave off! I implore you! Hush! Spare me!

HIRIN (*chasing* MADAME MERTCHUTKIN). Clear out! Catch her! Beat her! Cut her throat!

SHIPUTCHIN (*shouts*). Leave off! I beg you! I implore!

MADAME MERTCHUTKIN. Holy saints! . . . Holy saints! (*Squeals*) Holy saints!

TATYANA ALEXEYEVNA (*screams*). Save me! . . Ah! Oh! . . . I feel faint! I feel faint! (*jumps on to a chair, then falls on the sofa and moans as though in a swoon.*)

HIRIN (*chasing* MADAME MERTCHUTKIN). Beat her! Give it her hot! Kill her!

MADAME MERTCHUTKIN. Oh! Oh! . . . Holy saints! I feel dizzy! Oh! (*Falls fainting in* SHIPUTCHIN'S *arms.*)

(*A knock at the door and a voice behind the scenes:* "The deputation.")

SHIPUTCHIN. Deputation . . . reputation . . . occupation! . .

HIRIN (*stamps*). Get out, damn my soul! (*Tucks up his sleeves.*) Let me get at her! I could do for her!

(*Enter the* DEPUTATION, *consisting of five persons; all are in dress-coats. One holds in his hands the address in a velvet binding, another the silver tankard,* CLERKS *look in at the door.* TATYANA ALEXEYEVNA *on the sofa,* MADAME MERTCHUTKIN *in* SHIPUTCHIN'S *arms, both uttering low moans.*)

ONE OF THE DELEGATES (*reads aloud*). Dear and highly respected Andrey Andreyevitch! Casting a retrospective glance over the past of our financial institution, and taking a mental view of its gradual development, we obtain a highly gratifying impression. It is true that in the early years of its existence the limited amount of our original capital, the absence of any important transactions, and also the indefiniteness of our policy, forced into prominence

Hamlet's question: To be or not to be? And at one time voices were even raised in favour of closing the bank. But then you took the management. Your knowledge, your energy, and your characteristic tact have been the cause of our extraordinary success and exceptional prosperity. The reputation of the bank (*coughs*) . . . the reputation of the bank . . .

MADAME MERTCHUTKIN (*moans*). Oh! Oh!

TATYANA ALEXEYEVNA (*moans*). Water! Water!

THE DELEGATE (*continues*). The reputation . . . (*coughs*) the reputation of the bank has been raised by you to such a pinnacle that our bank may now rival the foremost institutions of the kind in foreign countries.

SHIPUTCHIN. Deputation . . . reputation . . . occupation! . . . Two friends one summer evening walked, and sagely of deep matters talked. . . . Tell me not thy youth is ruined, poisoned by my jealous love. . . .

THE DELEGATE (*continues in confusion*). Then, turning an objective eye upon the present we, dear, highly respected Andrey Andreyevitch . . . (*Dropping his voice*) Perhaps later . . . we'd better come again later . . . (*They walk out in confusion.*)

CURTAIN.

ON THE HIGH ROAD

A Dramatic Study in One Act

Performance forbidden by the Censor in 1885

CHARACTERS IN THE PLAY

TIHON YEVSTIGNEYEV (*keeper of an Inn on a high road*).
SEMYON SERGEYEVITCH BORTSOV (*a ruined Landowner*).
MARYA YEGOROVNA (*his wife*).
SAVVA (*an old Pilgrim*).
NAZAROVNA ⎫
YEFIMOVNA ⎭ (*Pilgrim women*).
FEDYA (*a Factory hand*).
YEGOR MERIK (*a Tramp*).
KUZMA (*a passing Traveller*).
POSTMAN.
DENIS (*Madame Bortsov's Coachman*).
PILGRIMS, DROVERS, WAYFARERS, *etc.*

The action takes place in one of the Southern Provinces of Russia.

ON THE HIGH ROAD

A DRAMATIC STUDY IN ONE ACT

Room in TIHON'S *Inn. On right a counter and shelves full of bottles. In the background a door opening on to the road, with a dirty red lantern hanging above it outside. The floor and the benches round the walls are crowded with* PILGRIMS *and* WAYFARERS. *Many unable to find space to lie down are asleep in a sitting posture. The middle of the night. As the Curtain goes up there is a clap of thunder, and a flash of lightning is seen through the open door.*

TIHON *is at the counter. On one of the benches* FEDYA *sits, half reclining, and playing softly on the concertina. By his side is sitting* BORTSOV, *dressed in shabby summer clothes.* SAVVA, NAZAROVNA *and* YEFIMOVNA *are lying on the floor near the benches.*

YEFIMOVNA (*to* NAZAROVNA). Give the poor old man a nudge, mother! I do believe he is dying!

NAZAROVNA (*raising the corner of* SAVVA's *coat from off his face*). Good Christian! Hey, good Christian! Are you alive or dead?

SAVVA. Why dead? I am alive, mother! (*Raises himself on his elbow.*) Cover up my legs, my good soul! That's it. More on the right one. That's it. God bless you!

NAZAROVNA (*covering* SAVVA's *legs*). Sleep, good man.

SAVVA. No chance of sleep! If only I have the patience to bear this agony, I don't mind about sleep, my good soul. A sinner does not deserve to be in peace. What is that noise, good pilgrim woman?

NAZAROVNA. God is sending us a storm. The wind's howling, and the rain is lashing and lashing. It's pattering like peas on the window-panes and on the roof. Do you hear? The flood-gates of heaven are opened . . . (*thunder*). Holy, holy, holy . . .

FEDYA. It thunders and roars and howls, and there is no end to it. . . . Goo-oo-oo! . . . It's like the roar of the forest. . . . Goo-oo-oo! . . . The wind is like a dog howling (*he shivers*). It's cold . . . my clothes are wet, you could wring them out. . . . The door is open . . (*plays softly*). My concertina has got wet, good Christians—there is no music in it, or I'd screw out of it a concert that would bowl you over! Glorious! A quadrille or a polka, let

201

us say . . . or a Russian dance-song. We can manage all that. When I was waiter at the Grand Hotel I did not save money, but I learnt all there was to learn on the concertina. And I can play the guitar, too. . . .

VOICE (*from the corner*). A fool and a fool's talk!

FEDYA. And it's from a fool I hear it. (*A pause.*)

NAZAROVNA (*to* SAVVA). You ought to be lying in the warm now, old man, and warming your poor leg (*a pause*). Old man! Good Christian! (*Nudges* SAVVA.) Are you going to die?

FEDYA. You had better have a drop of vodka, grandfather. You drink it off, it will burn for a while in your stomach, but it will draw it away from your heart a bit! Drink it!

NAZAROVNA. Don't talk lightly, lad! The old man, maybe, is giving up his soul to God and is repenting of his sins. And you say such things and play your concertina. . . . Give over the music, you impudent fellow!

FEDYA. Why do you pester him? He is not well, and you . . . Woman's silliness! . . . He is a saintly man and can't say a rude word to you, and you take advantage of it, pleased at his listening to your foolishness. . . . Sleep, grandfather—don't listen! Let her talk, but don't you heed. . . . A woman's tongue is a devil's broom—it will sweep the wise and the cunning out of the house. Never heed them . . . (*clasps his hands in horror*). But how thin you are, my dear! Awful! A regular dead skeleton! No live-stock in you! Are you really dying?

SAVVA. Dying? What for? The Lord spare me an untimely death. . . . I shall be bad for a bit, and then with God's help I shall get up again. . . . The Mother of God will not let me die in a strange land . . . I shall die at home. . . .

FEDYA. Do you come from far?

SAVVA. From Vologda. From the town itself. . . . I am a workman there. . . .

FEDYA. And where is this Vologda?

TIHON. Beyond Moscow . . . A province. . . .

FEDYA. Tut, tut, tut! . . . You've come a long way, old bushy-beard! And all on foot?

SAVVA. All on foot, lad. I've been at Saint Tihon's in Zadonsk, and I am going to the Holy Mountains . . . from the Holy Mountains, if it's the Lord's will, to Odessa. . . . From there, they say, they'll take you cheap to Jerusalem . . . for twenty-one roubles, so I'm told. . .

FEDYA. And have you been in Moscow?

SAVVA. To be sure! Five times. . . .

FEDYA. Is it a good town? (*Lights a cigarette.*) Worth seeing?

SAVVA. There are many holy shrines, lad. . . . Where there are many holy shrines there it is always good. . . .

BORTSOV (*goes up to the counter, to* TIHON). Once more I entreat you! Give it me, for Christ's sake!

FEDYA. The chief thing in a town is cleanliness. . . . If there's dust, they should water the streets; if there's mud, they should clean them. There must be tall houses . . a theatre . . . police . . . cabs. . . . I've lived in towns myself—I know.

BORTSOV. One little glass . . . this little glass here. You can put it down, you know! I'll pay you!

TIHON. We know all about that.

BORTSOV. Come, I beg you! Do me a kindness!

TIHON. Go along!

BORTSOV. You don't understand me. . . . Do understand, you ignorant dolt, if there is an ounce of brain in your wooden peasant skull, it isn't I that am asking, it's my inside asking—to talk like you, like a peasant! It's my illness that's asking! You must understand!

TIHON. There's nothing to understand. . . . Get along!

BORTSOV. Why, if I don't have a drink this minute—you must understand—if I don't satisfy my craving, I may do something dreadful! God knows what I may not do! You must have seen a lot of drinking people in your pothouse existence; surely you must by now have got a notion of what such people feel like? Why, they are ill! You may chain them up, you may beat them, stick knives into them, if only you give them vodka! Come, I beg you most humbly! Do me a kindness! I am humiliating myself. Good God, how I'm humiliating myself!

TIHON. Give me the money and then you shall have the vodka.

BORTSOV. Where can I get the money? Everything has gone for drink! There's nothing left! What can I give you? This overcoat here is all I have, but I can't give it to you. . . . I have nothing on underneath. . . . Will you have my cap? (Takes off cap and gives it to TIHON.)

TIHON (examining the cap). Hm. . . . There are caps and caps. . . . It's all in holes like a sieve. . . .

FEDYA (laughs). It's a gentleman's cap! One to walk out in the street in and to take off to the young ladies. "Good day, good day! How do you do!"

TIHON (gives the cap back to BORTSOV). I wouldn't take it as a gift. Filthy rubbish.

BORTSOV. You don't care for it? Then give me some on credit. I'll look in on my way back from the town and pay you your five kopeks. You may choke yourself with your five kopeks then! You may choke! I hope they will stick in your throat! (Coughs) I hate you!

TIHON (banging the counter with his fist). Why do you keep on? Who are you? A pickpocket, or what? What are you here for?

BORTSOV. I want a drink! It's not I want it, it's my illness. Can't you understand?

TIHON. Don't try my patience! You'll find yourself out on the steppe pretty quick!

BORTSOV. What am I to do? (Moves away from the counter.) What am I to do? (Ponders.)

YEFIMOVNA. It's the devil fretting you. Don't heed him, master! He, curse him! keeps whispering to you, "Drink, drink!" but you answer back, "I won' drink—I won't!" He'll give over.

FEDYA. I expect there's a hammer going in your head and your stomac pinches you! (*Laughs*) You are a crazy one, your honour! Lie down and go t sleep! It's no good standing up there like a scarecrow. It's not a kitche garden!

BORTSOV (*angrily*). Hold your tongue! Nobody asked your opinion, ass!

FEDYA. Mind what you are talking about! I know the likes of you! Ther are plenty of your sort tramping the high roads! As for asses, wait till I bo your ears, then you'll howl worse than the wind. You are an ass yoursel Silly fool! (*a pause*) Dirty cad!

NAZAROVNA. The holy man maybe is saying his prayers and giving up h soul to God. while these infidels are trying to pick a quarrel and saying a sorts of things. . . . Shameless fellows!

FEDYA. Don't go on canting, you old cabbage-stump! If you are in a po house, put up with pothouse ways.

BORTSOV. What is there for it? What am I to do? How can I appeal to him What words are needed more? (*To* TIHON) The blood is stagnant in my vein Uncle Tihon! (*Weeps*) Uncle Tihon!

SAVVA (*groans*). There is shooting in my leg like a bullet of fire. . . . Goo pilgrim woman, little mother!

YEFIMOVNA. What is it, good man?

SAVVA. Who is that crying?

YEFIMOVNA. The gentleman.

SAVVA. Ask the gentleman to shed a tear for me too, that I may die i Vologda. A prayer with tears is more acceptable.

BORTSOV. I am not praying, grandfather! These are not tears! My heart ha been wrung and the blood is running out! (*Sits down at* SAVVA's *feet.*) Th blood! But you won't understand! You can't grasp it, grandfather, with you dim understanding. You are people that sit in darkness!

SAVVA. Where are there any that have light?

BORTSOV. There are some that have light, grandfather. . . . They woul understand!

SAVVA. There are, there are, my son. . . . The saints had light. . . . The understood every sorrow. . . . Without your telling them, they would under stand. . . . They'll look into your eyes and understand. . . . And you are s comforted by their understanding you, it's as though you had had no sorrow —it's all gone!

FEDYA. And have you seen the saints, then?

SAVVA. Yes, I have, lad. . . . There are folks of all sorts on earth. Ther are sinners and there are servants of God.

BORTSOV. I don't understand . . . (*gets up quickly*). One must have som sense to understand what people say, and I haven't any now. I have nothin out an instinct, a thirst! (*Goes rapidly to the counter.*) Tihon, take my overcoat! Do you understand? (*Is about to take off his overcoat.*) The overcoat . . .

TIHON. And what have you got on under it? (*Looks under* BORTSOV's *coat.*) Your bare skin? Don't take it off, I won't have it. . . . I am not going to take a sin upon my soul.

(*Enter* MERIK.)

BORTSOV. Very good, I take the sin on myself. Do you agree?

MERIK (*in silence takes off his outer coat and remains in his jerkin. He has an axe stuck in his belt*). Some people are cold, but a bear and a man who is wanted are always hot. I am all in a sweat! (*Puts the axe on the floor and takes off his jerkin.*) You are wet through with sweat by the time you have pulled one leg out of the mud. As soon as one foot is free, the other is stuck.

YEFIMOVNA. That's true. . . . Tell me, good lad, is the rain giving over?

MERIK (*after looking at* YEFIMOVNA). I don't waste words on women (*a pause*).

BORTSOV (*to* TIHON). I take the sin on myself! Do you hear?

TIHON. I don't want to hear, leave off!

MERIK. It's as dark as though someone had been tarring the sky. You can't see your own nose. The rain cuts you in the face like snow (*picks up his clothes and his axe*).

FEDYA. For rascals like you, it's first-rate. The beast of prey takes shelter, but for you devils, it's a holiday.

MERIK. Who was it said that?

FEDYA. Just look. . . . I suppose you are not blind.

MERIK. We'll make a note of it. (*Goes up to* TIHON) Hullo, old fat face! Don't you know me?

TIHON. If I had to know all you drunken fellows that wander on the high road, I'd want a dozen eyes at least.

MERIK. Take a good look . . . (*a pause*).

TIHON. Well, I do declare, I know you! I knew you by your eyes! (*Offers his hand.*) Andrey Polikarpov?

MERIK. I was Andrey Polikarpov, but now I am Yegor Merik.

TIHON. What's that for?

MERIK. Whatever passport God sends me, that's my name. I've been Merik for two months now . . . (*Thunder*). Rr-rr-rr . . . thunder away, I am not afraid (*looks about*). No bloodhounds here?

TIHON. Bloodhounds, indeed! Midges and gnats, mostly. . . . A soft lot. . . . The bloodhounds are snoring in their feather-beds by now, I bet. . . . (*Aloud*) Good Christians, look out for your pockets and your clothes, if you mind about them. He is a smart fellow! He'll rob you.

MERIK. Well, they'd better take care of their money, if they've got any, but clothes I won't touch. I've no use for them.

TIHON. Where's the devil taking you?

MERIK. To Kuban.

TIHON. You don't say so!

FEDYA. To Kuban? Really? (*Sits up.*) It's a fine place. You might sleep for three years and never dream of as fine a place. So wide and free! They say there's no end to the birds and game and wild beasts of all sorts! Grass grows all the year round. People live like friends, there's such a lot of land they don't know what to do with it! The government they say . . . a soldier was telling me the other day . . . gives three hundred acres per head. That's the place to be happy, strike me dead!

MERIK. Happy. . . . Happiness is always behind you. . . . There's no seeing it. When you can bite your elbow you'll see happiness. . . . It's all foolishness. (*Looks round the benches and the people.*) It's like a convict station! . . . Good evening, poor folks!

YEFIMOVNA (*to* MERIK). You've such wicked eyes! The evil one is in you, lad. . . . Don't look at us.

MERIK. Good evening, poor people!

YEFIMOVNA. Turn away! (*Nudges* SAVVA.) Savva dear, the wicked man is looking at us. He'll do you harm, my dear! (*To* MERIK) Turn away, I tell you, serpent!

SAVVA. He won't touch us, mother; he won't touch us. . . . God will defend us. . . .

MERIK. Good evening, good Christians! (*Shrugs his shoulders.*) They say nothing! You are not asleep, are you, you clumsy beggars? Why don't you speak?

YEFIMOVNA. Turn your wicked eyes! Turn away your devilish pride!

MERIK. Hold your tongue, you old hag! It wasn't devilish pride, I meant to greet your hard lot with kind words and friendliness! You are huddling like flies with the cold—I felt sorry for you and wanted to say a kind word, to comfort you in your wretchedness, and you turn away your ugly faces! Very well, I don't care! (*Goes up to* FEDYA.) Where do you come from?

FEDYA. I belong to these parts, from the Hamonyevsky brickyards.

MERIK. Get up!

FEDYA (*sitting up*). Well?

MERIK. Stand up! Get up altogether! I'm going to lie there. . . .

FEDYA. I say. . . . Is it your place?

MERIK. Yes. . . . Go and lie on the floor.

FEDYA. Get along. . . . I am not afraid of you. . . .

MERIK. You are a smart chap. . . . Come, get along, don't talk! You'll be sorry for it, silly fellow.

TIHON (*to* FEDYA). Don't cross him, lad. Never mind.

FEDYA. What right have you? You roll your eyes like a shark and think I am frightened! (*Gathers up his belongings, goes and lies down on the floor.*) The devil! (*Lies down and covers his head.*)

MERIK (*making his bed on the bench*). You can't have seen the devil if you call me one. The devils are not like me (*lies down and lays his axe beside him*). Lie there, axe, my boy! Let me cover up your handle. I stole it . . . and now I fuss over it like a fool over a toy: I am sorry to throw it away and have nowhere to put it. Like a wife one is sick of. . . . Yes . . . (*covers himself over*). The devils aren't like me, lad. . . .

FEDYA (*poking his head out from under his coat*). What are they like then?

MERIK. They are like a vapour, a spirit. . . . Here you blow (*he blows*), they are like that. You can't see them.

A VOICE (*from the corner*). If you sit under a harrow, then you will see them.

MERIK. I've sat under one and I didn't see them. . . . The women talk nonsense . . . and so do silly peasants. . . . You won't see a devil nor a wood-goblin nor a ghost. . . . Our eyes aren't made to see everything. . . . When I was little I used to go on purpose into the woods at night to see the wood-goblin. . . . I'd shout and shout my loudest, I'd call the wood-goblin and not blink an eye. I seemed to see all sorts of nonsense, but I didn't see the wood-goblin. I used to go to the churchyard at night, I wanted to see a ghost— it's all old women's tales. I've seen all sorts of wild beasts, but as for anything terrible—it's all fiddlesticks. The eye is not made for that. . . .

A VOICE (*from the corner*). Don't say that, it sometimes happens that one does see things. . . . In our village a peasant was cutting up a pig . . . he cut open its belly and something jumped out!

SAVVA (*sitting up*). Lads, don't speak of the evil one! It's a sin, my dears!

MERIK. Aha, the greybeard! The skeleton! (*Laughs*) No need to go to the churchyard! Ghosts will creep up from the floor to preach to us. . . . A sin! . . . It's not for you to preach with your silly notions! You are an ignorant people, living in darkness . . . (*Lights a pipe.*) My father was a peasant, and he too was fond of preaching at times. One night he stole a sack of apples from a priest, brought it to us, and said "Mind, now, children, don't you touch an apple before the day of the blessing of apples in church, because it's a sin." It's just like you: one mustn't mention the devil, but one may play the devil. . . . For instance, take this hag here (*points to* YEFIMOVNA): she saw the evil one in me, but I'll bet she has given her soul over to the devil half a dozen times in her day with her womanish follies. . . .

YEFIMOVNA. Ough, ough, ough! . . . The power of the Cross be with us! (*Hides her face in her hands.*) Savva, dear!

TIHON. Why are you scaring them? A nice way to amuse yourself! (*The door bangs with the wind.*) Lord have mercy on us! What a wind!

MERIK (*stretches*). Oh, I should like to show my strength! (*The door bangs with the wind.*) To tussle with . . . that wind! He can't pull the door off, but I could pull the inn down, if I liked! (*Gets up and lies down again.*) I am so dreary!

NAZAROVNA. Say a prayer, you idol! What's the good of tossing about?

YEFIMOVNA. Don't touch him, bother him! He's looking at us again! (*To*

MERIK) Don't look at us, wicked man! His eyes! . . . His eyes are like the devil's before matins!

SAVVA. Let him look, pilgrim women! Say a prayer, and an evil eye cannot touch you. . . .

BORTSOV. No, I can't bear it. It's too much! (*Goes up to the counter.*) I say Tihon, for the last time I beg you. . . . Half a glass!

TIHON (*shakes his head*). Cash!

BORTSOV. My God, but I've told you already! Everything has gone on drink Where can I get it for you? And surely it won't ruin you to give me a drop of vodka on credit? A glass of vodka costs you a copper, but it will save me from agony. I'm in agony! It's not a whim: it's agony! Do understand!

TIHON. Go and tell that to somebody else, not to me. . . . Go and ask the good people here; let them treat you, for Christ's sake, if they want to, but I only give bread in charity.

BORTSOV. You may fleece them, poor things! But I—no thank you. It's not for me to rob them! Not for me! Do you understand that? (*Bangs the counter with his fist.*) It's not for me! (*a pause*) Hm! . . . Wait a minute . . (*Turning to the pilgrims*) But that's an idea! Good people, will you give me a copper? My inside craves it. I'm ill!

FEDYA. Anything else . . . you rascal? . . . You don't care for water, I suppose?

BORTSOV. How I degrade myself! How I degrade myself! I don't want it! I don't want anything. . . . I was joking!

MERIK. You won't get it out of him, master. . . . We all know he is a skin-flint. . . . Wait a bit! I've a copper somewhere about. . . We'll have a glass between us . . . (*Fumbles in his pockets.*) Damn it! . . . Have I lost it somewhere? I thought I heard a jingling in my pocket the other day. . . . No, I've nothing. . . . I've nothing, friend! It's your ill-luck! (*A pause*)

BORTSOV. I must have a drink, or I shall do something violent, or commit suicide! . . . My God! What am I to do? (*Looks towards the door.*) Shall I go? Go out into the darkness and go where chance takes me. . . .

MERIK. Why don't you preach him a sermon, you pilgrim women? And you, Tihon, why don't you turn him out? He has not paid you for his night's lodging, has he? Turn him out, give him a shove! Ah, people are cruel now-adays! There is no softness and kindness in them. . . . People are brutal. A man is drowning, and they shout to him, "Make haste and sink; we have no time to look at you—it's a working day." As for throwing him a rope!—there's no chance of that. . . . A rope cost money. . . .

SAVVA. Do not judge, good man!

MERIK. Hold your tongue, you old wolf! You are a cruel people! Herods! Judases! (*To* TIHON) Come here! Take off my boots! Look sharp!

TIHON. I say, isn't he going it? (*Laughs*) You are a terror!

MERIK. Come here, I tell you! Look sharp! (*a pause*) Do you hear? Am I speaking to the walls? (*Gets up.*)

TIHON. Come, come! . . . That's enough!

MERIK. I want you, you bloodsucker, to take my boots off, though I am a ~amp and a beggar.

TIHON. Come, come! . . . Don't be cross! Come and have a glass. . . . :omè and have a drink!

MERIK. Good people, what is it I want? That he should treat me to vodka, ~r that he should take off my boots? Didn't I speak plainly? Didn't I say ght? (*To* TIHON) I suppose you did not hear me? I'll wait a minute. Per~aps you will hear.

(*There is some perturbation among the* PILGRIMS *and* WAYFARERS. *They get up and look at* TIHON *and* MERIK *in silent expectation.*)

TIHON. It's an ill wind brought you! (*Comes out from behind the counter.*) ~ fine gentleman, indeed! Here, where are they? (*Pulls off* MERIK's *boots.*) 'ou brood of Cain! . . .

MERIK. That's it. Put them side by side. . . . That's right. . . . You can ~o!

TIHON (*after taking off* MERIK's *boots goes back to the counter*). You are ~o fond of swank. Give me any more of your swank, and you will be flying ~ut of the door pretty quick! Yes! (*To* BORTSOV, *who is approaching*) You ~ it again?

BORTSOV. You see, I could perhaps give you a thing of value. . . . If you ~ke, I will . . .

TIHON. Why are you shaking? Speak plainly!

BORTSOV. It's mean and nasty of me, but there's no help for it. I am not ~sponsible for doing it. . . . I should be acquitted if I were tried for it. . . . 'ake it, only on condition that you let me redeem it when I am on my way ~ack .from the town. I give it you before witnesses. . . . Friends, you'll be ·itnesses. (*Takes a gold locket out of his breast pocket.*) Here it is. . . . I ~ught to take the portrait out, but I have nowhere to put it; I am soaked ~hrough. . . . Well, take it with the portrait. Only, mind you . . . don't put ~our fingers on the face. Please . . . I was rude to you, my dear man. . . . ~was stupid, but you must forgive me, and . . . don't finger it. . . . I don't ~ant your eyes looking at it . . . (*gives* TIHON *the locket*).

TIHON (*examines the locket*). A stolen watch! Well, all right! Here is a drink *pours out vodka*) . . . Gulp it down. . . .

BORTSOV. Only don't you finger it . . . (*drinks slowly, with spasmodic ~auses*).

TIHON (*opens the locket*). Hm! . . . a madam. . . . Where did you get ~old of her?

MERIK. Show me! (*Gets up and goes to the counter.*) Let me have a look!

TIHON (*pushes away his hand*). Where are you shoving to? Look while I ~old it!

FEDYA (*gets up and goes to* TIHON). Let me have a look too!

(PILGRIMS *and* WAYFARERS *come round the counter, forming a group.*)

MERIK (*holds* TIHON's *hand with the locket firmly in both of his hand* *and looks at the portrait without speaking. A pause*). A handsome she-devi . . . A lady! . . .

FEDYA. A lady! . . . You can see from the cheeks and the eyes. . . . Tak your hand away; I can't see. Hair down to her waist. . . . For all the worl as though she were alive! She is just going to speak (*a pause*). . . .

MERIK. There's no surer ruin for a weak man. Once you are saddled with woman like that . . . (*waves his hand*) that's the end of you!

(*Voice of* KUZMA: "Wo-o-o! Stop, you deaf beasts!" *Enter* KUZMA.)

KUZMA (*coming in*). If there's an inn by the wayside, there is no passin it. You might pass your own father in daylight without seeing him, but yo see an inn a hundred miles off in the dark. Make way, if you are goo Christians! Hey, there! (*Taps with a copper on the counter.*) A glass of re Madeira! Look sharp!

FEDYA. He is a brisk devil!

TIHON. Don't wave your arms! You'll knock something over!

KUZMA. That's what we have them for, to wave. You are afraid of the rai you softies! You are made of sugar, I suppose! (*Drinks*)

YEFIMOVNA. One might well be afraid, good man, when one is overtake by a night like this on the road. Now, thank God! we are well off. There ar plenty of villages and houses on the roads; one can find shelter from th weather. But it's awful to think what it was in old days. You might walk fo a hundred miles and not see a chip of wood, let alone a house or a villag You had to sleep on the ground. . . .

KUZMA. Have you been knocking about in the world so long, old girl?

YEFIMOVNA. Getting on for eighty years.

KUZMA. Eighty years! You'll soon be as old as a ·raven. (*Looking a* BORTSOV) And what sort of queer fish is this? (*Looks steadily at* BORTSOV Master!

(BORTSOV *recognises* KUZMA *and, overwhelmed with confusion, retire into a corner and sits down on a bench.*)

KUZMA. Semyon Sergeyevitch! Can it be you? Eh? How on earth did yo come into this pothouse? This isn't a place for you!

BORTSOV. Hold your tongue!

MERIK (*to* KUZMA). Who is he?

KUZMA. An unhappy martyr! (*Walks nervously up and down by th counter.*) In a pothouse? Well, I never! In rags! Drunk! It's upset me, friend . . . it's upset me. (*To* MERIK *in a half-whisper*) It's our master, our land owner, Semyon Sergeyevitch, Mr. Bortsov. . . . You see what a state he is in What does he look like now? See what drunkenness can bring a man to! . . Fill my glass (*drinks*). I'm from his village, Bortsovka—maybe you've hear of it—a hundred and fifty miles from here in the Yergovsky district. We wer his father's serfs. . . . It's a pity!

MERIK. Was he rich?

KUZMA. A great man. . . .

MERIK. Frittered away his father's money?

KUZMA. No; it was his fate, my dear soul. . . . He was a grand gentleman, rich and sober. . . . (*To* TIHON) I bet you used to see him yourself sometimes, driving by on his way to the town. Fine, spirited horses, and a carriage with springs—all first class! He used to keep five troikas, my lad. . . . Five years ago, I remember, he drove by the Mikishkinsky ferry, and instead of a copper flung down a rouble. . . . "I haven't time to wait for change," says he. . . . There!

MERIK. He went out of his mind, I suppose?

KUZMA. He seems to have all his senses about him. . . . It all came from want of spirit. Softness! In the first place, lads, it was on account of a woman. . . . He fell in love, poor fellow, with a lady from the town, and fancied that there was nothing lovelier in the world. . . . Fall in love with a crow and she is finer than a falcon! She was a girl of good family. . . . Not one of these low-class women or anything in that way, but just . . . giddy . . . trailing her petticoats and making eyes! And always laughing and laughing! No sense. . . . The gentry like that; they think it's clever. But we peasants would have turned a giddy pate like that out of the house. . . . Well . . . he fell in love with her . . . and it was all up with him. He began dancing attendance on her, this and that, tea and sugar. . . . They'd be out all night in a boat, or playing the piano. . . .

BORTSOV. Don't talk of it, Kuzma. What's the use? What have they to do with my life?

KUZMA. Excuse me, your honour, I haven't said much. . . . I've just told them, and that's all. . . . I couldn't help speaking, because I was upset. . . . I was dreadfully upset! Fill up my glass (*drinks*).

MERIK (*in a half-whisper*). And did she love him?

KUZMA (*in a whisper, which gradually passes into ordinary talk*). I should think she did! He wasn't a gentleman of no consequence. . . . You may well love anyone who's got three thousand acres and more money than he can count. . . . And he was dignified, stately, sober. . . . He used to shake hands with all the government people, just like you and me now . . . (*takes* MERIK's *hand*), with "Good day" and "Good-bye," and "You are very welcome." . . . Well, I was walking one evening through the garden. . . . There were miles of garden! I was going along quietly, and I saw them sitting on a garden-seat and kissing each other (*makes sound of a kiss*). He gave her one, and she—the serpent!—gave him two. . . . He took her white hand, and she flushed up and squeezed up to him, damn her! "I love you, Senya!" said she. . . . And Senya, as though he were crazed, rushed about and boasted of his joy in his foolishness, with a rouble to one and two to another. . . . He gave me enough for a horse. . . . He forgave all his debtors in his joy. . . .

BORTSOV. Oh, why go on telling? These people have no feeling. . . . It's painful, you know!

KUZMA. I've not said much, sir! They keep asking. Why not tell them little? There, there! I won't if you are angry. . . . I won't. I'll take no notice of them.

(*There is the sound of the* POSTMAN'S *bells.*)

FEDYA. Don't shout! Speak quietly. . . .

KUZMA. I am speaking quietly. . . . He says I mustn't, so there's nothing to be done. . . . And indeed there is nothing more to tell. They were married that was all. . . . There was nothing more. . . . Fill my glass (*drinks*). don't like drunkenness! Just when the gentle-folk were to sit down to supper after the wedding, she takes and runs off in a carriage . . . (*in a whisper*) To the town, to a lawyer who was her lover. . . . Eh, what do you say to that? Just that very moment! . . . Why, killing's too good for her!

MERIK (*dreamily*). Well . . . what happened to him?

KUZMA. Went crazy. . . . As you see, he began by taking a drop, and now it's come to buckets. . . . First a drop, then buckets. . . . And still he loves her. There you are: he loves her! He must be on his way now to the town to try and get a peep at her . . . to get a peep and back again. . . .

(*The mail-cart drives up to the inn. The* POSTMAN *comes in and drinks.*)

TIHON. The post's late to-day.

(*The* POSTMAN *pays without speaking and goes out. The mail-cart drives away with the jingle of bells.*)

A VOICE (*from the corner*). This is the weather for robbing the post. It would be nothing to do.

MERIK. I've lived thirty-five years in the world and never once robbed the post (*a pause*). . . . Now it's gone. . . . It's too late . . . it's too late. . .

KUZMA. Want a sniff of prison?

MERIK. Plenty of folk rob without getting a sniff. And what if it did come to prison? (*Abruptly*) And what then?

KUZMA. You mean about the poor gentleman?

MERIK. Why, whom else?

KUZMA. The next thing is how he came to ruin . . . it was his brother-in-law . . . his sister's husband. . . . He took it into his head to stand security for his brother-in-law with a bank . . for thirty thousand or so. . . The brother-in-law was fond of borrowing . . . he knew which side his bread was buttered and never turned a hair, the swine. . . . Borrowed, but did not trouble to pay back. . . . So our master had to pay the whole thirty thousand (*sighs*). A foolish man has to suffer for his foolishness. His wife has children by the lawyer and his brother-in-law has bought an estate near Poltava. Our master like a fool hangs about in pothouses complaining to peasants like us "I've lost my faith, lads! There's nothing I can believe in now!" Weak heartedness I call it! Every man has his sorrow, some snake gnawing at his heart, but that's no reason for drinking. Take the elder in our village, now His wife is openly carrying on with the schoolmaster, spends her husband' money on drink, and the elder goes about with a scornful grin. . . . He's gone a bit thin in the face though. . . .

TIHON (*sighs*). Men bear their troubles as God gives them strength.

KUZMA. Everyone hasn't the same strength, that's true enough. . . . Well, how much is it? (*Pays*) There, take my hard-earned wages! Good-bye, lads! Good night to you and pleasant dreams! I must run, it's late. . . I am fetching the midwife for my mistress from the hospital. . . . I expect she's tired of waiting and wet through, poor dear . . . (*runs out*).

TIHON (*after a pause*). Hi you! What's your name! Have a drink, poor fellow! (*Fills his glass.*)

BORTSOV (*comes up to the counter irresolutely and drinks*). So now I owe you for two glasses.

TIHON. That's nothing. Drink. Drown your grief in ruin!

FEDYA. Have a glass from me too! Ough! (*Throws a copper on the counter.*) You'll die if you drink, and die if you don't. It's a good thing not to drink, but by God, vodka frees the heart! Even grief's not grief when you're drunk. . . . Swill it up!

BORTSOV. Foo! it's hot!

MERIK. Give it here! (*Takes the locket from TIHON and looks at the portrait.*) Hm. . . . Ran off on her wedding day. . . . What a woman!

A VOICE (*from the corner*). Pour him out a glass on my account, too, Tihon!

MERIK (*flings the locket violently on the ground*). Damn her! (*Goes quickly to his place and lies down with his face to the wall.*)

(*Sensation.*)

BORTSOV. How's this? What's the meaning of that? (*Picks up the locket.*) How dare you, you beast? What right have you? (*Tearfully*) You want me to kill you, do you? You ignorant peasant!

TIHON. Don't be angry, master. . . . It's not made of glass, it's not broken. . . . Have another glass and then go to sleep (*fills another glass*). I've been listening to you here and it's time to shut the inn (*goes and shuts outer door*).

BORTSOV (*drinks*). How dare he? What a fool! (*To MERIK*) Do you know that you are a fool, an ass?

SAVVA. Good friends! Put a curb on your tongues! What's the use of making a row? Let folks sleep!

TIHON. Lie down, lie down. . . . That's enough! (*Goes behind the counter and locks the till.*) It's bedtime.

FEDYA. It is! (*Lies down.*) Good night, friends!

MERIK (*gets up and spreads his coat on the bench*). Come, master, lie here.

TIHON. Where are you going to lie, then?

MERIK. Anywhere . . . on the floor . . . (*spreads jerkin on the floor*). It's all one to me (*lays the axe beside him*). It would be misery for him to sleep on the floor. . . . He's used to silks and down. . . .

TIHON (*to BORTSOV*). Lie down, your honour! You've looked at the portrait long enough (*puts out the candle*). Give her up!

BORTSOV (*staggering*). Where am I to lie?

TIHON. In the tramp's place! Didn't you hear? He's offered it to you.

BORTSOV (*goes to the bench*). I'm . . . I'm . . . drunk. . . This . . . this it? . . . Am I to lie here? . . .

TIHON. Yes, yes, don't be afraid, lie down . . . (*stretches himself on the counter*).

BORTSOV (*lies down*). I'm . . . drunk. . . . Everything is going round . . . (*opens the locket*). Haven't you a bit of candle? (*a pause*) You're a queer girl, Masha. . . . You look at me out of the frame and laugh . . . (*laughs*). Drunk! You oughtn't to laugh at a drunken man! You disregard everything, as Schastlivtsev says . . . and love a drunken man. . . .

FEDYA. How the wind howls! It's terrifying.

BORTSOV (*laughs*). What a girl you are . . . How can you go whirling round like that? There's no catching you!

MERIK. He's wandering. He keeps looking at the portrait (*laughs*). It's a queer start! These learned gentry have invented machines and medicines of all sorts, and yet no one has been clever enough to find a cure against the female sex. . . . They try to find how to cure every sort of disease, and they never seem to have a notion that more are ruined by womenfolk than by any disease. . . . Sly, money-loving, no mercy and no sense. . . . The old women lead their sons' wives an awful life, the wives think of nothing but how to deceive their husbands. . . . And there's no end to it!

TIHON. The women have pulled the cock's comb and now he is ruffling up his feathers.

MERIK. I am not the only one. . . . From time immemorial, as long as there has been a world, men have been weeping. . . . It's not for nothing that in all the tales and songs woman is reckoned with the devil. . . . It's not for nothing! It's more than half true anyway (*a pause*). . . . Here's this gentleman playing the fool, and it's not through wisdom that I've turned tramp, left my mother and father. . . .

FEDYA. Was it women?

MERIK. Just the same as the gentleman here. I went about like one possessed, bewitched. Boasted of my happiness. . . . Day and night as though on fire, but the time came when my eyes were opened. . . . It wasn't love, but only a cheat. . .

FEDYA. What did you do to her?

MERIK. That's not your business . . . (*a pause*). Killed her, do you suppose? My hand failed. . . . One doesn't kill them. . . . One even feels for them. . . . Live and be . . . happy! If only you are not before my eyes and I can forget you, snake in the grass! (*A knock at the door.*)

TIHON. Who the devil's there? Who is it? (*a knock*) Who's knocking? (*Gets up and goes to the door.*) Who's knocking? You must go on! We're shut!

VOICE (*at door*). Let me in. Tihon, for goodness' sake! A spring's broken in the carriage! Help me, be a father to me! If only we had a bit of cord to tie it up, then somehow we could get home. . . .

TIHON. Who is it?

VOICE (*at door*). My lady's driving from town to Varsonofyevo. . . . We've only four miles to go! Help me, for goodness' sake!

TIHON. Tell your lady if she gives us ten roubles there will be a cord, and we'll mend the spring. . . .

VOICE (*at door*). Are you crazy? Ten roubles! You mad dog, you are glad of other people's troubles.

TIHON. You know best. . . . You needn't give it if you don't want to. . . .

VOICE (*at door*). Well, all right then, wait a bit (*pause*). My lady says, very good.

TIHON. Walk in then! (*Opens the door and admits* DENIS.)

DENIS. Good evening, good Christian people! Here, give me the rope! Make haste! Lads, who'll come out and help? There'll be something for you!

TIHON. No need of anything. . . . Let them sleep. We'll manage it together!

DENIS. Ough! I'm regular worn out! Cold, muddy, not a dry thread on me. . . . Another thing, my good man. . . . Haven't you a little room here where my lady can get warm? The carriage is all on one side, there's no sitting in it. . . .

TIHON. She wants a room, too? Let her get warm here if she's cold . . . we'll find room for her! (*Goes up to* BORTSOV *and clears a space.*) Get up, get up! You can lie just for one hour on the floor while the lady's getting warm. (*To* BORTSOV) Get up, your honour! Sit up a bit! (BORTSOV *sits up.*) Here's a place for you!

(DENIS *goes out.*)

FEDYA. Here's a visitor now, plague take her! Now there'll be no sleeping till morning.

TIHON. It's a pity I didn't ask fifteen. . . She'd have given it (*stands before the door in expectant attitude*). . . . And you must be on your best behaviour, all of you. . . . No rude words now. . . .

(*Enter* MARYA YEGOROVNA, *followed by* DENIS. TIHON *bows.*)

TIHON. Pray walk in, your Excellency! Our poor abode, only fit for peasants and blackbeetles. . . . Don't disdain it!

MARYA YEGOROVNA. I can't see anything . . . where am I to go?

TIHON. This way, your Excellency. (*Leads her to seat beside* BORTSOV.) Pray come this way! (*Blows on the seat.*) You must excuse me, I've no room apart. But don't you be uneasy, madam: they are good, quiet folks. . . .

MARYA YEGOROVNA (*sits down beside* BORTSOV). How fearfully stuffy! You might at least open the door!

TIHON. Yes, madam! (*Runs and opens the door wide.*)

MERIK. People are cold and they open the doors (*gets up and slams the door.*) Who's she to give orders? (*Lies down.*)

TIHON. You must excuse it, your Excellency, he's a simpleton . . . a bit cracked. . . . But don't be frightened. . . . He won't hurt you. . . . Only excuse me, lady, I didn't agree for ten roubles . . . for fifteen if you like.

MARYA YEGOROVNA. Very well, only make haste.

TIHON. This minute; we'll do it in a twinkling . . . (*hauls out rope from under counter*). This minute . . . (*a pause*).

BORTSOV (*looks intently at* MARYA YEGOROVNA). Marie . . . Masha. . . .

MARYA YEGOROVNA (*looking at* BORTSOV). What next?

BORTSOV. Marie . . . is it you? Where have you come from?

(MARYA YEGOROVNA, *recognising* BORTSOV, *utters a shriek and dashes away from him into the middle of the room.*)

BORTSOV (*follows her*). Marie . . . it's me . . . it's me . . . (*laughs*). My wife! Marie! But where am I? Somebody, light a candle!

MARYA YEGOROVNA. Go away! You are lying! It's not you! It's impossible! (*Hides her face in her hands.*) It's a lie! It's silly!

BORTSOV. Her voice, her movements . . . Marie, it's me! I shan't be . . . drunk . . . in a minute. . . . My head's going round. . . . My God! Wait a bit . . . wait a bit. . . . I can't understand (*cries out loud*). Wife! (*Falls at her feet and sobs.*)

(*A group forms round the husband and wife.*)

MARYA YEGOROVNA. Go away! (*To* DENIS) Denis, let us go! I can't stay here!

MERIK (*leaps up and looks intently into her face*). The portrait! (*Clutches her arm.*) It's the same! Hey folks! The gentleman's wife!

MARYA YEGOROVNA. Hands off, peasant! (*Tries to pull her arm away.*) Denis, what are you waiting for? (DENIS *and* TIHON *run up to her and seize* MERIK *under the arms.*) This is a robbers' den! Let go my arm! I am not afraid of you! . . . Go away!

MERIK. Stop a bit, I'll let you go directly. Only let me say something to you. . . . One thing, so you may understand. . . . Wait a bit . . . (*turns to* TIHON *and* DENIS). Keep off, you louts, don't hold me! I won't let her go till I've told her something. Wait a bit . . . in a minute (*strikes his forehead with his fist*). No. God has given me no sense! I can't think of the word to say to you!

MARYA YEGOROVNA (*pulls away her arm*). Go away! They are drunk. . . . Let us go, Denis! (*Tries to move towards door.*)

MERIK (*bars the way*). Come, you might give him just one look! Comfort him with one kind word! For God's sake!

MARYA YEGOROVNA. Take this . . . crazy man away from me.

MERIK. Then go to the devil, you damned woman! (*Swings the axe.*)

(*Terrible commotion. They all leap up with noise and outcries of horror.* SAVVA *stands between* MARYA YEGOROVNA *and* MERIK. DENIS *violently pulls* MERIK *away and carries his lady out of the inn. After this all stand rooted to the spot. A prolonged pause.*)

BORTSOV (*clutches at the air with his hands*). Marie. . . . Where are you, Marie?

NAZAROVNA. Oh dear, oh dear. . . . You've wrung my heart, you murderers. And what a fearful night!

MERIK (*dropping the hand which holds the axe*). Have I killed her?

TIHON. Thank God, your life's safe this time. . .

MERIK. I didn't kill her then . . . (*goes staggering to his place*). It was not my luck to die from a stolen axe . . . (*sinks down on his coat and sobs*). Oh, misery! cruel misery! Have pity on me, good Christians!

CURTAIN.

THE WEDDING

A Farce in One Act

CHARACTERS IN THE PLAY

YEVDOKIM ZAHAROVITCH ZHIGALOV (*retired Collegiate registry-clerk*).
NASTASYA TIMOFEYEVNA (*his wife*).
DASHENKA (*their daughter*).
EPAMINOND MAXIMOVITCH APLOMBOV (*her bridegroom*).
FYODOR YAKOVLEVITCH REVUNOV-KARAULOV (*retired Naval Captain of the second rank*).
ANDREY ANDREYEVITCH NYUNIN (*Insurance Agent*).
ANNA MARTYNOVNA ZMEYUKIN (*a Midwife, about thirty, in a bright magenta dress*).
IVAN MIHAILOVITCH YAT (*a Telegraph Clerk*).
HARLAMPY SPIRIDONOVITCH DYMBA (*a Greek keeper of a confectioner's shop*).
DMITRY STEPANOVITCH MOZGOVOY (*a Sailor in the Volunteer fleet*).
BEST MEN, DANCING GENTLEMEN, WAITERS, *etc*.

The action takes place in one of the rooms of a second-class restaurant.

THE WEDDING

A FARCE IN ONE ACT

A brilliantly lighted room. A big table laid for supper. WAITERS *in swallow-tails are busy at the tables. Behind the scenes a band is playing the last figure of the quadrille.*

MADAME ZMEYUKIN, YAT, *and the Bridegroom's* BEST MAN *walk across the stage.*

MADAME ZMEYUKIN. No, no, no!

YAT (*following her*). Have pity on me!

MADAME ZMEYUKIN. No, no, no!

THE BEST MAN (*hastening after them*). I say, you can't go on like that! Where are you off to? And the *Grand-rond? Grand-rond*, silvoo-play! (*They go out*).

(*Enter* NASTASYA TIMOFEYEVNA *and* APLOMBOV.)

NASTASYA. Instead of worrying me, saying all sorts of things, you had much better go and dance.

APLOMBOV. I am not a Spinoza, to go twirling my legs like a top. I am a practical man and a man of character, and I find no entertainment in idle diversions. But dancing is not what I am talking about. Forgive me, *maman*, but there's a great deal I can't make out in your conduct. For instance, apart from objects of household utility, you promised to give me two lottery tickets with your daughter. Where are they?

NASTASYA. I've got a shocking headache. . . . It must be the weather. . . . There's going to be a thaw!

APLOMBOV. Don't try to put me off. I found out to-day that your tickets are pawned. Excuse me, *maman*, no one but an exploiter would do a thing like that. I don't say this from egoisticism—I don't want your lottery tickets—but it's a matter of principle, and I won't allow anyone to do me. I've made your daughter's happiness, and if you don't give me the tickets to-day, I'll make it hot for her! I am a man of honour!

NASTASYA (*looking round the table and counting the places laid*). One, two, three, four, five . . .

A WAITER. The cook told me to ask you how you will have the ices served: with rum, with Madeira, or with nothing.

221

APLOMBOV. With rum. And tell the manager there is not enough wine. Tell him to send some Haut-Sauterne as well. (*To* NASTASYA TIMOFEYEVNA) You promised, too, and it was an agreed thing, that at supper to-night there should be a general. And where is he, I should like to know?

NASTASYA. That's not my fault, my dear.

APLOMBOV. Whose then?

NASTASYA. Andrey Andreyevitch's. He was here yesterday and promised to bring a real general (*sighs*). I suppose he could not find one anywhere, or he would have brought him. As though we were mean about it! There's nothing we'd grudge for our child's happiness. A general by all means, if you want one.

APLOMBOV. And another thing. . . . Everybody knows, and so do you, *maman*, that that telegraph clerk Yat was courting Dashenka before I made her an offer. Why have you invited him? Surely you must have known I should dislike it?

NASTASYA. Oh, what's your name? Epaminond Maximitch, here you have not been married one day, and already you've worn me out, and Dashenka too, with your talk. And what will it be in a year? You are a trying man, you really are!

APLOMBOV. You don't like to hear the truth? A-ha! So that's how it is. But you should behave honourably. All I want of you is to be honourable!

(*Couples dancing the Grand-rond come in at one door, cross the stage, and go out at another. The first couple are* DASHENKA *and the* BEST MAN, *the last* YAT *and* MADAME ZMEYUKIN. *The last couple drop behind and remain in the room.* ZHIGALOV *and* DYMBA *enter and go up to the table.*)

THE BEST MAN (*shouts*). Promenade! Messieurs, promenade! (*Behind the scenes*) Promenade!

(*The couples dance out.*)

YAT (*to* MADAME ZMEYUKIN). Have pity, have pity, enchanting Anna Martynovna!

MADAME ZMEYUKIN. Oh, what a man! . . . I have told you already that I am not in voice to-day.

YAT. I entreat you, do sing! If it's only one note! Have pity! If only one note!

MADAME ZMEYUKIN. You worry me . . . (*sits down and waves her fan*).

YAT. Yes, you really are pitiless! To think of such a cruel creature, if I may use the expression, having such a lovely voice! With such a voice you oughtn't to be a midwife, if you'll allow me to say so, but to sing at public concerts! How divine is your rendering of this phrase, for instance . . . this one . . . (*hums*) . . . "I loved you, love that was in vain" . . . Exquisite!

MADAME ZMEYUKIN (*hums*). "I loved you, and still it may be love" . . . Is that it?

YAT. Yes, that's it. Exquisite!

MADAME ZMEYUKIN. No, I am not in voice to-day. . . . There, fan me

. . . it's hot! (*To* APLOMBOV) Epaminond Maximitch, why are you so melancholy? That's not the thing on your wedding day! You ought to be ashamed, you horrid man! Why, what are you thinking about?

APLOMBOV. Marriage is a serious step. It needs serious consideration from every point of view.

MADAME ZMEYUKIN. What hateful sceptics you all are! I cannot breathe in your society. . . . Give me atmosphere! Do you hear? Give me atmosphere! (*Hums*)

YAT. Exquisite! exquisite!

MADAME ZMEYUKIN. Fan me, fan me! I feel as though my heart were going to burst. . . . Tell me, please, why is it I feel suffocated?

YAT. It's because you are in a sweat. . . .

MADAME ZMEYUKIN. Ough, what vulgarity! Don't dare to use such expressions!

YAT. I beg your pardon! Of course you are used to aristocratic society, if you'll excuse the expression. . . .

MADAME ZMEYUKIN. Oh, let me alone! Give me poetry, raptures! Fan me, fan me! . . .

ZHIGALOV (*to* DYMBA). Shall we repeat? (*Fills glasses.*) One can drink at any minute. The great thing is not to neglect one's business, Harlampy Spiridonitch. Drink, but keep your wits about you! . . . But as for drinking, why not drink? There's no harm in a drink. . . . To your good health! (*They drink.*) And are there tigers in Greece?

DYMBA. Dere are.

ZHIGALOV. And lions?

DYMBA. Yes, lions too. In Russia dere's noding, but in Greece dere's everyding. Dere I have fader, and uncle, and broders, and here I have noding.

ZHIGALOV. Hm. . . . And are there whales in Greece?

DYMBA. Dere's everyding.

NASTASYA (*to her husband*). Why are you eating and drinking all anyhow? It's time for everyone to sit down. Don't stick your fork into the tinned lobster. . . . That's for the general. Perhaps he may come yet. . . .

ZHIGALOV. And are there lobsters in Greece, too?

DYMBA. Yes . . . dere's everyding dere.

ZHIGALOV. Hm. . . . And collegiate registry clerks too?

MADAME ZMEYUKIN. I can imagine what the atmosphere is in Greece!

ZHIGALOV. And I expect there's a lot of roguery. . . . Greeks are much the same as Armenians or gypsies. They sell you a sponge or a goldfish, and are all agog to fleece you over it. Shall we repeat?

NASTASYA. What's the good of repeating? It's time we were all sitting down. It's past eleven. . . .

ZHIGALOV. Well, let us sit down, then. Ladies and gentlemen, pray come to supper! (*Shouts*) Supper! Young people!

NASTASYA. Dear friends, please come! Sit down!

MADAME ZMEYUKIN (*sitting down at the table*). Give me poetry! "His restless spirit seeks the storm as though in tempest there were peace!" Give me tempest!

YAT (*aside*). A remarkable woman! I am in love! head over ears in love!

(*Enter* DASHENKA, MOZGOVOY, *the* BEST MAN, *gentlemen and ladies. They all sit down noisily; a moment's pause; the band plays a march.*)

MOZGOVOY (*getting up*). Ladies and gentlemen, I have something to say. . . . We have a great many toasts to drink and speeches to make. Don't let us put them off, but begin at once. Ladies and gentlemen, I propose the toast of the bride and bridegroom!

(*The band plays a flourish. Shouts of "Hurrah!" and clinking of glasses.*)

MOZGOVOY. It needs sweetening!

ALL. It needs sweetening!

(APLOMBOV *and* DASHENKA *kiss.*)

YAT. Exquisite! exquisite! I must declare, ladies and gentlemen—and it's only paying credit where credit is due—that this room and the establishment generally is magnificent! Superb, enchanting! But, you know, there's one thing wanting to complete it: electric lighting, if you will excuse the expression! In all countries they have electric light now, and only Russia lags behind.

ZHIGALOV (*with an air of profundity*). Electric light. . . . Hm. . . . But to my mind electric light is nothing but roguery. . . . They stick a bit of coal in, and think they will hoax you with that! No, my good man, if you are going to give us light, don't give us a little bit of coal, but give us something substantial, something solid that you can get hold of! Give us light—you understand—light that's natural and not intellectual!

YAT. If you had seen an electric battery, and what it's made of, you'd think differently.

ZHIGALOV. I don't want to see it. It's roguery. They take simple folks in. . . . Squeeze the last drop out of them. . . . We know all about them. . . . Instead of sticking up for roguery, young man, you had better have a drink and fill other people's glasses. Yes, indeed!

APLOMBOV. I quite agree with you, Pa. What's the use of trotting out these learned subjects? I am quite ready to talk of all sorts of discoveries in the scientific sense, but there's a time for everything! (*To* DASHENKA) What do you think about it, *ma chère?*

DASHENKA. He wants to show off his learning, and always talks of things no one can understand.

NASTASYA. Thank God, we have lived all our lives without learning, and this is the third daughter we are marrying to a good husband. And if you think we are so uneducated, why do you come to see us? You should go to your learned friends!

YAT. I've always had a respect for your family, Nastasya Timofeyevna. and if I did say a word about electric lighting, it doesn't mean I spoke out of conceit. I am ready enough to have a drink! I have always wished Darya Yevdokimovna a good husband with all the feelings of my heart. It's difficult to find a good husband nowadays, Nastasya Timofeyevna. Nowadays everybody is keen on marrying for money. . . .

APLOMBOV. That's a hint at me!

YAT (*scared*). Not the slightest hint intended. . . . I was not speaking of present company. . . . I meant it as a general remark. . . . Upon my word! Everyone knows you are marrying for love. . . . The dowry is not worth talking about!

NASTASYA. Not worth talking about, isn't it? You mind what you are saying, sir. Besides a thousand roubles in cash, we are giving three pelisses, the bedding and all the furniture. You try and find a dowry to match that!

YAT. I didn't mean anything. . . . The furniture is certainly nice . . . and . . . and the pelisses, of course; I only spoke in the sense that they're offended as though I'd dropped a hint.

NASTASYA. Well, you shouldn't drop hints. It's out of regard for your parents we asked you to the wedding, and you keep saying all sorts of things. And if you knew that Epaminond Maximovitch was after her money, why didn't you speak before? (*Tearfully*) I have reared and nurtured her. . . . I've watched over her like a diamond or an emerald, my sweet child. . . .

APLOMBOV. And you believe him? Much obliged, I am sure! Very much obliged. (*To* YAT) And as for you, Mr. Yat, though you are a friend, I won't allow you to behave so disgracefully in other people's houses! Kindly take yourself off!

YAT. What do you mean?

APLOMBOV. I could wish you were as much of a gentleman as I am! In fact, kindly take yourself off.

(*The band plays a flourish.*)

GENTLEMEN (*to* APLOMBOV). Oh, stop it! Leave off! It doesn't matter! Sit down! Let him alone!

YAT. I wasn't saying anything . . . why, I . . . In fact, I don't understand it. . . . Certainly, I'll go. . . . But first pay me the five roubles you borrowed from me a year ago to buy yourself a piqué waistcoat; excuse the expression. I'll have another drink and I'll . . . I'll go, only first pay me what you owe me.

GENTLEMEN. Come, stop it, stop it! That's enough! Making such a fuss about nothing!

THE BEST MAN (*shouts*). To the health of the bride's parents, Yevdokim Zaharitch and Nastasya Timofeyevna!

(*The band plays a flourish. Shouts of* "Hurrah!")

ZHIGALOV (*touched, bows in all directions*). Thank you, good friends! I am very grateful to you for not forgetting us and not being too proud to come! . . . Don't think that I am a knave or that it's roguery. I speak merely as I feel! In the simplicity of my heart! For my friends I grudge nothing! I thank you sincerely! (*Kisses those near him.*)

DASHENKA (*to her mother*). Ma, why are you crying? I am so happy.

APLOMBOV. Maman is upset at the approaching separation. But I would advise her to think over our conversation.

YAT. Don't cry, Nastasya Timofeyevna! Think what human tears are! Neurotic weakness, that's all!

ZHIGALOV. And are there mushrooms in Greece?

DYMBA. Yes, dere is everyding dere.

ZHIGALOV. But, I bet, there are no brown ones, like ours.

DYMBA. Yes, dere are.

MOZGOVOY. Harlampy Spiridonitch, it's your turn to make a speech! Ladies and gentlemen, let him make a speech!

ALL. A speech! a speech! It's your turn.

DYMBA. Why? What for? I not understand what it is. . . .

MADAME ZMEYUKIN. No, no! Don't dare to refuse! It's your turn! Get up!

DYMBA (*stands up, in confusion*). I can say dis. . . . Dere's Russia and dere's Greece. Dere's people in Russia and dere's people in Greece. . . . And *caravies* floating on de sea, dat is in Russia, ships, and on de earth de different railways. I know very well. . . . We Greeks, you Russians, and not want noding. I can tell you . . . dere's Russia and dere's Greece.

(*Enter* NYUNIN.)

NYUNIN. Stay, ladies and gentlemen, don't eat yet! Wait a bit! Nastasya Timofeyevna, one minute; come this way! (*Draws* NASTASYA TIMOFEYEVNA *aside, breathlessly.*) I say, the general is just coming. . . . At last I've got hold of him. . . . I am simply worn out. . . . A real general, so dignified, elderly, eighty I should think, or perhaps ninety. . . .

NASTASYA. When is he coming?

NYUNIN. This minute! You will be grateful to me to the end of your days. Not a general but a peach, a Boulanger! Not a common general, not an infantry man, but a naval one! In grade he is a captain of the second rank, but in their reckoning, in the fleet, it's equal to a major-general, or, in the civil service, to an actual civil councillor. It's exactly the same; higher, in fact.

NASTASYA. You are not deceiving me, Andryushenka?

NYUNIN. What next! Am I a swindler? Set your mind at rest.

NASTASYA (*with a sigh*). I don't want to spend my money for nothing, Andryushenka. . . .

NYUNIN. Set your mind at rest! He is a perfect picture of a general! (*Raising his voice.*) I said to him: "You have quite forgotten us, your Excellency! It's too bad, your Excellency, to forget your old friends! Nastasya Timofeyevna," I said, "is quite huffy!" (*Goes to the table and sits down.*) And he said to me: "Upon my soul, my boy, how can I go when I don't know the bridegroom?" "What next, your Excellency! why stand on ceremony? The bridegroom is a splendid fellow, an open-hearted chap. He is a valuer in a pawnbroker's shop," I told him, "but don't imagine, your Excellency, that he is a paltry beggar or a cad. Even well-born ladies serve in pawnshops nowadays."

He slapped me on the shoulder, we each had a Havana cigar, and here he is coming now. . . . Wait a minute, ladies and gentlemen, don't eat. . . .

APLOMBOV. And when will he be here?

NYUNIN. This minute. He was putting on his goloshes when I came away.

APLOMBOV. Then we must tell them to play a march.

NYUNIN (shouts). Hey, bandmaster! A march! (The band plays a march for a minute.)

A WAITER (announces). Mr. Revunov-Karaulov!

(ZHIGALOV, NASTASYA TIMOFEYEVNA, and NYUNIN hasten to meet him. Enter REVUNOV-KARAULOV.)

NASTASYA (bowing). You are very welcome, your Excellency! Delighted to see you!

REVUNOV. Delighted!

ZHIGALOV. We are not distinguished or wealthy people, your Excellency, we are plain folks; but don't think there's any roguery on our part. We grudge nothing for nice people, nothing is too good for them. You are very welcome!

REVUNOV. Delighted!

NYUNIN. Allow me to introduce, your Excellency! The bridegroom Epaminond Maximitch Aplombov, with his new born . . . I mean newly married bride! Ivan Mihailitch Yat, of the telegraph department. Harlampy Spiridonitch Dymba, a foreigner of Greek extraction, in the confectionery line! Osip Lukitch Babelmandebsky! and so on . . . and so on. . . . The rest are not much account. Sit down, your Excellency.

REVUNOV. Delighted! Excuse me, ladies and gentlemen, I want to say a couple of words to Andryusha (leads NYUNIN aside). I feel rather awkward, my boy. . . . Why do you call me "your Excellency"? Why, I am not a general! A captain of the second rank; it isn't even as good as a colonel.

NYUNIN (speaks into his ear as to a deaf man). I know, but, Fyodor Yakovlevitch, be so good as to let us say "your Excellency"! They are a patriarchal family here, you know; they honour their betters, and like to show respect where respect is due. . . .

REVUNOV. Well, if that's how it is, of course . . . (going to the table). Delighted!

NASTASYA. Sit down, your Excellency! Do us the honour! What will you take, your Excellency? Only you must excuse us, you are accustomed to dainty fare at home, while we are plain people!

REVUNOV (not hearing). What? Hm. . . . Yes. . . . (a pause). Yes. . . . In old days people all lived plainly and were satisfied. I am a man of rank in the service, but I live plainly. . . . Andryusha came to me to-day and invited me here to the wedding. "How can I go," said I, "when I don't know them? That would be awkward!" But, he said, "They are plain people, a patriarchal family, always glad to see a visitor." "Oh well, of course if that is how it is . . . Why not? I am delighted. It's dull for me at home all alone, and if my being at the wedding can give pleasure to anyone, well, by all means," I said.

ZHIGALOV. So it was in the kindness of your heart, your Excellency? I honour you! I am a plain man, with no sort of roguery about me, and I respect those that are the same. Pray take something, your Excellency.

APLOMBOV. Have you long left the service, your Excellency?

REVUNOV. Eh? Yes, yes . . . to be sure. That's true. Yes. . . . But how is this? The herring is bitter and the bread is bitter, I can't eat it.

ALL. It needs sweetening!

(APLOMBOV and DASHENKA kiss.)

REVUNOV. He-he-he! . . . Your health! (a pause) Yes. . . . In old days everything was plain, and everyone was satisfied. . . . I like plain ways. . . . I am an old man. Of course, I retired from the service in 1865. I am seventy-two. . . . Yes. In old days to be sure, they liked, too, on occasion to make a show, but . . . (seeing MOZGOVOY). You . . . er . . . are a sailor, aren't you?

MOZGOVOY. Yes, sir.

REVUNOV. Aha! . . . To be sure. . . . Yes. . . . The naval service was always a hard one. You've something to think about and rack your brains over. Every trivial word has, so to say, a special meaning. For instance: Mast-hands, to the top-sail lifts and the mainsail braces! What does that mean? A sailor understands, no fear about that! Ha-ha! It's as hard as any mathematics.

NYUNIN. To the health of his Excellency, Fyodor Yakovlevitch Revunov-Karaulov!

(Band plays a flourish.)

ALL. Hurrah!

YAT. Well, your Excellency, you've just been pleased to tell us something about the difficulties of the naval service. But is the telegraph service any easier? Nowadays, your Excellency, no one can go in for the telegraph service unless he can read and write French and German. But the hardest job for us is transmitting the telegrams! It's awfully difficult! Just listen (taps with his fork on the table, imitating the telegraph code).

REVUNOV. And what does that mean?

YAT. That means: I respect you, your Excellency, for your noble qualities. Do you suppose that's easy? And now listen (taps).

REVUNOV. A little louder. . . . I don't hear.

YAT. That means: Madam, how happy I am to hold you in my arms.

REVUNOV. What madam are you talking about? Yes . . . (to MOZGOVOY). And now if you are sailing with a strong wind and want to hoist the top-gallant sail and the royal, then you must shout: Sail hands, on the cross-trees to the top-gallant sail and the royal sail! . . . and while they pay out the sails on the yards below, they are at the top-gallant and royal halyards, stays and braces. . . .

THE BEST MAN (getting up). Ladies and gentle . . .

REVUNOV (interrupting). Yes . . . there are all sorts of orders to be given. . . . Yes. . . . Top-gallant sheets and royal sheets taut, let go the lifts!

Sounds fine, doesn't it? But what does it mean? Oh, it's very simple. They pull the top-gallant and royal sheets and raise the lifts. . . . All at once! And at the same time as they raise them, level the royal sheets and the royal lifts, and, where necessary, slacken the braces of those sails, and when the sheets are taut and all the lifts have been raised to their places, the top-gallant braces and the royal braces are taut and the yards are turned the way of the wind. . . .

NYUNIN (to REVUNOV). Fyodor Yakovlevitch! our hostess begs you to talk of something else. Our guests can't understand this, they are bored. . . .

REVUNOV. What? Who is bored? (To MOZGOVOY) Young man! Now, if the ship is lying with the wind on the starboard tack, under full sail, and you want to bring her round before the wind, what order must you give? Why, pipe all hands on deck, bring her round before the wind.

NYUNIN. Fyodor Yakovlevitch, that's enough, eat your supper!

REVUNOV. As soon as they have all run up, you give the command at once: Stand to your places, bring her round before the wind! Ah, what a life! You give the command and see the sailors run like lightning to their places and pull the stays and the braces, then you can't help shouting, Bravo, lads! (Chokes and coughs.)

THE BEST MAN (hastening to take advantage of the ensuing pause). On this, so to speak, festive occasion, on which we, all gathered together here, to do honour to our beloved . . .

REVUNOV (interrupting). Yes! And you have to remember all that! For instance: let out the fore-top-sail-sheet, top-gallant-sail sheet! . . .

THE BEST MAN (offended). Why does he interrupt? At this rate we shan't get through a single speech!

NASTASYA. We are ignorant people, your Excellency, we don't understand a word of all this. If you would tell us something that would amuse . . .

REVUNOV (not hearing). Thank you, I have had some. Did you say goose? Thank you. . . . Yes. I was recalling old days. It's a jolly life, young man! You float over the sea without a care in your heart and . . . (In a shaking voice) Do you remember the excitement of tacking? What sailor isn't fired by the thought of that manœuvre! Why, as soon as the command is given: Pipe all hands on deck, it's like an electric shock running through them all. From the commanding officer to the lowest sailor they are all in a flutter. . . .

MADAME ZMEYUKIN. I am bored, I am bored! (A general murmur).

REVUNOV (not hearing). Thank you, I have had some. (With enthusiasm) Everyone is ready and all eyes are fixed on the senior officer. . . . "Fore-topsail and mainsail braces to starboard, mizzen-braces to larboard, counter-braces to port," shouts the senior officer. Every order is carried out instantly. "Slacken fore-sheet and jib-stay . . . right to starboard!" (Gets up.) Then the ship rolls to the wind and the sails begin to flap. The senior officer shouts "To the braces! to the braces! look alive!" While he fixes his eyes on the topsail and when at last it begins to flap, that is, when the ship begins to turn, a terrific yell is heard: "Loose the mainsail-stays, let go the braces!" Then everything is flying and creaking—a regular tower of Babel! it's all done without a break. The ship is turned!

NASTASYA (*flaring up*). For all you are a general, you've no manners! You should be ashamed at your age!

REVUNOV. Greengage? No, I have not had any. . . . Thank you.

NASTASYA (*aloud*). I say, you ought to be ashamed at your age! You are a general, but you have no manners!

NYUNIN (*in confusion*). Come, friends! . . . why make a fuss? . . . really.

REVUNOV. To begin with, I am not a general, but a captain of the second rank, which corresponds to a lieutenant-colonel of military rank.

NASTASYA. If you are not a general, what did you take the money for? We did not pay you money to be rude to us!

REVUNOV (*in perplexity*). What money?

NASTASYA. You know very well what money. You got the twenty-five roubles from Andrey Andreyevitch right enough . . . (*to* NYUNIN). It's too bad of you, Andryusha! I didn't ask you to engage a fellow like this.

NYUNIN. Oh, come. . . . Drop it! Why make a fuss?

REVUNOV. Engaged . . . Paid . . . What does it mean?

APLOMBOV. Allow me. . . . You've received twenty-five roubles from Andrey Andreyevitch, haven't you?

REVUNOV. Twenty-five roubles? (*Grasping the situation*) So that's how it is! Now I understand it! What a dirty trick! What a dirty trick!

APLOMBOV. Well, you had the money, hadn't you?

REVUNOV. I've had no money! Get away with you! (*Gets up from the table.*) What a dirty trick! What a mean trick! To insult an old man like this—a sailor—an officer who has seen honourable service! . . . If these were decent people I might challenge someone to a duel, but as it is, what can I do? (*Distractedly*) Where is the door? Which way do I go? Waiter! show me out! Waiter! (*Going*) What a mean trick! What a dirty trick! (*Goes out.*)

NASTASYA. Andryusha, where is that twenty-five roubles, then?

NYUNIN. Oh, don't make a fuss about such a trifle! As though it matters! Here everyone is rejoicing, while you keep on about this silly business. (*Shouts*) To the health of the happy pair! Band, a march! (*The band plays a march.*) To the health of the happy pair!

MADAME ZMEYUKIN. I am stifling! Give me atmosphere! At your side I am suffocated!

YAT (*delighted*). Exquisite creature!

(*Hubbub.*)

THE BEST MAN (*trying to shout above the rest*). Ladies and gentlemen! On this, so to say, festive occasion . . .

CURTAIN.

ON THE HARMFULNESS OF TOBACCO

A Stage Monologue in One Act[1]

[1]Originally published in 1886.

THE CHARACTER

IVAN IVANOVICH NYUKHIN, a hen-pecked husband, whose wife keeps a music school and boarding-school for girls.

The scene represents a platform in a provincial club.

ON THE HARMFULNESS OF TOBACCO

Nyukhin. [*With long side whiskers and clean-shaven upper lip, in an old, well-worn frock coat, entering with great dignity, bowing and adjusting his waistcoat.*] Ladies and gentlemen, so to say! [*Smoothing down his whiskers.*] It has been suggested to my wife that I should read here, for a charitable object, a popular lecture. Well, if I must lecture, I must—it is absolutely no matter to me. Of course, I am not a professor and hold no learned degrees, yet and nevertheless for the last thirty years, without stopping, I might even say to the injury of my own health and so on, I have been work-ing on questions of a strictly scientific nature. I am a thinking man, and, imagine, at times even I compose scientific contributions; I mean, not pre-cisely scientific, but, pardon my saying so, they are almost in the scientific line. By the way, the other day I wrote a long article entitled 'On the Harmful-ness of Certain Insects.' My daughters like it immensely, especially the references to bugs; but after reading it I tore it to pieces. Surely, no matter how well you write, dispense with Persian powder[2] you cannot. We have got bugs even in our piano. . . . For the subject of my present lecture I have taken, so to say, the harm caused to mankind by the consumption of tobacco. I myself smoke, but my wife ordered me to lecture to-day on the harmfulness of tobacco, and therefore there is no help for it. On tobacco, well, let it be on tobacco—it is absolutely no matter to me; but to you, gentlemen, I suggest that you should regard my present lecture with all due seriousness, for fear that something unexpected may happen. Yet those who are afraid of a dry, scientific lecture, who do not care for such things, need not listen to it and may even leave. [*Adjusting his waistcoat.*] I particularly crave the attention of the members of the medical profession here present, who may gather from my lecture a great deal of useful information, since tobacco, apart from its harmful effects, is also used in medicine. Thus, for instance, if you place a fly in a snuff-box, it will probably die from derange-ment of the nerves. Tobacco, essentially, is a plant. . . . When I lecture I usually wink my right eye, but you must take no notice: it is through sheer nervousness. I am a very nervous man, generally speaking; and I started to wink my eye as far back as 1889, to be exact, on 13th September, on the very day when my wife gave birth to our, so to say, fourth daughter, Bar-

[2] An insecticide, like Keating's.

bara. All my daughters were born on the 13th. Though [*looking at his watch*], in view of the short time at our disposal, I must not digress from the subject of the lecture. I must observe, by the way, that my wife keeps a music school and a private boarding-school; I mean to say, not exactly a boarding-school, but something in the nature of one. Between ourselves, my wife loves to complain of straitened circumstances; but she has put away in a safe nook some forty or fifty thousand roubles; as to myself, I have not a penny to bless myself with, not a *sou*—but, well, what's the good of dwelling on that? In the boarding-school it is my duty to look after the housekeeping. I buy the provisions, keep an eye on the servants, enter the expenses in a ledger, stitch together the exercise-books, exterminate bugs, take my wife's pet dog for a walk, catch mice. . . . Last night I had to give out flour and butter to the cook, as we were going to have pancakes to-day. Well, to be brief, to-day, when the pancakes were ready, my wife came into . the kitchen to say that three of her pupils would have no pancakes, as they had swollen glands. So it happened that we had a few pancakes extra. What would you do with them? My wife first ordered those pancakes to be taken to the larder but then she thought for a while, and after deliberation she said: 'You can have those pancakes, you scarecrow. . . .' When she is out of humour, she always addresses me like that: 'scarecrow' or 'viper' or 'Satan.' You see what a Satan I am. She's always out of humour. But I didn't masticate them properly, I just gulped them down, for I am always hungry. Yesterday, for instance, she gave me no dinner. 'It's no use,' she says, 'feeding you, scarecrow that you are . . .' However [*looking at his watch*], I have strayed from my subject, and have digressed somewhat from my theme. Let us continue. Though, of course, you would rather hear now a romance, or symphony, or some aria. . . . [*Singing.*] 'In the heat of the battle we shan't budge. . . .' I don't remember where that comes from. . . . By the way, I have forgotten to tell you that in my wife's music school, apart from looking after the housekeeping, my duties also include the teaching of mathematics, physics, chemistry, geography, history, solfeggio, literature, etc. For dancing, singing, and drawing my wife charges an extra fee, although it is I who am the dancing and singing master. Our music school is at No. 13 Five Dogs' Lane. That is probably why my life has been so unlucky, through living in a house numbered thirteen. Again, my daughters were born on the thirteenth, and our house has thirteen windows. . . . But, well, what's the good dwelling on all this? My wife is at home at any hour for business interviews, and the prospectus of the school can be had from the porter here, at sixpence a copy. [*Taking a few copies from his pocket.*] And, if you please, I myself can let you have some. Each copy sixpence! Any one like a copy? [*A pause.*] No one? Well, make it fourpence. [*A pause.*] How very annoying! Yes, the house is number thirteen. I am a failure at everything; I have grown old, stupid. Now, I am lecturing, and to look at me I am quite jolly, but I have such a longing to shout at the top of my

voice or to run away to the ends of the earth. . . . And there is no one I
can complain to, I even want to cry. . . . You may say, You have your
daughters. . . . But what are daughters? I speak to them, and they only
laugh. . . . My wife has seven daughters. . . . No, I'm sorry, I believe
only six. . . . [*Vivaciously.*] Sure it's seven! The eldest, Anna is twenty-
seven; the youngest seventeen. Gentlemen! [*Looking round.*] I am miserable,
I have become a fool, a nonentity, but, after all, you see before you the
happiest of fathers. After all, it ought to be like that, and I dare not say it
is not. But if only you knew! I have lived with my wife for thirty-three
years, and, I can say, those were the best years of my life; I mean not precisely the best, but generally speaking. They have passed, in a word, like
one happy moment; but strictly speaking, curse them all. [*Looking round.*]
I think, though, she has not come yet; she is not here, and therefore I may
say what I like. . . . I am terribly afraid. . . . I am afraid when she looks
at me. Well, as I was just saying; my daughters don't get married, probably
because they are shy, and also because men never have a chance of seeing
them. My wife does not want to give parties, she never invites any one to
dinner, she's a very stingy, ill-tempered, quarrelsome lady and therefore no
one comes to the house, but . . . I can tell you in confidence [*Coming close
to the footlights.*] . . . My wife's daughters can be seen on great feast days
at the house of their aunt, Natalie Semionovna, that very same lady who
suffers from rheumatism and always wears a yellow dress with black spots,
as though she were covered all over with black beetles. There you get real
food. And if my wife happens not to be there, then you can also. . . .
[*Raising his elbow.*] I must observe that I get drunk on one wineglass, and
on account of that I feel so happy and at the same time so sad that I cannot
describe it to you. I then recall my youth, and for some reason I long to
run away, to run right away. . . . Oh, if only you knew how I long to do
it! [*Enthusiastically.*] To run away, to leave everything behind, to run without ever looking back. . . . Where to? It does not matter where . . . pro-
vided I could run away from that vile, mean, cheap life, which has turned
me into a miserable old fool, into a miserable old idiot; to run away from
that stupid, petty, ill-tempered, spiteful, malicious miser, my wife, who
has been tormenting me for thirty-three years; to run away from the music,
from the kitchen, from my wife's money affairs, from all those trifles and
banalities. . . . To run away and then to stop somewhere far, far away
in a field, and to stand stock-still like a tree, like a post, like a garden scarecrow, under the wide heaven, and to look all night long at the still, bright
moon over my head, and to forget, to forget. . . . Oh, how much I long
not to remember! . . . How I long to tear off this old, shabby coat, which
thirty-three years ago I wore at my wedding . . . [*tearing off his frock coat*]
in which I always give lectures for charitable objects. . . . Take that!
[*Stamping on the coat.*] Take that! I am old, poor, wretched, like this waistcoat, with its patched, shabby, ragged back. . . . [*Showing his back.*] I

want nothing! I am better and cleaner than that; I was once young, I studied at the university, I had dreams, considered myself a man. . . . Now I want nothing! Nothing but rest . . . rest! [*Looking back, he quickly puts on his frock coat.*] Behind the platform is my wife. . . . She has come and is waiting for me there. . . . [*Looking at his watch.*] The time is now over. . . . If she asks you, please, I implore you, tell her that the lecturer was . . . that the scarecrow, I mean myself, behaved with dignity. [*Looking aside, coughing.*] She is looking in my direction. . . . [*Raising his voice.*] Starting from the premise that tobacco contains a terrible poison, of which I have just spoken, smoking should in no circumstance be permitted, and I venture to hope, so to say, that this my lecture 'On the Harmfulness of Tobacco' will be of some profit to you. I have finished. Dixi et animam levavi!

[*Bows and walks off with dignity.*

THE BEAR

CHARACTERS

ELENA IVANOVNA POPOVA, *a landowning little widow, with dimples on her cheeks*

GRIGORY STEPANOVITCH SMIRNOV, *a middle-aged landowner*

LUKA, *Popova's aged footman*

I

A drawing-room in POPOVA's *house.*

POPOVA *is in deep mourning and has her eyes fixed on a photograph.* LUKA *is haranguing her.*

LUKA. It isn't right, madam. . . . You're just destroying yourself. The maid and the cook have gone off fruit picking, every living being is rejoicing, even the cat understands how to enjoy herself and walks about in the yard, catching midges; only you sit in this room all day, as if this was a convent, and don't take any pleasure. Yes, really! I reckon it's a whole year that you haven't left the house!

POPOVA. I shall never go out. . . . Why should I? My life is already at an end. He is in his grave, and I have buried myself between four walls. . . . We are both dead.

LUKA. Well, there you are! Nicolai Mihailovitch is dead, well, it's the will of God, and may his soul rest in peace. . . . You've mourned him—and quite right. But you can't go on weeping and wearing mourning for ever. My old woman died too, when her time came. Well? I grieved over her, I wept for a month, and that's enough for her, but if I've got to weep for a whole age, well, the old woman isn't worth it. [*Sighs*] You've forgotten all your neighbours. You don't go anywhere, and you see nobody. We live, so to speak, like spiders, and never see the light. The mice have eaten my livery. It isn't as if there were no good people around, for the district's full of them. There's a regiment quartered at Riblov, and the officers are such beauties—you can never gaze your fill at them. And, every Friday, there's a ball at the camp, and every day the soldier's band plays. . . . Eh, my lady! You're young and beautiful, with roses in your cheek—if you only took a little pleasure. Beauty won't last long, you know. In ten years' time you'll want to be a pea-hen yourself among the officers, but they won't look at you, it will be too late.

POPOVA. [*With determination*] I must ask you never to talk to me about it! You know that when Nicolai Mihailovitch died, life lost all its meaning for me. I vowed never to the end of my days to cease to wear mourning, or to see the light. . . . You hear? Let his ghost see how well I love him. . . . Yes, I know it's no secret to you that he was often unfair to me, cruel, and . . .

239

and even unfaithful, but I shall be true till death, and show him how I can love. There, beyond the grave, he will see me as I was before his death.

Luka. Instead of talking like that you ought to go and have a walk in the garden, or else order Toby or Giant to be harnessed, and then drive out to see some of the neighbours.

Popova. Oh! [*Weeps*]

Luka. Madam! Dear madam! What is it? Bless you!

Popova. He was so fond of Toby! He always used to ride on him to the Korchagins and Vlasovs. How well he could ride! What grace there was in his figure when he pulled at the reins with all his strength! Do you remember? Toby, Toby! Tell them to give him an extra feed of oats.

Luka. Yes, madam. [*A bell rings noisily*]

Popova. [*Shaking*] Who's that? Tell them that I receive nobody.

Luka. Yes, madam. [*Exit*

Popova. [*Looks at the photograph*] You will see, *Nicolas*, how I can love and forgive. . . . My love will die out with me, only when this poor heart will cease to beat. [*Laughs through her tears*] And aren't you ashamed? I am a good and virtuous little wife. I've locked myself in, and will be true to you till the grave, and you . . . aren't you ashamed, you bad child? You deceived me, had rows with me, left me alone for weeks on end. . . .

Luka *enters in consternation.*

Luka. Madam, somebody is asking for you. He wants to see you. . . .

Popova. But didn't you tell him that since the death of my husband I've stopped receiving?

Luka. I did, but he wouldn't even listen; says that it's a very pressing affair.

Popova. I do not re-ceive!

Luka. I told him so, but the . . . the devil . . . curses and pushes himself right in. . . . He's in the dining-room now.

Popova. [*Annoyed*] Very well, ask him in. . . . What manners! [*Exit* Luka] How these people annoy me! What does he want of me? Why should he disturb my peace? [*Sighs*] No, I see that I shall have to go into a convent after all. [*Thoughtfully*] Yes, into a convent. . . .

Enter Luka *with* Smirnov.

Smirnov. [*To* Luka] You fool, you're too fond of talking. . . . Ass! [*Sees* Popova *and speaks with respect*] Madam, I have the honour to present myself, I am Grigory Stepanovitch Smirnov, landowner and retired lieutenant of artillery! I am compelled to disturb you on a very pressing affair.

Popova. [*Not giving him her hand*] What do you want?

Smirnov. Your late husband, with whom I had the honour of being acquainted, died in my debt for one thousand two hundred roubles, on two bills of exchange. As I've got to pay the interest on a mortgage to-morrow, I've come to ask you, madam, to pay me the money to-day.

Popova. One thousand two hundred. . . . And what was my husband in debt to you for?

SMIRNOV. He used to buy oats from me.

POPOVA. [*Sighing, to* LUKA] So don't you forget, Luka, to give Toby an extra feed of oats. [*Exit* LUKA] If Nicolai Mihailovitch died in debt to you, then I shall certainly pay you, but you must excuse me to-day, as I haven't any spare cash. The day after to-morrow my steward will be back from town, and I'll give him instructions to settle your account, but at the moment I cannot do as you wish. . . . Moreover, it's exactly seven months to-day since the death of my husband, and I'm in a state of mind which absolutely prevents me from giving money matters my attention.

SMIRNOV. And I'm in a state of mind which, if I don't pay the interest due to-morrow, will force me to make a graceful exit from this life feet first. They'll take my estate!

POPOVA. You'll have your money the day after to-morrow.

SMIRNOV. I don't want the money the day after to-morrow, I want it to-day.

POPOVA. You must excuse me, I can't pay you.

SMIRNOV. And I can't wait till after to-morrow.

POPOVA. Well, what can I do, if I haven't the money now?

SMIRNOV. You mean to say, you can't pay me?

POPOVA. I can't.

SMIRNOV. Hm! Is that the last word you've got to say?

POPOVA. Yes, the last word.

SMIRNOV. The last word? Absolutely your last?

POPOVA. Absolutely.

SMIRNOV. Thank you so much. I'll make a note of it. [*Shrugs his shoulders*] And then people want me to keep calm! I meet a man on the road, and he asks me: "Why are you always so angry, Grigory Stepanovitch?" But how on earth am I not to get angry? I want the money desperately. I rode out yesterday, early in the morning, and called on all my debtors, and not a single one of them paid up! I was just about dead-beat after it all, slept, goodness knows where, in some inn, kept by a Jew, with a vodka-barrel by my head. At last I get here, seventy versts from home, and hope to get something, and I am received by you with a "state of mind"! How shouldn't I get angry.

POPOVA. I thought I distinctly said my steward will pay you when he returns from town.

SMIRNOV. I didn't come to your steward, but to you! What the devil, excuse my saying so, have I to do with your steward!

POPOVA. Excuse me, sir, I am not accustomed to listen to such expressions or to such a tone of voice. I want to hear no more.

SMIRNOV. Well, there! "A state of mind." . . . "Husband died seven months ago!" Must I pay the interest, or mustn't I? I ask you: Must I pay, or must I not? Suppose your husband is dead, and you've got a state of mind, and nonsense of that sort. . . . And your steward's gone away somewhere, devil take him, what do you want me to do? Do you think I can fly away from my creditors in a balloon, or what? Or do you expect me to go and run my head into a brick wall? I go to Grusdev and he isn't at home, Yaroshe-vitch has hidden himself, I had a violent row with Kuritsin and nearly threw him out of the window, Mazugo has something the matter with his bowels, and this woman has "a state of mind." Not one of the swine wants to pay me! Just because I'm too gentle with them, because I'm a rag, just weak wax in their hands! I'm much too gentle with them! Well, just you wait! You'll find out what I'm like! I shan't let you play about with me, confound it! [*Exit* Popova] I shall jolly well stay here until she pays! Brr! . . . How angry I am to-day, how angry I am! All my inside is quivering with anger, and I can't even breathe. . . . Foo, my word, I even feel sick! [*Yells*] Waiter!

Enter Luka.

Luka. What is it?

Smirnov. Get me some kvass or water! [*Exit* Luka] What a way to reason! A man is in desperate need of his money, and she won't pay it because, you see, she is not disposed to attend to money matters! . . That's real silly feminine logic. That's why I never did like, and don't like now, to have to talk to women. I'd rather sit on a barrel of gunpowder than talk to a woman. Brr! . . . I feel quite chilly—and it's all on account of that little bit of fluff! I can't even see one of these poetic creatures from a distance without breaking out into a cold sweat out of sheer anger. I can't look at them.

Enter Luka *with water.*

Luka. Madam is ill and will see nobody.

Smirnov. Get out! [*Exit* Luka] Ill and will see nobody! No, it's all right, you don't see me. . . . I'm going to stay and will sit here till you give me the money. You can be ill for a week, if you like, and I'll stay here for a week. . . . If you're ill for a year—I'll stay for a year. I'm going to get my own, my dear! You don't get at me with your widow's weeds and your dimpled cheeks! I know those dimples! [*Shouts through the window*] Simeon, take them out! We aren't going away at once! I'm staying here! Tell them in the stable to give the horses some oats! You fool, you've let the near horse's leg get tied up in the reins again! [*Teasingly*] "Never mind. . . ." I'll give it you. "Never mind." [*Goes away from the window*] Oh, it's bad. . . . The heat's frightful, nobody pays up. I slept badly, and on top of everything else here's a bit of fluff in mourning with "a state of mind." . . . My head's aching. . . . Shall I have some vodka, what? Yes, I think I will. [*Yells*] Waiter!

Enter Luka.

Luka. What is it?

Smirnov. A glass of vodka! [*Exit* Luka] Ouf! [*Sits and inspects himself*] I must say I look well! Dust all over, boots dirty, unwashed, unkempt, straw on my waistcoat. . . . The dear lady may well have taken me for a brigand. [*Yawns*] It's rather impolite to come into a drawing-room in this state, but it can't be helped. . . . I am not here as a visitor, but as a creditor, and there's no dress specially prescribed for creditors. . . .

Enter Luka *with the vodka.*

LUKA. You allow yourself to go very far, sir. . . .

SMIRNOV. [*Angrily*] What?

LUKA. I . . . er . . . nothing . . . I really . . .

SMIRNOV. Whom are you talking to? Shut up!

LUKA. [*Aside*] The devil's come to stay. . . . Bad luck that brought him. . . . [*Exit*

SMIRNOV. Oh, how angry I am! So angry that I think I could grind the whole world to dust. . . . I even feel sick. . . [*Yells*] Waiter!

Enter POPOVA.

POPOVA. [*Her eyes downcast*] Sir, in my solitude I have grown unaccustomed to the masculine voice, and I can't stand shouting. I must ask you not to disturb my peace.

SMIRNOV. Pay me money, and I'll go.

POPOVA. I told you perfectly plainly; I haven't any money to spare; wait until the day after to-morrow.

SMIRNOV. And I told you perfectly plainly I don't want the money the day after to-morrow, but to-day. If you don't pay me to-day, I'll have to hang myself to-morrow.

POPOVA. But what can I do if I haven't got the money? You're so strange!

SMIRNOV. Then you won't pay me now? Eh?

POPOVA. I can't. . . .

SMIRNOV. In that case I stay here and shall wait until I get it. [*Sits down*] You're going to pay me the day after to-morrow? Very well! I'll stay here until the day after to-morrow. I'll sit here all the time. . . . [*Jumps up*] I ask you: Have I got to pay the interest to-morrow, or haven't I? Or do you think I'm doing this for a joke?

POPOVA. Please don't shout. This isn't a stable!

SMIRNOV. I wasn't asking you about a stable, but whether I'd got my interest to pay to-morrow or not?

POPOVA. You don't know how to behave before women!

SMIRNOV. No, I do know how to behave before women!

POPOVA. No, you don't! You're a rude, ill-bred man! Decent people don't talk to a woman like that!

SMIRNOV. What a business! How do you want me to talk to you? In French, or what? [*Loses his temper and lisps*] Madame, je vous prie. . . . How happy I am that you don't pay me. . . . Ah, pardon. I have disturbed you! Such lovely weather to-day! And how well you look in mourning! [*Bows*]

POPOVA. That's silly and rude.

SMIRNOV [*Teasing her*] Silly and rude! I don't know how to behave before women! Madam, in my time I've seen more women than you've seen sparrows! Three times I've fought duels on account of women. I've refused twelve women, and nine have refused me! Yes! There was a time when I played the fool, scented myself, used honeyed words, wore jewellery, made beautiful bows. . . . I used to love, to suffer, to sigh at the moon, to get sour, to thaw, to freeze. . . . I used to love passionately, madly, every blessed way, devil take me; I used to chatter like a magpie about emancipation, and wasted half my wealth on tender feelings, but now—you must excuse me! You won't get round me like that now! I've had enough! Black eyes, passionate eyes, ruby lips, dimpled cheeks, the moon, whispers, timid breathing—I wouldn't give a brass farthing for the lot, madam! Present company always excepted, all women, great or little, are insincere, crooked, backbiters, envious, liars to the marrow of their bones, vain, trivial, merciless, unreasonable, and, as far as this is concerned [taps his forehead], excuse my outspokenness, a sparrow can give ten points to any philosopher in petticoats you like to name! You look at one of these poetic creatures: all muslin, an ethereal demi-goddess, you have a million transports of joy, and you look into her soul—and see a common crocodile. [He grips the back of a chair; the chair creaks and breaks] But the most disgusting thing of all is that this crocodile for some reason or other imagines that its chef d'œuvre, its privilege and monopoly, is its tender feelings. Why, confound it, hang me on that nail feet upwards, if you like, but have you met a woman who can love anybody except a lapdog? When she's in love, can she do anything but snivel and slobber? While a man is suffering and making sacrifices all her love expresses itself in her playing about with her scarf, and trying to hook him more firmly by the nose. You have the misfortune to be a woman, you know from yourself what is the nature of woman. Tell me truthfully, have you ever seen a woman who was sincere, faithful, and constant? You haven't! Only freaks and old women are faithful and constant! You'll meet a cat with a horn or a white woodcock sooner than a constant woman!

POPOVA. Then, according to you, who is faithful and constant in love? Is it the man?

SMIRNOV. Yes, the man!

POPOVA. The man! [Laughs bitterly] Men are faithful and constant in love! What an idea! [With heat] What right have you to talk like that? Men are faithful and constant? Since we are talking about it, I'll tell you that of all the men I knew and know, the best was my late husband. . . . I loved him passionately with all my being, as only a young and imaginative woman can love, I gave him my youth, my happiness, my life, my fortune, I breathed in him, I worshipped him as if I were a heathen, and . . . and what then? This best of men shamelessly deceived me at every step! After his death I found in his desk a whole drawerful of love-letters, and when he was alive— it's an awful thing to remember!—he used to leave me alone for weeks at a time, and make love to other women and betray me before my very eyes; he wasted my money, and made fun of my feelings. . . . And, in spite of all that, I loved him and was true to him. . . . And not only that, but, now that he is dead, I am still true and constant to his memory. I have shut myself for ever within these four walls, and will wear these weeds to the very end. . . .

SMIRNOV. [*Laughs contemptuously*] Weeds! . . . I don't understand what you take me for? As if I don't know why you wear that black domino and bury yourself between four walls! I should say I did! It's so mysterious, so poetic! When some junker* or some tame poet goes past your windows he'll think: "There lives the mysterious Tamara who, for the love of her husband, buried herself between four walls." We know these games!

POPOVA. [*Exploding*] What? How dare you say all that to me?

SMIRNOV. You may have buried yourself alive, but you haven't forgotten to powder your face!

POPOVA. How dare you speak to me like that?

SMIRNOV. Please don't shout, I'm not your steward! You must allow me to call things by their real names. I'm not a woman, and I'm used to saying what I think straight out! Don't you shout, either!

POPOVA. I'm not shouting, it's you! Please leave me alone!

SMIRNOV. Pay me my money and I'll go.

POPOVA. I shan't give you any money!

SMIRNOV. Oh, no, you will.

POPOVA. I shan't give you a farthing, just to spite you. You leave me alone!

SMIRNOV. I have not the pleasure of being either your husband or your fiancé, so please don't make scenes. [*Sits*] I don't like it.

POPOVA. [*Choking with rage*] So you sit down?

SMIRNOV. I do.

POPOVA. I ask you to go away!

SMIRNOV. Give me my money. . . . [*Aside*] Oh, how angry I am! How angry I am!

POPOVA. I don't want to talk to impudent scoundrels! Get out of this! [*Pause*] Aren't you going? No?

SMIRNOV. No.

POPOVA. No?

SMIRNOV. No!

POPOVA. Very well then! [*Rings, enter* LUKA] Luka, show this gentleman out!

LUKA [*Approaches* SMIRNOV] Would you mind going out, sir, as you're asked to! You needn't . . .

SMIRNOV. [*Jumps up*] Shut up! Who are you talking to? I'll chop you into pieces!

LUKA. [*Clutches at his heart*] Little fathers! . . . What people! . . . [*Falls into a chair*] Oh, I'm ill, I'm ill! I can't breathe!

POPOVA. Where's Dasha? Dasha! [*Shouts*] Dasha! Pelageya! Dasha! [*Rings*]

LUKA. Oh! They've all gone out to pick fruit. . . . There's nobody at home! I'm ill! Water!

POPOVA. Get out of this, now.

SMIRNOV. Can't you be more polite?

*So in the original.

POPOVA [*Clenches her fists and stamps her foot*] You're a boor! A coarse bear! A Bourbon! A monster!

SMIRNOV. What? What did you say?

POPOVA. I said you are a bear, a monster!

SMIRNOV. [*Approaching her*] May I ask what right you have to insult me?

POPOVA. And suppose I am insulting you? Do you think I'm afraid of you?

SMIRNOV. And do you think that just because you're a poetic creature you can insult me with impunity? Eh? We'll fight it out!

LUKA. Little fathers! . . . What people! . . . Water!

SMIRNOV. Pistols!

POPOVA. Do you think I'm afraid of you just because you have large fists and a bull's throat? Eh? You Bourbon!

SMIRNOV. We'll fight it out! I'm not going to be insulted by anybody, and I don't care if you are a woman, one of the "softer sex," indeed!

POPOVA. [*Trying to interrupt him*] Bear! Bear! Bear!

SMIRNOV. It's about time we got rid of the prejudice that only men need pay for their insults. Devil take it, if you want equality of rights you can have it. We're going to fight it out!

POPOVA. With pistols? Very well!

SMIRNOV. This very minute.

POPOVA. This very minute! My husband had some pistols. . . . I'll bring them here. [*Is going, but turns back*] What pleasure it will give me to put a bullet into your thick head! Devil take you! [*Exit*

SMIRNOV. I'll bring her down like a chicken! I'm not a little boy or a sentimental puppy; I don't care about this "softer sex."

LUKA. Gracious little fathers! . . . [*Kneels*] Have pity on a poor old man, and go away from here! You've frightened her to death, and now you want to shoot her!

SMIRNOV. [*Not hearing him*] If she fights, well that's equality of rights, emancipation, and all that! Here the sexes are equal! I'll shoot her on principle! But what a woman! [*Parodying her*] "Devil take you! I'll put a bullet into your thick head." Eh? How she reddened, how her cheeks shone! . . . She accepted my challenge! My word, it's the first time in my life that I've seen . . .

LUKA. Go away, sir, and I'll always pray to God for you!

SMIRNOV. She is a woman! That's the sort I can understand! A real woman! Not a sour-faced jellybag, but fire, gunpowder, a rocket! I'm even sorry to have to kill her!

LUKA. [*Weeps*] Dear . . . dear sir, do go away!

SMIRNOV. I absolutely like her! Absolutely! Even though her cheeks are dimpled, I like her! I'm almost ready to let the debt go . . . and I'm not angry any longer. . . . Wonderful woman!

Enter POPOVA *with pistols.*

POPOVA. Here are the pistols. . . . But before we fight you must show me how to fire. I've never held a pistol in my hands before.

LUKA. Oh, Lord, have mercy and save her. . . . I'll go and find the coachman and the gardener. . . . Why has this infliction come on us? . . . [*Exit*

SMIRNOV. [*Examining the pistols*] You see, there are several sorts of pistols. . . . There are Mortimer pistols, specially made for duels, they fire a percussion-cap. These are Smith and Wesson revolvers, triple action, with extractors. . . . These are excellent pistols. They can't cost less than ninety roubles the pair. . . . You must hold the revolver like this. . . . [*Aside*] Her eyes, her eyes! What an inspiring woman!

POPOVA. Like this?

SMIRNOV. Yes, like this. . . . Then you cock the trigger, and take aim like this. . . . Put your head back a little! Hold your arm out properly. . . . Like that. . . . Then you press this thing with your finger—and that's all. The great thing is to keep cool and aim steadily. . . . Try not to jerk your arm.

POPOVA. Very well. . . . It's inconvenient to shoot in a room, let's go into the garden.

SMIRNOV. Come along then. But I warn you, I'm going to fire in the air.

POPOVA. That's the last straw! Why?

SMIRNOV. Because . . . because . . . it's my affair.

POPOVA. Are you afraid? Yes? Ah! No, sir, you don't get out of it! You come with me! I shan't have any peace until I've made a hole in your forehead . . . that forehead which I hate so much! Are you afraid?

SMIRNOV. Yes, I am afraid.

POPOVA. You lie! Why won't you fight?

SMIRNOV. Because . . . because you . . . because I like you.

POPOVA. [*Laughs*] He likes me! He dares to say that he likes me! [*Points to the door*] That's the way.

SMIRNOV. [*Loads the revolver in silence, takes his cap and goes to the door. There he stops for half a minute, while they look at each other in silence, then he hesitatingly approaches* POPOVA] Listen. . . . Are you still angry? I'm devilishly annoyed, too . . . but, do you understand . . . how can I express myself? . . . The fact is, you see, it's like this, so to speak. . . . [*Shouts*] Well, is it my fault that I like you? [*He snatches at the back of a chair; the chair creaks and breaks*] Devil take it, how I'm smashing up your furniture! I like you! Do you understand? I . . . I almost love you!

POPOVA. Get away from me—I hate you!

SMIRNOV. God, what a woman! I've never in my life seen one like her! I'm lost! Done for! Fallen into a mousetrap, like a mouse!

POPOVA. Stand back, or I'll fire!

SMIRNOV. Fire, then! You can't understand what happiness it would be to die before those beautiful eyes, to be shot by a revolver held in that little, velvet hand. . . . I'm out of my senses! Think, and make up your mind at

once, because if I go out we shall never see each other again! Decide now.
. . . I am a landowner, of respectable character, have an income of ten
thousand a year. . . . I can put a bullet through a coin tossed into the air as
it comes down. . . . I own some fine horses. . . . Will you be my wife?

POPOVA. [*Indignantly shakes her revolver*] Let's fight! Let's go out!

SMIRNOV. I'm mad. . . . I understand nothing. . . . [*Yells*] Waiter, water!

POPOVA. [*Yells*] Let's go out and fight!

SMIRNOV. I'm off my head, I'm in love like a boy, like a fool! [*Snatches her
hand, she screams with pain*] I love you! [*Kneels*] I love you as I've never
loved before! I've refused twelve women, nine have refused me, but I never
loved one of them as I love you. . . . I'm weak, I'm wax, I've melted. . . .
I'm on my knees like a fool, offering you my hand. . . . Shame, shame! I
haven't been in love for five years, I'd taken a vow, and now all of a sudden
I'm in love, like a fish out of water! I offer you my hand. Yes or no? You
don't want me? Very well! [*Gets up and quickly goes to the door*]

POPOVA. Stop.

SMIRNOV. [*Stops*] Well?

POPOVA. Nothing, go away. . . . No, stop. . . . No, go away, go away! I
hate you! Or no. . . . Don't go away! Oh, if you knew how angry I am, how
angry I am! [*Throws her revolver on the table*] My fingers have swollen because of all this. . . . [*Tears her handkerchief in temper*] What are you
waiting for? Get out!

SMIRNOV. Good-bye.

POPOVA. Yes, yes, go away! . . . [*Yells*] Where are you going? Stop. . . .
No, go away. Oh, how angry I am! Don't come near me, don't come near me!

SMIRNOV. [*Approaching her*] How angry I am with myself! I'm in love like
a student, I've been on my knees. . . . [*Rudely*] I love you! What do I want
to fall in love with you for? To-morrow I've got to pay the interest, and begin
mowing, and here you . . . [*Puts his arms around her*] I shall never forgive
myself for this. . . .

POPOVA. Get away from me! Take your hands away! I hate you! Let's go and
fight!

A prolonged kiss. Enter LUKA *with an axe, the* GARDENER *with a rake,
the* COACHMAN *with a pitchfork, and* WORKMEN *with poles.*

LUKA. [*Catches sight of the pair kissing*] Little fathers! [*Pause*]

POPOVA. [*Lowering her eyes*] Luka, tell them in the stables that Toby isn't
to have any oats at all to-day.

CURTAIN.

Breinigsville, PA USA
11 December 2010
251154BV00002B/2/A